**Class Cultures and
Social Mobility**

Critical Issues in American Education
Lisa M. Nunn, Series Editor

Taking advantage of sociology's position as a leader in the social scientific study of education, this series is home to new empirical and applied bodies of work that combine social analysis, cultural critique, and historical perspectives across disciplinary lines and the usual methodological boundaries. Books in the series aim for topical and theoretical breadth. Anchored in sociological analysis, Critical Issues in American Education features carefully crafted empirical work that takes up the most pressing educational issues of our time, including federal education policy, gender and racial disparities in student achievement, access to higher education, labor market outcomes, teacher quality, and decision making within institutions.

Paul Dean, *Class Cultures and Social Mobility: The Hidden Strengths of Working-Class First-Generation Graduates*

Judson G. Everitt, *Lesson Plans: The Institutional Demands of Becoming a Teacher*

Karey Harwood, *Wake: Why the Battle over Diverse Public Schools Still Matters*

Megan M. Holland, *Divergent Paths to College: Race, Class, and Inequality in High Schools*

Katie Kerstetter, *How Schools Meet Students' Needs: Inequality, School Reform, and Caring Labor*

Laura Nichols, *The Journey Before Us: First-Generation Pathways from Middle School to College*

Lisa M. Nunn, *College Belonging: How First-Year and First-Generation Students Navigate Campus Life*

Daisy Verduzco Reyes, *Learning to Be Latino: How Colleges Shape Identity Politics*

Sophia Rodriguez, *Undocumented in the U.S. South: How Youth Navigate Racialization and Immigration Status in Policy and School Contexts*

Class Cultures and Social Mobility

The Hidden Strengths of Working-Class First-Generation Graduates

PAUL DEAN

Rutgers University Press
New Brunswick, Camden, and Newark, New Jersey
London and Oxford

Rutgers University Press is a department of Rutgers, The State University of New Jersey, one of the leading public research universities in the nation. By publishing worldwide, it furthers the University's mission of dedication to excellence in teaching, scholarship, research, and clinical care.

Library of Congress Cataloging-in-Publication Data

Names: Dean, Paul, 1980– author.
Title: Class cultures and social mobility: the hidden strengths of working-class first-generation graduates / Paul Dean.
Description: New Brunswick, New Jersey: Rutgers University Press, [2025] | Series: Critical issues in American education | Includes bibliographical references and index.
Identifiers: LCCN 2025005265 (print) | LCCN 2025005266 (ebook) | ISBN 9781978845800 (paperback) | ISBN 9781978845817 (hardcover) | ISBN 9781978845824 (epub)
Subjects: LCSH: First-generation college students—United States. | Working class—United States. | Social mobility—United States.
Classification: LCC LC4069.6 .D43 2025 (print) | LCC LC4069.6 (ebook) | DDC 331.7/930926230973—dc23/eng/20250225
LC record available at https://lccn.loc.gov/2025005265
LC ebook record available at https://lccn.loc.gov/2025005266

A British Cataloging-in-Publication record for this book is available from the British Library.

Copyright © 2026 by Paul Dean
All rights reserved

No part of this book may be reproduced or utilized in any form or by any means, electronic or mechanical, or by any information storage and retrieval system, without written permission from the publisher. Please contact Rutgers University Press, 106 Somerset Street, New Brunswick, NJ 08901. The only exception to this prohibition is "fair use" as defined by U.S. copyright law.

References to internet websites (URLs) were accurate at the time of writing. Neither the author nor Rutgers University Press is responsible for URLs that may have expired or changed since the manuscript was prepared.

⊚ The paper used in this publication meets the requirements of the American National Standard for Information Sciences—Permanence of Paper for Printed Library Materials, ANSI Z39.48-1992.

rutgersuniversitypress.org

To Tia, for endless support on this project and in life. Love always.

Contents

Introduction: Climbing the Class Ladder
Is an Emotional Journey ... 1

Part I Class Cultures and Social Mobility

1. The Differences Between Working-Class and Middle-Class Cultures ... 19
2. Classism and Cultural Mismatches Faced by Upwardly Mobile Working-Class People ... 36

Part II The Hidden Strengths of Working-Class Cultural Capital

3. Cultural Empathy ... 57
4. Working-Class Norms, Language, and Communication ... 73
5. Translating, Code-Switching, Mediating, and Bridge-Building ... 86
6. Working-Class Dispositions: Hard Work, Practicality, Authenticity, Resilience, and Ingenuity ... 102

Part III Lessons Learned

7. Managing the Threats of Assimilation, Complicity, and Co-Optation ... 117

8	Applying the Lessons to First-Gen Students, Working Straddlers, and Our Workplaces	133
	Appendix: Research Methodology	147
	Acknowledgments	153
	Notes	157
	References	165
	Index	181

**Class Cultures and
Social Mobility**

Introduction

Climbing the Class Ladder Is an Emotional Journey

When I was a working-class kid growing up, the message I got was that with hard work I could accomplish whatever I wanted. But they left out a couple of important details. First, for many people, hard work alone is not enough to overcome the barriers we face in life. Second, even when we do overcome those hurdles and move up the class ladder, the more we feel like a cultural outsider. This is because straddlers like me live in two different cultural worlds. We have one foot in the working-class culture in which we were raised. And we have another foot in the professional world and its middle-class culture. We straddle working-class and middle-class cultures.

When you are a first-generation student or a straddler, it's hard to know where you fit in. There is often a cultural mismatch between the world in which we are raised and the world we increasingly inhabit. We ask ourselves questions like, Do I belong here in my new social class? How do I relate to my roots? Who do I want to become? It's a journey filled with excitement because of the opportunities it could bring. But we have been taught not to discuss class while also looking down on the poor and working class. As a result, the nagging voices of self-doubt are impossible to ignore.

Despite the American Dream proclaiming that class and race do not affect our life journey, people whom I spoke with for this book described myriad ways in which they dramatically shaped their lives. While they all came from the working class and moved into middle-class life, they had to learn the rules of a new world. At the same time, they were proud of their working-class roots and did not want to forget their working-class culture or community. This book tells the stories of the cultural experience of upward mobility, the inevitable classism and cultural mismatches that emerge, and how straddlers find ways to turn their working-class roots into an asset. It further shows how these experiences are shaped by race, as well as gender, sexuality, and the region in which we live. Ashley's story offers a glimpse of this balancing act and some pitfalls that upwardly mobile people face along the way. Like this book, her story reveals hidden elements of social class in America, how culture shapes inequality, and how cultural outsiders can flip the script.

Ashley's Emotional Journey of Upward Mobility

Ashley grew up in southeast Ohio, an area known as Ohio's Hill Country. When she was a child, Ashley's family moved to a new home every two or three years. Sometimes it was trailers, sometimes old farmhouses, and one time it was even a church parsonage (the housing normally provided to a minister). Ashley explained that the houses themselves were not fancy and were "always houses that we had to go into and do a lot of cleanup and repair to make them pretty livable." Nonetheless, her mother always kept a clean house and took pride in decorating and turning each new place into a home.

When I asked Ashley about her upbringing, she described the values with which she was raised. I could sense great pride in how she characterized "the community and family orientation, the work ethic," adding, "There's always an emphasis on doing kind of the right thing, even though that might look different for people or people don't always live by that." Ashley fondly explained learning that "you should always try to help one another and be there for each other. So, I have a very strong sense of integrity. If I say I'm going to do something, it's really important to me to do it." These values of family, community, a strong work ethic, and commitment came up time and time again in my interviews. These are core to working-class culture.

Ashley's father was a union boilermaker. Boilermakers produce, install, and maintain the large tanks or vats that heat liquids to generate electricity and provide heat to buildings. It is grueling work requiring significant physical strength and stamina, often in confined spaces or at great heights. It can also be intellectually demanding, requiring the ability to read blueprints for installation or diagnose and troubleshoot problems. Because of the skills required and because it was a unionized job, it paid a decent wage—significantly more than what her mother earned as a medical transcriptionist for a local hospital. Both her parents graduated high school, and her mother started attending nursing school four or five times, but it never worked out.

The difference in her parents' income was important because when Ashley was thirteen, her father left the family and stopped contributing financially. As she put it, "When he left, like he *left*." Her mother struggled with mental illness and it had worsened. Eventually, her mother went on disability, leaving Ashley and her mother with a small monthly income. During those teenage years, when children are trying to figure out who they are and constantly comparing themselves to others, she remembers feeling ashamed of their class position. It was the early 2000s, "around the time in high school when everybody was getting cool new cars or at least newer cars, I got an '88 Beretta GT, stick shift in the floor. The CD player would slide out of the dash when you hit the brakes hard. . . . I remember feeling really ashamed and knowing that we were too poor to even get a car loan." Ashley went on to recount how she and her mom would shop at second-hand stores, which she associated with feelings of embarrassment, frustration, and anger. She would come to view thrift stores more positively later in life, but as a child she viewed them as an unpleasant experience.

Despite a wealth of research showing that moving frequently has negative effects on childhood learning, Ashley performed well in school and set her sights on college.[1] Her mother had taken an occasional class at a local college, but she knew little about the admission and college selection process. When it came to picking a college, applying, and paying for it, Ashley was on her own. She explained that she "didn't even understand the cost of higher education when I was a senior in high school." She also had doubts about her academic abilities, painfully recalling that "I didn't think that I was good enough." And it stuck with her: "I still fight this some today although it eases over time—this perception of myself. Ya know, some little girl from a small town that nobody knows about or cares about. . . . Why would they look at me?"

Ashley enrolled at the Ohio State University (OSU) because "growing up in Ohio, it's kinda a pinnacle school." She was excited for the opportunities it would bring. But when Ashley went away to college, her class background continued to shape her experiences socially, financially, and academically. Her "roommates had a lot more clothing" and money to spend on going out to eat. Based on how they spoke, Ashley "could just tell that they grew up in more suburban places with better schools." She was intimidated. It seemed that the girls she met "all participated in like cheer and dance and all of these different things," traveling for spring break, "or being able to study abroad." Like many working-class students, Ashley felt like she was fumbling her way through college with no one to guide her. She added that "now that I know how higher ed works, I probably could have figured out how to study abroad, but at that time it seemed so expensive." She "just didn't understand how financial aid worked. And my mother was so fearful. I was forbidden from leaving the country." Because she did not understand how the system worked, Ashley missed out on many opportunities like studying abroad. But she persevered and graduated from OSU, majoring in English. She was the first in her family to graduate college and would eventually go on to finish a master's and a PhD.

Ashley's background continued to shape her professional career. On the one hand, she was aware that her racial and ethnic background meant other people would give her the benefit of the doubt. She shared that "I know that I have a very English-sounding name and I'm white," so people wouldn't discriminate against her because of that. On the other hand, people did discriminate against her class background, which continued shaping her professional journey. In one of her first jobs after graduating with her bachelor's degree, Ashley attended CPR training. The woman leading the training evoked stereotypical images of poverty in her region of Appalachia:

> She went on to say that, for various reasons, different cultural groups practice hygiene differently. . . . She was like, "People in Southeast Ohio, they don't bathe regularly like we do. They take a bath maybe once a month, and if they're lucky in the summertime, it'll be once a week. They don't have access to running water, and they take bouts in a tub in the yard." And here I was Appalachian. So I was just sitting there feeling an inch tall, and I remember going out and calling my mom and crying because it was my first . . . experience of having somebody say something blatantly negative and untrue about the place and the people where I grew up.

In that moment, Ashley felt a deep sense of shame. She thought she "made it" and proved herself by graduating college and getting a professional job. In an instant, she was cut down.

Ultimately, Ashley found that at each step of her upward journey—growing up, in high school and college, and in the professional world—Ashley's class background shaped her experiences. It came in many forms, including different experiences (high school activities), missing out on opportunities (study abroad), and other times having people look down on her or people from her background (using negative stereotypes of Appalachia).

Those of us who were raised in the working class and move into the middle class don't simply *forget* who we are and spontaneously fit into this new world. As Ashley entered the professional middle class, she remembered feeling "like you're straddling and you have one foot in two camps that are almost in opposition to one another." They don't tell you about this part of the American Dream. She further elaborated, "When I was younger, I often felt like my class background was super obvious. So, I always felt a little bit conspicuous. And going back to that whole like 'holding a foot in two camps' kind of feeling—like I don't fully belong here. I'm just a girl from a working-class, you know, poor background, and people can look at me and they can tell that. So I think there was a level of discomfort or embarrassment."

Our class experiences are inherently emotional experiences. On the one hand, Ashley was proud of her mother's ability to transform run-down spaces into a home. She treasured the values upon which she was raised. And she reveled in the accomplishment of not just being the first in her family to graduate college but having gone all the way for her PhD. On the other hand, she felt that others looked down on her because of her background. She knew there was so much about the world she did not know because of where she came from, and these feelings did not entirely disappear as she became a professional. At the same time, she was excited how her education and middle-class job could open new doors for her. She wanted the opportunities but also wanted to maintain her working-class roots.

Ashley's experience is a common one. Journalist Alfred Lubrano wrote about it beautifully in his book, *Limbo: Blue Collar Roots, White Collar Dreams*, in which he coined the term "straddlers."[2] It refers to upwardly mobile first-gen college grads with a foot in both the working-class and professional middle-class worlds. He talks about this as a "duality" and as a "never-ending struggle with identity." It is certainly the case that straddlers have various strategies for overcoming this duality—which can lead to radically different life choices and lifestyles. For example, some are so ashamed of their roots that they run as fast as they can to the materialism that upper-middle-class life affords and don't talk about their humble beginnings. They push it deep down and wall themselves off from the memories of struggling (or worse yet, they look down on others who didn't make it out like they did). Others may reject middle-class life and focus on the more familiar comfortability of the working-class life that they know. But in this book, I focus on a third strategy for managing upward mobility—an attempt to balance working-class roots and the new middle-class life.

When I interviewed Ashley, she described largely overcoming the oppositional feelings she initially encountered and had a fulfilling career in student services at a university. In fact, she not only found a way of balancing these two seemingly contradictory selves, but she also learned how to turn her working-class roots into an asset in her professional career. How do straddlers like Ashley do it? How do she and others draw upon their working-class roots in navigating this new life of straddling classes? This book reveals a variety of ways that straddlers leveraged the cultural resources of their working-class roots in ways that have not yet been identified in scholarly research. But first, we should pause to take a closer look at some key terms.

Defining Class and Your Place in the Hierarchy

Class is a messy topic, especially in a country like the United States where we are taught to believe it does not exist. It can be tricky to define class and our place in the hierarchy. While there is much debate on how many classes there are and where we draw the boundaries, there are some basic definitions to get us started.

A class is a grouping of individuals with similar economic positions. The economic positions are largely determined by our job; level of education; property or wealth (the physical and financial assets we own, like houses or stocks); and workplace authority (if we take orders or give orders). Class positions are also related to income, which is more intuitively associated with class but not always the best way to define to which class we belong. We often think of families as belonging to a class, with children's or students' class positions defined by their parents' class location.

Things start getting messy as we map these onto different class categories. In everyday language, we often greatly simplify things into the rich and the poor, or the 1 percent and the 99 percent. Experts divide classes into three, four, five, or up to nine categories. For example, a typical four-tiered class hierarchy has the upper class at its peak. They own significant wealth (usually inherited wealth), have college or advanced degrees, and hold occupations controlling large companies (although many of them need not work to remain wealthy), which yield high incomes. The middle class holds modest amounts of property and wealth, has bachelor's degrees or advanced degrees, works as professionals, and has mid-level positions of workplace authority. They tend to work more with symbols and mental processes, have fair amounts of autonomy at work, and may have people below them whom they supervise, but they also take orders from those above. The working class has no or very little wealth and property, lower levels of education (which can include some high school, high school graduates, technical school, or some college), and works at manual labor that can include work with both their head and hands. Their occupations include blue-collar, service, and clerical occupations that have little or no workplace authority, and they largely take orders from others. Finally, the poor have no property or wealth, low levels of education, work part-time or menial jobs with no authority, and may experience periods of unemployment and/or periods of living on public assistance.

Sometimes our experiences neatly map onto these class categories, but often they do not. For example, an electrician who owns her own small business has a blue-collar occupation, which requires both physical labor and significant intellectual skill in diagnosing and troubleshooting issues. By owning their own small business, people in this occupation won't take orders from others and could earn incomes greater than some white-collar occupations, such as college professors. Professors have the highest degrees within their fields (usually a doctorate), but their incomes are often less than jobs held by people with bachelor's degrees. But despite their middling incomes, professors have significant job autonomy and social status. Sociologist Erik Olin Wright referred to such positions as "contradictory class locations" because they share properties with different class positions—such as the electrician having characteristics of both the working and middle classes.[3] Others talk about the "fuzzy boundaries" between classes because it is not always clear where the working class ends and the middle class begins.[4] It is also common to move between classes—especially between the poor and working class—during one's lifetime.

Things get even messier when we think about the racial effects on class categories and experiences. However we divide up the class categories, it is almost always the case that, on average, white people in a particular class will fare better socially and economically than Black, Latine,[5] and Native American people in the same class.[6] For example, white people in a particular occupation tend to earn higher incomes and have significantly more wealth than people of color in the same occupation with the same level of schooling. In the labor market, people of color will likely experience discrimination in hiring when searching for a job. In our communities, Black middle-class neighborhoods tend to be closer geographically to poor neighborhoods and exposed to higher levels of crime than white middle-class neighborhoods with similar homes and household incomes.[7] We will continue exploring many other racial effects on class as we unpack the world of class cultures.

The vast majority of research on class cultures compares middle-class culture with working-class culture, and I will therefore use this focus throughout the book. The people whom I interviewed used a variety of terms to refer to their class backgrounds. They included terms like "blue-collar," "working class," "lower class," "working poor," "middle class," "lower middle class," "working middle class," and "poor, but not that poor." These self-identities are shaped by a variety of factors that include the fuzziness of the categories mentioned above. For many people, they are wary of self-identifying with some terms, such as "poor," because of the stigma they carry—even if they fit the official definition of poverty.[8] There is a lot of pressure in the United States to consider yourself as "middle class." For some, even the term "working class" carries this stigma, while for others it is a term of great pride.

Regardless of their self-identities, all the people I spoke with can be described as coming from working-class and poor families who climbed the class ladder into middle-class life but with varying degrees of racial consciousness. Like Ashley, their parents all held working-class jobs and lacked a college education. So, Ashley and my respondents became first-generation college graduates because their parents did not have a four-year college degree. Some white respondents were quite aware of having been advantaged by their race, while others believed race has not impacted their lives or those around them. My Black, Asian American, Latine, and multiracial respondents tended to have more racial awareness, but not in all cases. Nonetheless, they all now work professional jobs with better working conditions and advanced education, with growing levels of workplace authority and *usually* higher incomes. But how common is this type of upward mobility? Is Ashley's trajectory and those of others in this book unique? And how is it affected by their race and other social backgrounds?

Pick Your Parents Well

The promise of the American Dream is that it is your individual effort and intelligence that determines where you end up in the class hierarchy. Indeed, Ashley worked hard and attained that dream. But as we scratch at the surface, it doesn't take long to see the reality is much more complicated.

In the race to economic prosperity, people have different starting points in life. Children born into wealthy families, on average, attend schools that have two-to-three times more money per pupil than children born into poor and working-class families.[9] They are more likely to have higher-quality teachers and better educational resources. They live in safer neighborhoods and are exposed to less crime.[10] Children from wealthier families are healthier in every way measurable, and better health is associated with better educational outcomes. They come from families with college-educated professionals who can better assist them with applying for college, afford tutors for standardized exams, and help them navigate the college experience. Their parents are more likely to have connections to other professionals, helping them to get summer jobs and internships and support them financially if the internship is unpaid. If you want to get ahead in life, pick your parents well, they say.

So, it is no surprise that children from rich families are more likely to stay rich as adults. Children born into the top 20 percent of the income ladder have over a 31 percent chance of reaching the top as adults, whereas children born into the bottom 20 percent of the income ladder have only a 9 percent chance of making it into the top 20 percent as adults.[11] In other words, children born at the bottom are far more likely to remain at, or near, the bottom. While some have claimed that the children from these rich families are more intelligent, the reality is that they are not more or less intelligent than those born into other classes.[12] Instead, such outcomes are a result of social systems that help to preserve advantages for the children from rich families. It is as if everyone is running the 100-meter dash, but some people start at the beginning, others at 20 meters out, and still others 50 meters out. It doesn't mean kids who start further ahead will win the race every time, but it sure helps.

These experiences in life are further shaped by our racial background. For every dollar in household wealth that a typical white family has, an average Latine family has only ten cents, and a Black family today has only nine cents in wealth.[13] These enormous differences in wealth provide very different opportunities for acquiring stable housing in a safe neighborhood or the ability to pay for a college education. Children of color are far less likely to attend good-quality schools, and they receive much less in school funding. While there has been some progress since the civil rights era, studies consistently show people of color continue to be discriminated against in hiring. For example, two economists sent fake job resumes to real job ads in the United States.[14] They made the candidates comparable in every way except the names—some had traditional white-sounding names (Emily Baker or Greg Walsh) while others had traditional Black-sounding names (Jamal Jones or Lakisha Washington). Despite having equally qualified resumes, the applicants with Black-sounding names had to send out 50 percent more resumes to get the same number of callbacks from real employers.

Mobility patterns also vary by race.[15] Among poor children (from the bottom 20 percent), white boys are 31 percent more likely to remain among the poorest, but 48 percent of Black boys will remain the poorest. Poor white boys are five times more likely than poor Black boys to climb to the top one-fifth. While Black girls fare better than Black boys, poor white and Black girls are also unlikely to move up substantially as adults. Only 7 percent of poor white girls will make it to the top compared with 5 percent of poor Black girls. When you compare white children with Black, Latine, or Native American children in the same economic circumstances at any level, white children will fare better as adults on average. Asian American children—whose parents and relatives tend to migrate to the United States with far higher levels of wealth and education than other minority groups—are the exception. But their life prospects also vary significantly depending on their country of origin and how many generations their family has been in the United States. Accordingly, to understand the experience of social mobility, we must also examine race.

What makes our cultural narrative of the American Dream even more puzzling is how the United States compares to other countries. Data collected by the World Economic Forum reveals some startling findings.[16] Its research shows the United States ranks relatively low (number twenty-seven) compared to many other countries in terms of mobility. Despite the promise of the American Dream, class origins matter much more for shaping life outcomes here in the United States. In contrast, many European countries—especially the Scandinavian countries like Denmark (number one in social mobility)—have far higher rates of mobility. Who your parents are in Denmark has much less impact on where you end up on the class ladder as an adult. As a result, mobility researchers joke that if you want the American Dream, go to Europe.

In 2023, I checked out what these mobility researchers had to say and traveled to Europe (Denmark specifically) with working-class, first-gen students to investigate how these countries have been so successful. We learned a lot about how the United States and Denmark create different rules of society as they relate to economic opportunity. For example, Denmark funds its schools evenly, while the United States spends more on wealthy kids' schools than those attended by poor kids. Denmark has a much more generous social safety net to keep people afloat when they fall on hard times. Its workforce is far more unionized (64 percent in Denmark compared to 10% in the United States) so workers have more power negotiating for wages and electing politicians that represent their interests.[17] In the United States, the economic power of the wealthy translates much more effectively into political power, and the upper class here uses that political power to rig the system to benefit themselves more so than in Denmark. But I am interested in those that do climb that class ladder—what is the experience like for them? How do these straddlers draw on their working-class origins in their new middle-class life?

Class-Based Cultures Are Different Worlds

Class is not just about the economic resources we have (or don't have). It is also about the people we hang around, our sense of belonging, our shared values, how we speak, and what we do for fun. Class is as much cultural as it is economic, as much social as it is financial. For this reason, people also talk about *social* classes and not only *economic* classes.

The term *culture* refers to people's beliefs, language, norms that shape behavior, and values. There are many forms of culture, including class culture, which I will explore in greater depth in chapter 1. For example, class culture affects how parents raise their children.[18] Middle-class parents enlist their children in many organized activities, instill a broader vocabulary in their children, reason with their children more when disciplining them, and are more likely to speak with their children's teachers or intervene on their behalf in institutional settings. Working-class parents provide their children with love, food, and safety but allow them more autonomy in how they organize their days, their children spend more time with extended family, and the family uses a more limited vocabulary in the home. These childrearing strategies are further shaped by race and gender.[19]

Class culture impacts how we build our sense of self and how we interact with others. As Lubrano describes it, class "tells us how to talk, how to dress, how to hold ourselves, how to eat, and how to socialize."[20] Middle-class people express a greater degree of individuality (using more "I" statements) and have a sense of entitlement when interacting with people in positions of authority. Working-class people are more likely to build group agreement (using more "we" statements) and avoid situations where they interact with people with authority over them. Class culture affects how we relate to each other over shared tastes.[21] Lubrano explained that class affects "the books we read; the movies we see; the restaurants we pick; how we decide to buy houses, carpets, furniture, and cars; where our children are educated; what we tell our children at the dinner table (conversations about the Middle East, for example, versus the continuing sagas of the broken vacuum cleaner or the half-wit neighbors); whether we have a dinner table, or a dinner time."[22] To note some contrasts, middle- and upper-middle-class people with college educations are more likely to enjoy yoga, international foods, abstract art, theater, museums, tennis, and spending vacations abroad. Working-class people tend to enjoy pasta and foods from their own ethnic group, mainstream television shows and crime dramas, contemporary pop music, casual clothes and workwear, and spending time at family gatherings.

Class also shapes our values, how we differentiate right from wrong, and how we believe people should (or should not) behave.[23] For example, middle-class people place greater value on individuality, productivity, socioeconomic achievement, self-actualization, and conflict avoidance. Working-class people tend to value community, hard work, resilience, integrity, straightforwardness, sincerity, and humility. These divergent values can create problems when middle-class people might look down on working-class people for their values, or when working-class people view middle-class strategies to avoid conflict as being two-faced. But because middle-class people hold higher positions of status and their values are what shape college and professional workplaces, they have advantages over working-class people in those settings.

While there are common elements of working-class culture, it is often more accurate to describe working-class culture*s* (plural). Working-class culture varies by region, race, ethnicity, gender, sexuality, which age group we are a part of, and if we're from the city or the country, among other factors. Therefore, it is important to adopt an intersectional perspective that looks at how working-class people's experiences vary based on their other social experiences and backgrounds.[24] In addition to encountering different types of discrimination, we are also socialized in culturally distinct ways. Whether we raise our children to greet others with "sir"/"ma'am," if we like mudding or basketball, if we listen to Bruce Springsteen or Kendrick Lamar, or the kind of slang we use—these are all different elements of diverse working-class cultures. Nonetheless, there are some common dimensions found among working-class culture and common elements among middle-class culture.

Finally, these elements of class culture function as resources for navigating the world. Building on the foundational work of Pierre Bourdieu, sociologists refer to these resources as *cultural capital*.[25] They include skills for navigating a particular context, attitudes like a sense of entitlement or constraint, manners of speech that help us fit in, tastes that affect how we relate to others, and knowledge of how colleges and other institutions work. Like economic resources, these cultural resources affect how we manage different situations, and they give some people advantages over others.

In studies of cultural capital and social mobility, the focus has almost entirely been on the ways that middle-class cultural capital is needed to be successful in professional occupations and upward mobility. Such a perspective frames working-class cultural capital as a weakness and a working-class background as a deficit. It is an important—indeed essential—body of work for understanding how social inequality is reproduced from generation to generation.

Middle-class children grow up learning the skills, attitudes, and cultural capital that are demanded by professional occupations and help give them an advantage over working-class people later in life. In chapters 1 and 2, I will demonstrate how my respondents were socialized into working-class culture and encountered cultural barriers as they tried climbing the class ladder, noting how existing research informs our understanding of class culture and social mobility.

But that story of cultural capital is not the entire story. Indeed, a few rare studies have identified working-class cultural capital as a strength or asset but in a narrow way. For example, studies have shown how working-class cultural capital exists in limited forms, such as care work.[26] Working-class culture is more oriented around caring for others, which can be an asset in tasks where care work is required. Other studies have looked at working-class cultural capital in a specific occupation, such as academia, where upwardly mobile professors can support working-class college students.[27] This reflects a broader limitation among existing research that has undertheorized the cultural capital of marginalized groups, such as feminized cultural capital, Black cultural capital, and cultural wealth, as being a strength in navigating education, labor markets, and upward mobility.[28]

This book is the first of its kind to present a systematic framework of working-class cultural capital and the ways that straddlers can leverage their class background as a strength in their professional work. Of course, these cultural resources do not function the same way in all circumstances. Furthermore, they do not lessen the need for upwardly mobile straddlers to acquire middle-class cultural capital as well. But this framework does provide a more nuanced picture of the roles that a working-class background can play and suggests sources of pride and strength for straddlers who wish to maintain a connection to their working-class roots. Understanding working-class cultural capital in these ways is both a tool for individual empowerment and a means by which straddlers can lift up others in their working-class communities.

My Class Journey and the Stories in This Book

I grew up working-class. My father has spent his life as a mechanic working with the machinery used to make bricks. He graduated from high school and developed on-the-job skills in fixing heavy machinery. I have always been awed by his mechanical abilities. I did learn how to change my own oil, but I would probably be walking if I actually had to fix anything that broke down on my car. My father is of a different generation in that he started working at a factory at age twenty and stayed there until he retired—corporations simply don't provide jobs with that kind of stability anymore.

My mother had worked occasional service jobs—like a cashier at McDonald's or working on the line in a box factory. But she was mostly a stay-at-home mom because her schizophrenia often prevented her from holding down a job. She was a brilliant artist and even took a couple of college-level classes but could never transition that into a paid job, let alone a career. I wish I had inherited her artistic skills, too, because students get a good laugh out of the stick figures I draw on the whiteboard.

When I was six years old, we moved from a trailer to the first house my parents ever owned. It was a small, three-bedroom house where my sister and I could each have our own room. Despite my parents' modest education levels, my father's union job provided some stability. It meant the mortgage could be paid and the utilities were always on. But we did not have much more. We did not take vacations, except to nearby campgrounds. New clothes or shoes were rare, and eating out meant a trip to McDonald's or the local diner. We spent a lot of time playing outdoors with cousins and other extended family. I usually did not mind it because nearly everyone around us was in a similar position. But there were times I became painfully aware that we did not have much. I remember being made fun of for not having the newer, trendier clothes, and when I would get hungry at school, I felt like I couldn't ask for more. When money is so tight, getting more means someone else in the family gets less.

College was a foreign world to me and my family. I had no idea about college or how to pick one, so I started at the local community college literally on the same street where my father lived. My parents couldn't help me financially, community college was free, and I was terrified of accumulating debt. At the time, I thought you only go to college to get a good-paying job. While it is natural for people to want more economic security, I see college as much more than that now and hope that I can help my students see it differently as well. But I started off as a business major, thinking that was my ticket to a more stable life.

As part of my business major, I interned at a local corporate headquarters that made ready-to-assemble furniture (think: Ikea-type furniture minus the giant showrooms). I was working in the accounting department when I took my first-ever sociology class. I started to read theories about economic inequality, and it pushed me to think about my own class experiences. I also began seeing other differences more clearly, like the dynamics between the Latine workers on the hot-and-noisy factory floor, compared with the white workers in the air-conditioned offices above. Where my business classes failed to inspire me, the insights of sociology grabbed me to my core. I changed my major a few times and eventually landed on sociology. I came to learn class helped me to make sense of who I am. It helped me to understand experiences in my life, including what I struggled with and what I was proud of, my anxieties and dreams, and the social forces shaping my life.

College also helped me to develop a racial consciousness. American towns and cities remain highly segregated places by both class and race. My high school was almost entirely white, with just a few people of color in my graduating class of 120. But in college, I met and made friends with people from other racial and ethnic backgrounds. As a graduate student, I would eventually study class and race with some of the world's leading scholars. Along the way, I had to unlearn much of what society taught me about whiteness, race, and what it means to be a person of color—an educational journey that will never end.

Now, as a college professor, my teaching and research focus on issues of class, race, the economy, and inequality. While I love working with students of all backgrounds, I find that working-class, first-gen students are especially drawn to my classes. I am passionate about helping them succeed, and I hope to help them avoid the many mistakes I made along the way. Like Ashley whose story is presented above, I fumbled my way through college. Neither of us had a guide for the obstacles in our way, but we had people who helped us and supported us.

The more I have come to explore class and race with people around me, the more connected to them I have felt. With friends, I have shared many beers discussing our fathers' strategies for numbing the pain from another twelve-hour shift in the factory (my dad preferred to put a bag of frozen peas on his neck). It is no surprise that many of my closest friends share my working-class background. When I traveled to Denmark with my working-class students, we squirmed over trying pickled herring open-faced sandwiches and vented about the turmoil brought about when a parent lost their job. In my office, students have shed tears as we strategized how they could pay their semester's tuition, wondering if they would have to drop out of the school that they have come to love and at which they had found their mentors. Through discussing our journeys with students, colleagues, and friends, we have found deeper bonds—as collaborators, as allies, and as brothers and sisters.

The more I discussed these topics with friends and did my own research, the more interested I became in how upwardly mobile straddlers navigate the working world. So, I set out to find people who have taken that journey in a variety of occupational fields. I created a call for participants, and I shared it all over social media and sent it to email lists where I could speak not just to fellow educators but also to engineers, nurses, marketing experts, elected politicians, social workers, and climate scientists.

In total, I interviewed thirty-seven people across a wide variety of occupational fields. A few of them are people I know, but the vast majority of them came from those invitations sent to email lists and social media. I sat down with each of them for an in-depth conversation, which averaged over one hundred minutes each. I wanted to know about their class backgrounds, their journeys through college and into the professional world, and how they draw upon their working-class roots in the work that they do. People opened up about intimate details of their lives. They shared inspiring stories but sometimes unexpected tears—both of joy but also of heartache from difficult memories of what they and their families have endured. They came from different regions of the country, diverse racial backgrounds, and different genders and sexual orientations. Some of them preferred to be anonymous and have been given pseudonyms, while some requested that I use their real names. The research appendix provides more details on my methodology.

But there is an inherent difficulty in presenting the stories of people in this book. As you will see, chapter 1 presents important cultural differences in how people are socialized into working-class and middle-class cultures. Chapter 2 shows how schools and professional workplaces are dominated by middle-class culture, and classism and cultural mismatches experienced by upwardly mobile working-class people make climbing the ladder more difficult. And yet, the people in this book overcame sometimes terrible odds to be the first in their family to attend and graduate from college, climb into the middle class, and now proudly leverage their working-class roots in their professional jobs. But we must be wary of romanticizing working-class life or of using these as exemplars of the American Dream that only requires individual effort to move up. The people throughout these pages sometimes suffered greatly, like when Nina remembers her mother crying herself to sleep each night around Christmas because she could not afford gifts for her children. Furthermore, many of these straddlers made it because they had supportive people enter their lives, often found mentors, and frequently benefited from government programs or free tuition to lift them up. Not everyone is so fortunate, and for each story of someone who made it, there are many more for whom the obstacles were too high. Rather than stories that confirm the power of the individual, these stories further reinforce the need for societal support. They each developed an awareness of that, and it shaped the people they would become and the work they would pursue.

The people throughout this book did seek out some degree of comfort and economic security (not to mention safer working conditions and more fulfilling work) that a college degree, professional job, and upward mobility could bring. They became social workers, engineers, lawyers, journalists, nurses, therapists, musicians, community organizers, chaplains, and managers, just to name a few. But in addition to learning the ways of middle-class culture, we found ways to draw upon cultural resources from our upbringing to be more effective in our jobs.

In chapters 3 through 6, I will present this set of cultural resources, or working-class cultural capital. These chapters present a new contribution, and readers familiar with existing theory and research on class cultures may wish to jump to this section. In chapter 3, I show how cultural empathy enables straddlers to shift their perspectives and imparts important career-oriented skills.

In chapter 4, I discuss the ways that middle-class culture can lead people astray and how knowing working-class cultural norms, language, and communication styles are better suited for working with certain groups. In chapter 5, I demonstrate how mastering both working-class and middle-class cultures helps straddlers to become effective at translating and decoding unwritten cultural rules, code-switching, mediating class conflicts, and building bridges across classes. Finally, in chapter 6, I reveal how dispositions like hard work, practicality, ingenuity, and resilience become important cultural resources in our journey upward.

While not all straddlers strive to help lift up others in the working class, it is something that my respondents share. In chapter 7, I show how these lifting straddlers put this into action and how they sought to avoid assimilation, complicity, and co-optation into a system that so often disadvantages those at the bottom of society. In chapter 8, I conclude with lessons learned for first-gen students and working straddlers in lifting up others and rising with one's class. While acknowledging the real difficulties of upward mobility, this book shows the strength, pride, and opportunity that our working-class roots can offer along the way.

Part 1

Class Cultures and Social Mobility

1
The Differences Between Working-Class and Middle-Class Cultures

Khalid grew up in two different class worlds. His mother, with a high school education, worked as a nurse's aide and supplemented her low wages with periods of public assistance. He was raised in the 1970s in the Bronx, which was ground zero for the emergence of rap, inspiring Khalid's lifelong interest in making music.[1] Once a vibrant and racially integrated working-class neighborhood, the Bronx experienced decades of divestment from redlining and white flight. The neighborhood became infamous through an "epidemic" of burned-down buildings that stretched for entire blocks (fires were started by landlords to collect insurance money). Because the borough had largely been abandoned by the city government, gangs controlled the garbage-strewn streets and brought rampant crime, including a tripling of the murder rate. While his local school was "one of the most notoriously dangerous high schools in the Bronx, in the city really," Khalid showed great intellectual potential. He was awarded a full scholarship to an elite private school in the suburbs.

Khalid remembered having a "positive experience" at his private school. But he explained to me that what happened *outside* the classroom—especially in the home—powerfully shaped his class journey:

> Looking back, I thought because I was in the same school as these kids who are coming from more privileged backgrounds and getting the same education that I was going to have all the same opportunities. . . . I think that I had a false

sense that, "Okay, now I'm good, right?" I know there's obstacles and hurdles but I think, "Hey, look, I'm getting the same education, same classroom as these students." . . . I think it was only in retrospect that I realized that there was a whole bunch of other stuff that they were getting—had already gotten before they got there.

As Khalid moved between the streets of the Bronx and the elite suburbs, he came to realize he was navigating very different worlds. Despite sitting side by side in the classroom, his classmates had far more opportunities to help them succeed.

The two worlds that Khalid navigated reflected vastly different *class cultures*. These cultures include divergent beliefs, language, norms, behaviors, and values. Furthermore, these dimensions of class function as a specific set of cultural resources that prepared Khalid and his peers differently for making it in the world. Sociologists refer to these resources as *cultural capital*. They include skills, attitudes, manners of speech, and institutional knowledge (e.g., understanding the college admissions process, knowing the steps to complete a college degree, and knowing the appropriate clothing for a job interview) that help people manage different situations. Like economic resources, these cultural resources give some people advantages over others.

In this chapter, I will show differences in class-based culture and cultural capital. These differences begin with a child's upbringing and are reinforced through social networks and institutions. In contrast to working-class children, middle-class children are equipped with cultural resources that will overall better prepare them for success in school, college, and the professional workplace—although these vary in important ways by race as well. Khalid and other working-class children will eventually have to learn this cultural capital if they want to climb into the middle class. However, these advantages are not totalizing, and later chapters will show how working-class cultural capital can also be used in strategic ways.

How Our Parents Raise Us

When I asked Khalid what types of experiences his more privileged peers had outside of the classroom, his responses echoed the research on class and child-rearing. He talked of a "whole world of other things" such as travel, competitive sports, and parents who would talk about the businesses they owned. It reminded me of my time as a graduate student working on my PhD when I took a course titled Family and Class with renowned sociologist Annette Lareau. Among our readings were her most famous book, *Unequal Childhoods: Class, Race, and Family Life*, and the subsequent scholarship that built upon it.[2] By observing numerous families, Lareau found that middle-class parents (both white and Black) raised their children using different strategies than working-class and poor families.

Lareau argues that middle-class parents adopted a strategy she called *concerted cultivation* in which parents actively cultivate opportunities for their children. First, they organize daily life with a busy schedule of competitive sports and structured activities nearly every single day. The days are packed with swim and soccer practices, piano lessons, private tutoring sessions, school field trips, and more. While such schedules require a great deal of labor for the parents and sometimes add stress on the family, middle-class parents view these organized activities as helping to develop important skills. For example, children learn to effectively work as part of a team, manage their time, set and work toward goals, and practice interacting with adults and looking them in the eye. Second, middle-class parents speak with a broader vocabulary in the home and use more reasoning when speaking with their children. They are more likely to explain their reasoning for decisions with children ("Do this because it will help you learn X"). This helps children like Khalid's former classmates develop skills in using language to negotiate and construct arguments while building comfort in interacting with adults as authority figures. Third, middle-class parents (usually mothers) use their professional expertise to actively intervene in their children's interactions within institutions, such as schools and doctor's offices. For example, middle-class parents actively involve themselves in school while dealing with behavioral issues that would lead to less strict punishments,[3] acquire diagnoses and accommodations to help their children's learning,[4] and intervene in school conflicts to get their children more second chances.[5]

In contrast, working-class and poor parents like Khalid's mother use a child-rearing strategy Lareau termed *the accomplishment of natural growth*. This strategy involves providing children with love, food, and safety, expecting this approach will allow their children to grow and thrive. There is limited time in organized and structured activities because there is less cultural emphasis placed on their importance. Khalid's mother also explained to him: "This is really nice that you're making friends and they are able to take you places. But I can't really do that." She wanted him not to expect those "same experiences" because "she couldn't afford that." Instead, working-class children tend to spend more time (and build stronger ties) with extended family. Through "hanging out," children develop richer bonds with more family members, learn to be creative with informal play, and become resourceful in unstructured settings. On the other hand, they develop far fewer experiences in organized settings, remaining less familiar with the unwritten rules and norms that shape professional environments. Working-class and poor parents have less formal education and talk less with their children. A higher proportion of parent-child speech is directives for the children to do something ("do this because I said so"). Children learn to accept these directives, and it leads to less whining than in middle-class homes. But it establishes much clearer boundaries between adults and children. Children get less practice in using the language needed to navigate college and other professional settings—which will make it harder for these children to succeed in these environments. Finally, parents have less knowledge of how these institutions work. As a result, they are unlikely to intervene in school conflicts or medical appointments and rely more on the advice and decisions of professionals regarding their children.

While each of these different childrearing strategies has its own strengths, the strategies used by middle-class parents better equip their children to climb the class ladder. Khalid's classmates received advantages like spending significant time in organized activities with adults, being coached to reason and negotiate with parents and other authority figures, developing skills needed in the professional environment (e.g., working on a team), and broadening their vocabulary to be useful in these encounters. These forms of cultural capital are helpful to succeed in school and score higher on standardized tests. Children have models to draw upon for advocating for themselves to get second chances and later navigate the professional office. All this time spent with adults and authority figures also has important consequences for how children develop certain attitudes. Specifically, through a process of concerted cultivation, middle-class children were more likely to grow a *sense of entitlement*. This helps them feel that they are worth the time that adults spend with them and that it is legitimate to ask for things and get what they want. They are much more likely to have confidence and take action when going after their wants/needs.[6]

This sense of entitlement was unmistakable in a story relayed to me by Alfred Lubrano, author of *Limbo*. When I interviewed Al, he recounted a powerful memory from a journalism class where the professor regularly hosted "luminaries from the world of arts and journalism" as guest speakers. One day the head of *Time* magazine visited the class, and one of Al's classmates (a fellow sophomore) told their esteemed guest during the discussion, "Your magazine is only television. It's just television. You're not achieving anything." The student meant to dismiss the popular magazine by comparing it to what he believed to be a lower form of media. Al described being dumbfounded: "I was thunderstruck. I could not believe that a student could talk to such an accomplished person that way, but that anybody would have the sense of entitlement." He was intimidated by his classmate's audacious comment to someone of such high status. It "kicked off this incredible inferiority complex" and made him feel like he didn't belong. Similar to Lubrano, Khalid remarked that "I didn't develop a sense of entitlement" that he observed in his peers, which made it more difficult to advocate for himself.

In contrast to the middle class, working-class and poor children like Alfred Lubrano and Khalid are more likely to develop a *sense of constraint*. Lareau explains they have fewer opportunities to learn vocabulary, reasoning, or skills gained from organized formal settings, less opportunity to practice them with adults and authority figures, and tend to observe family members as more outwardly deferential to authority figures (even when they distrust these authority figures). On the one hand, allowing their children to grow naturally led to other positive outcomes, such as resourcefulness in informal play, stronger relationships with extended family, and greater respect shown to parents and other adults. On the other hand, given this sense of constraint, Khalid and other working-class children don't tend to have the same level of confidence in organized settings and don't aggressively pursue opportunities or actively advocate for themselves. These working-class strengths do not translate the same way into conventionally successful behaviors in college and professional settings. As a result, individuals from the working class will face more challenges as they move up the class hierarchy.

When I interviewed Marie, she explained that, in college, "I felt like the kids around me had grown up in professional career families, and I felt very out of place coming from a working-class family." This was exemplified by an exchange she had with a classmate. Marie recounted, "I said something about my dad not having a coat, a nice winter dress coat, overcoat." Her classmate responded, "Well, he wears one every day to work, doesn't he?" I was like, "My dad works in a paper mill." Marie was taken aback by "his assumption that every dad wears a suit and tie to work every day and in the winter has this nice, warm, button-up overcoat," whereas her "dad wears a uniform and comes home sweaty." Its effect was twofold. First, "At the time, I felt very intimidated that all of these kids around me grew up with parents who were accountants and lawyers and whatever." This sense of intimidation or inferiority leads working-class children to speak up less often and not advocate for themselves when needed. This sense of constraint means that they get fewer second chances and opportunities both as children and adults. Second, Marie internalized this feeling as being her own fault. Marie went on to say, "Now looking back on it, that was me doing that." She explained the event, not as a result of her class culture or the way that we are raised but in individual terms. American culture socializes us to view our successes and failures as a result of our individual efforts, not as being shaped by the systems of which we are a part. But still, she felt unsure of her interpretation, immediately adding, "But it was just a new experience for me being around kids that were different from where I had grown up. I don't know."

A variety of other factors also affect the cultural capital we develop growing up. By building on Lareau's groundbreaking work, a wide range of studies show how Black families and other families of color raise their children in different ways than white families.[7] For example, Khalid explains having developed cultural resources for navigating white America as a Black man. He and other children of color "become conscious of it because the adults around you and who are raising you are conscious of it." Like Khalid's mother, both working-class and middle-class Black parents help facilitate their children's racial identity, build their awareness that social spaces are racialized, and equip them with skills for navigating racial encounters.[8] There are further distinctions, such as middle-class parents of color with professional jobs using concerted cultivation to structure leisure time strategically to build a racial and ethnic identity that is distinct from both working-class families of color and white middle-class families.[9] In these instances, children learn racial and ethnic cultural capital that helps them navigate the social world.

Gender also shapes practices of concerted cultivation and the accomplishment of natural growth in the development of cultural capital. In general, parents using concerted cultivation invest more time and resources in girls than boys.[10] Black and Latine middle-class families specifically are more involved in their daughters' schooling than their sons' schooling. Gender further shapes the types of activities children do, with girls more likely to participate in music, drama, and art.[11] Boys are encouraged to participate more in sports and activity clubs (e.g., Boy Scouts vs. Girl Guides). Compared with working-class girls, working-class boys tend to be given more unstructured time with friends outside of school and spend more time playing video games. Together, these alter the ways that girls and boys of different classes and racial groups are raised and the cultural capital they develop. This is important for understanding the different cultural resources children acquire, which affects how well they might be able to navigate school, college, and the professional office.

While child-rearing strategies of concerted cultivation do disproportionately advantage middle-class children, working-class and poor children are able to acquire middle-class cultural capital through other means. For example, schools can support students in building their cultural capital by exposing them to new cultural experiences.[12] But it means that upwardly mobile working-class people have to play catch up—and working-class children of color have to learn middle-class cultural skills plus how to navigate the predominantly white middle-class world. Indeed, Khalid was able to do this to some degree through his private school education although he was clear that his private schooling was not sufficient relative to the middle-class cultural resources that his peers had acquired.[13] For many straddlers, much of the valued cultural capital they described obtaining was developed in college or later in life through work experience.

Finally, working-class children develop their own cultural resources that can be useful in upward mobility in their own ways and in certain contexts. This working-class cultural capital has not yet been explored in previous studies. In chapters 3 through 6, I will show the myriad ways in which upwardly mobile straddlers can strategically leverage working-class culture in professional contexts. This does not come close to leveling the playing field, but it does reveal unacknowledged strengths of a working-class upbringing—and how upwardly mobile straddlers can apply it to their professional work.

Building Our Sense of Self and Group Belonging

How we build our sense of self and others represents a fundamental part of human development: Who am I? And with whom do I belong? We can begin to answer these questions in many different ways, but our class and racial backgrounds have important influences on how we respond—even though we are often unaware of it. By building on the previous section on how we are raised, I will further explore how communication, language, and tastes reveal class differences in the way we build our sense of self and group membership. I will show how middle-class people learn and demonstrate a heightened sense of individuality and independence, while working-class people develop more pro-social attitudes. Members of all social classes start becoming more comfortable with people like themselves.

Middle-class people build a strong sense of individuality with a greater degree of *independence* from others. This is demonstrated by the classic studies of British sociologist Basil Bernstein, who observed how working-class and middle-class groups communicate their opinions on social issues like capital punishment.[14] For example, Bernstein observed that middle-class people often begin their sentences with "I think," as in, "I think the evidence shows that capital punishment is not actually a deterrent," or "I think, in crimes of passion, the offender is unlikely to be thinking about the future."[15] By beginning sentences with "I think," the speaker differentiates themselves from listeners, inviting debate (and "I think . . .") from others. It asserts their individuality, which helps them feel more comfortable standing out from others. It also encourages a precise and explicit use of language to identify points where people hold similar or different positions to display their individual abilities. This individual sense of self will become valuable in schools and professional offices, where people are encouraged to differentiate themselves, compete with others, and stand out.

Working-class people tend to orient themselves more toward others, which social scientists refer to as *interdependence*. Both their speech patterns and behavior reflect this interdependence. At the end of their sentences, Bernstein found working-class people are much more likely to add phrases such as "you know?" "wouldn't she?" or "isn't it?" For example, they voiced their opinions as, "Well, what if it was the wrong guy, you know?" or "Sometimes they find evidence later on that can change things, right?" In his study, not a single working-class person began a sentence with "I think." The effect of "you know?" or "wouldn't he?" invites agreement, often with nodding heads or an "mhmm." It makes the speaker feel more at ease. Rather than differentiate the speaker as an individual with an "I statement," it seeks to establish agreement within the group. These "we statements" build emotional connections among the speaker and others in the group. Experimental research findings support this conclusion that working-class behaviors are more focused on and tend to the needs of others.[16]

Other patterns of communication also establish different degrees of comfort within and across class lines. For example, middle-class groups tend to speak using more abstract terms, which are learned through formal schooling and professional work. Working-class groups tend to speak with more concrete terms. In one study, people were asked where they usually purchased candy.[17] A middle-class person most likely responded, "At a cashier's counter or in a grocery store" (an abstract location). A working-class person would be more likely to say a specific store, such as "at the National" (a specific, concrete location). In another study, "working-class people tended to make their points using examples, metaphors, and especially analogies," rather than abstract concepts.[18] It's not that working-class people are incapable of abstract thought or speech, but they have less practice with it, and it simply feels less natural to them. It is also a learned habit of speech, and working-class speech tends to have less vocabulary. Members of the working-class use more hand gestures, variations in tone and volume, and glances and are freer to speak in parallel with someone rather than waiting for them to explicitly finish their statement. These habits also shape who we are comfortable with (people who speak more similarly to us) and those whom we might be less comfortable with (people who speak differently and with words we don't understand). This can make it more difficult for upwardly mobile working-class people to find a sense of belonging at college or to relate to middle-class professionals at the office.

How we relate to others is deeply shaped by class belonging. In *Reading Classes: On Culture and Classism in America*, Barbara Jensen argues that working-class people have "a tendency toward peer relationships (where power is equal)" and "to shy away from hierarchical relationships."[19] For example, working-class "children play with other children," and "workers talk together when the supervisor isn't around." In these types of relationships, equality invites playful and relaxed human interaction. This type of interaction differs from "middle-class life, where negotiating across and within established hierarchies of power is common." It is not that middle-class people don't have concern for others or strong personal connections, but their sense of belongingness in a group is different. They are more likely to pursue status and value others based on their belongingness in higher-status groups. Working-class people are less likely to pursue social gatherings where they may spend time with those who have authority over them, whereas middle-class people tend to invite these opportunities. This can also make it more difficult for straddlers to develop ties to people above them who can help open doors for them.

Tastes such as the types of movies, clothing, food, music, and art that we enjoy also shape how we relate to others.[20] While some tastes are shared across classes (e.g., love of pizza and rock music), our class background influences many tastes. For example, middle- and upper-middle-class people value goods and activities as a means of expressing themselves, purchase comfortable but individualized and aesthetically appealing furniture, pursue leisure activities to learn new skills and competencies, and enjoy entertaining films and television but express more interest in the quality of the writing or acting.[21] They are more likely to enjoy abstract art, international travel, yoga, tennis, cycling, golf, craft beer, organic food, and international food, and to be vegetarian, listen to world music, and not be religious.[22] They spend heavily on home renovations where they express themselves with their individualized tastes and use of space.[23]

In contrast, working-class people tend to value goods and activities for their practicality, purchase comfortable and functional furniture, and pursue leisure activities for their intrinsic enjoyment. They enjoy films and television that feel "real,"[24] such as hit television crime and hospital dramas.[25] In general, they have more "localized" tastes,[26] such as pasta and food from their own ethnic group, music from their own ethnic group (e.g., hip-hop), casual clothes and workwear, and are also more likely to be Christian.[27] They are less likely to enjoy more "highbrow" tastes, such as classical music, live theater, and high fashion. While middle- and upper-middle class people have more "highbrow" tastes, research shows that they are often cultural omnivores who also have "middlebrow" and "lowbrow" tastes as well.[28]

Class-based differences in tastes affect how we connect with people and whether we feel welcomed and comfortable in social settings. People often gravitate toward what they know. Accordingly, if universities and professional offices are characterized by more middle-class tastes, people with those tastes may feel more welcomed there and develop a deeper sense of belonging. Middle-class people may have more in common with one another, thus forming stronger bonds with people who can help them get ahead. Working-class people trying to fit in at the office or getting to know a hiring manager in an interview may find they have less in common to establish a connection. An instructor, hiring manager, or supervisor may not perceive the person with whom they have less in common and a weaker connection to be as strong of a fit.

The patterns discussed here do reflect broad class differences in American society, but there is even more variation under the surface. Class cultures, especially working-class cultures, also differ in terms of race and ethnicity, region (e.g., Appalachia vs. New England), gender, sexuality, and urban vs. rural. There are particularly well-documented differences in working-class cultures for different racial and ethnic groups, especially among new migrants or foreign-born students. Many East Asian cultures, such as Japanese and Chinese, emphasize being an interdependent member of the family as most important for a sense of oneself.[29] Putting the community first and the individual second is also a defining feature of many cultures from Central and South America, Africa, and southern Europe.

What helps someone have a sense of working-class belonging within white Appalachian culture is not the same as what would feel at home in an urban Black culture. In one of the few studies of the cultural capital of marginalized groups, Prudence Carter examines the ways that Black working-class youths signal their status as "culturally competent African Americans."[30] This includes familiarity with hip-hop and R&B artists, codes of speech (e.g., "Where you at?" rather than "Where are you?"), and culturally relevant activities (e.g., "stepping"—a type of dance used to build solidarity in Black sororities and fraternities). Black youths use these tastes and codes to signal their identity and racial authenticity (and avoid being accused of both "acting white" and being "uppity"). Furthermore, it serves as a means of constructing "a coherent, positive self-image (or set of images) in the face of hardship and subjugation." Such diverse examples abound within working-class cultures, with further variation within and across Appalachian working-class cultures, working-class women, working-class lesbians and other sexual identities, immigrant groups, national contexts, and more.[31]

The term "bougie" illustrates this tension between individualistic and group-based culture. Bougie is a common term within Black culture, but it has become more popularized recently and its meaning continues to evolve. It is originally derived from the French word "bourgeoisie," which means middle class. Bougie must be understood, however, in the context of Black oppression within the United States. Because of centuries of continued racism against Black Americans and their need to fight against ongoing discrimination, racial solidarity has been an important value within the Black community. In contrast to this group orientation, some Black people have aspired to the financial success, higher status, and individualism of the dominant middle-class culture. Bougie emerged as a putdown to refer to upwardly mobile or wealthy Black people perceived as "uppity," materialistic, and thinking that they are better than others.[32] It is the idea that you are leaving your people, or your community, behind, as you pursue something more for yourself. Instead, many in the Black community encourage helping others around you by lifting up those among your racial group—the idea of "lifting as we climb."[33] This book promotes a similar ethic of lifting up one's class. It is the notion that as you climb the class ladder and do well for yourself, you can lift others up with you.

Values and Morality

When people think of culture, they frequently think about values and morality. Social scientists here are interested in how our class positions shape what we believe to constitute right from wrong or a good way of life, how people should or should not behave, and how it shapes our worldviews.[34] To better understand the straddler experience, I was interested how working-class values shape our sense of right and wrong as well as behaviors, and especially how it affects experiences integrating into middle-class culture.

The working-class values that my respondents identified included hard work, resilience, responsibility, integrity, practicality, straightforwardness, sincerity, authenticity, providing for one's family, humility, and doing whatever it takes to get a job done. Perhaps above any other value, they emphasized hard work, or a "tremendous work ethic," as one educational administrator described it to me. When I asked Khalid, now a training manager, he said, "I would say there's a resilience. I think that when you've had to come up having less, I think you can take less for granted. When you haven't had certain advantages, I think maybe you're not quite as devastated when things don't go your way because you don't expect things to always go your way. And you learn how to adapt . . . if you already know going in the system may be working against you. So there's all kinds of survival mechanisms that you learn." Similarly, Suzanne, a judge whom I interviewed, emphasized a "stick-to-it-ness whether it's committed to a relationship, committed to work, just that you take it seriously." Another professor said that "there's no job that's beneath you. If you want to put food on the table and a roof over your head, you have to work." Cody, who works in international development, noted, "I feel like in my blue-collar background, people are honest. They're brutally honest. They use humor a lot to mask the cut of the honesty." Sage, an external relations manager, shared that her colleagues started calling her "Swiss" because she was "like a Swiss Army knife. . . . You can get it all done. You're resourceful. You can make it happen."

Working-class values are part of a "disciplined self" that is needed to overcome the economic uncertainty and physical dangers associated with working-class lives and jobs.[35] This is how sociologist Michèle Lamont famously described morality from a class perspective through several books.[36] She notes that many working-class jobs do not pay wages sufficient to maintain basic needs because minimum wage laws have not kept up with inflation, and relentless efforts by business owners have made workers more replaceable (either by other workers, machines, or artificial intelligence). Unionized jobs provide significantly higher levels of security and pay, but American unions have been on the decline for decades. In comparison to other developed countries, a weak social safety net in the United States leaves workers to fend for themselves. Just as Khalid had to survive life on the streets of the Bronx, working-class and poor people live in poorer neighborhoods with higher levels of crime. All of these factors together make life more unpredictable and help to explain why workers stress values like responsibility, hard work, integrity, resilience, and providing for one's family. In the face of these challenges, working-class people explain persevering to "make it through," sometimes arguing that "being a survivor means a lot." These core moral values reflect a "disciplined self" that is part of Khalid's "survival mechanisms." As Lamont explains it, "They don't let go, they don't give up, and it's largely through work and responsibility that they assert control over uncertainty." They have a strong orientation to others, in part, because their everyday lives depend on it. With fewer financial resources, less physical space at both work and home, and fewer buffers from crime and undesirable people, their lives are shaped more by the actions of others. Middle-class people, by contrast, have more freedom to move neighborhoods, have more physical space at work and home, and can move jobs more easily.

In contrast, middle-class people value self-sufficiency, productivity,[37] self-actualization, socioeconomic achievement, flexibility, team orientation, and conflict avoidance.[38] Their emphasis on self-actualization is documented by Lamont's interview with Bob Wilson, a computer specialist from Indianapolis. Active in both sports and the arts, he values "people who are accomplishing things." He states he is more comfortable with people who move in the direction of self-actualization or "the ability to find a problem worth solving and solve it." People who emphasize self-actualization "have active and structured activities, their long-term goal being to develop their potential to its maximum: they play chess, learn a musical instrument, exercise, diet, go to the museum, get involved in the PTA, save the rain forest, take classes, and so forth." When asked about people they dislike, middle-class people "are more likely to point to people who 'are mediocre and don't develop their minds' (in the words of a labor arbitrator) . . . and who are 'not as successful' as they might be (hospital controller)." While an interest in self-actualization does appear among the working class, further research confirms it is emphasized significantly more among the middle class, who embrace therapy and schooling to accomplish it.[39] They also feel a greater need to pass these qualities on to their children and have far greater financial resources to explore intellectual curiosities, motivating their children to pursue more educational and career opportunities.

The middle class also puts much greater value on socioeconomic achievement. Lamont interviewed a radio station owner in New York who described it this way: "If I look at somebody, no matter what field they're in, and I think that they've done it successfully, I admire that because, somehow, they had a sense of direction that made them succeed." Lamont argued that her middle-class respondents were much more likely to equate "moral character" with success—that morality and financial achievement go hand in hand. While working-class people also appreciated how higher incomes could bring greater security and opportunity, they tended to separate financial success from moral worth, often rejecting the values they perceived to be held by those above them. Lamont quoted a firefighter who criticized "the suits" driving in their Jaguars to show off. A mechanic believed that professionals "power-play people. [They think] they're better than them.... I have no time for it all." Many (but certainly not all) in the working class view this emphasis on flashing one's wealth as a reflection of their snobbery, lack of sincerity, or competitiveness. Indeed, Lareau's research confirms that middle-class parents' childrearing values are more focused on achievement, ambition, and competitiveness.

Upwardly mobile straddlers I interviewed had mixed feelings about middle-class values and integrating into middle-class culture. Some of my respondents especially appreciated the middle-class value of self-actualization. For example, Katrina worked advising college students, and she stated her goal for her students "would be for them to be able to open up their horizon to wanting more." Katrina believed "sometimes students of low economic backgrounds ... kind of have a small-minded frame. I want them, through their interactions with me, to see the sky is the limit ... not just wanting to maintain, but to achieve greatness." Indeed, this focus on self-actualization, and the middle-class focus on socioeconomic achievement, can help one's ambition to achieve occupational and material success.

Many upwardly mobile straddlers often experience a clash of values when integrating into middle-class life. For example, adjusting to middle-class values like conflict avoidance can create difficulties for straddlers. Anthony was a researcher whom I interviewed, and his straightforwardness got him into trouble. In an interview, he explained, "At first, I found myself often in meetings or whatever, just blurting out what I thought." He found that did not go over well and that "you have to learn to engage in this kind of genteel middle-class dancing around the problem." Sydney, who works in career development, described a similar situation, adding, "We literally all know the problem. Why don't we just say it and then deal with it?" She griped that there was an issue in a staff meeting but instead of coming out and addressing it, "everyone just gossips about the person behind their back.... It's just very passive-aggressive," which she equated with being a "middle-class" thing. She added, "It hinders productivity too." Similarly, Lamont found that an upwardly mobile data manager in New York explained that his superiors perceived his straightforwardness as "intense" and "aggressive," so he had to learn "to be a team player." This shift meant that "I've learned to let other people take the credit for [the] solution.... The advantage from my personal point of view is not to be disliked by others. If you're disliked, I think you're not going to do as well." A banker on Wall Street explained that he "always felt pressured [to be a yes-man]." For the working class, these moments at work can be perceived as insincerity, being "fake," or "two-faced." However, for the middle class, these values are viewed as necessary for meeting goals and professional accomplishment.

Of course, such values are further shaped by other factors, including racial differences. While workers in Lamont's study were generally interested in helping others, white workers most often expressed this through interpersonal altruism, such as helping family, community, or neighbors. In part because of their experiences with racial discrimination, Black workers expressed these prosocial values more as collective solidarity. This collective solidarity was learned through the Black church, a central institution in Black life and culture—as demonstrated by their higher emphasis on religious participation. Workers who were in labor unions were also more likely to emphasize class solidarity. However, the steady decline of unions has meant that white workers are less likely to learn collective solidarity through union rhetoric, thus leaving them with more individualistic expressions of helping others.[40] In that vein, Black workers are more willing than white workers to call out mistreatment and exploitation in the workplace or to believe that profits come at the expense of workers.

Finally, one other class difference in values represents a moral difference related to forms of inequality. Specifically, research shows that the working class tends to place higher emphasis on traditional morality, religion, and the military.[41] As Lamont describes it, "High school graduates generally uphold more rigid moral norms than college graduates: they are less supportive of freedom of choice and self-expression," and "their child-rearing values can also be described as more rigid." These traditional moral values span views on divorce, abortion, gender roles, and very tough positions on crime and drugs.

For the poor and working class, whose lives are more insecure and uncertain (and exposure to crime and violence is higher), holding strong and often uncompromising moral positions is a strategy for asserting control. Religious and military institutions offer a stable footing with a clear view of the world amid instability. But it can also mean they hold more conservative views on sexuality and gender norms and are somewhat more wary of social changes brought about by immigration. When these views of traditional morality combine with common racist, anti-immigrant, sexist, homophobic, and/or transphobic social messaging, they can bolster feelings of righteousness in times of change and be used to keep others down. While many in the middle class also hold traditional moral positions, their experiences in college, travel, and other activities help expose them to other forms of human experience and diversity. Accordingly, the middle class tends to be somewhat more open and pragmatic in these particular values. They are more likely to adjust such values to different contexts and experiences and to be more open to such views or experimentation within their children.

How Class Culture Shapes Social Mobility

There is nothing inherently better about middle-class cultures or working-class cultures (see Table 1 for a summary of class cultures). But the culture that we are socialized into has significant impacts on the people we become and can affect where we end up in life. First, we tend to develop a comfort with the

Table 1
Summary of Class Culture Differences

	Working-class culture	Middle-class culture
Organization of daily life	Emphasis on time with family and extended family; more unstructured time "hanging out"; limited time in structured activities	A busy daily schedule of organized and structured activities; children more involved in competitive sports
Language and communication	Communicate using fewer words, more gestures, and implied meanings; speak more with concrete examples, metaphors, and analogies; a higher proportion of parent-child interactions involve directives	Broader vocabulary used at home; speak more in generalizations and abstractions; a higher proportion of parent-child interactions communicate the reasoning involved
Predominant attitudes	Sense of constraint that is dependent on institutions and the decisions of experts; less likely to self-advocate and negotiate with experts	A sense of entitlement helps them view themselves as worthy of attention and advocate for themselves; more likely to negotiate for what they want
Sense of self	The individual is a member of the group, and the self should be aligned with group belonging	Strong sense of the individual self, which is to be actively cultivated
Group engagement	Tend toward group settings with peers and equals; less comfortable interacting with people of higher status	Group settings often involve members of different statuses; more comfortable interacting across status hierarchies
Examples of typical tastes	Value goods and activities for their practicality; pursue leisure activities for their intrinsic enjoyment; prefer functional furniture; enjoy hit TV crime and hospital dramas, pasta and food from their own ethnic group, casual clothes and workwear, and music from their own ethnic group	Value goods and activities for the means of expressing oneself; pursue leisure activities to learn new skills; prefer aesthetically appealing furniture; enjoy abstract art, international travel, yoga, tennis, cycling, golf, craft beer, organic food, international food, and listening to world music
Dominant values	Hard work, resilience, responsibility, integrity, practicality, straightforwardness, sincerity, authenticity, providing for one's family, humility	Self-actualization, productivity, socioeconomic achievement, flexibility, a team orientation, conflict avoidance
Durability of values	Relatively more rigid norms and values	Relatively more likely to adjust values to different contexts

culture we are socialized into, and it just feels more natural or better to us. Second, the institutions most responsible for socioeconomic advancement—specifically educational settings and professional workplaces—are much more characterized by middle-class culture.[42] Indeed, elites intentionally promote their own cultural norms and tastes in these institutions to preserve their own advantages.[43]

Because the institutions of upward mobility are dominated by middle-class culture, these institutions favor and reward those people for whom middle-class culture feels more natural. Skills associated with organized activities, a broader vocabulary, an ability to reason and assert your position, confidence and a sense of entitlement for going after what you want, prioritizing individual achievement, advocating effectively for yourself, and middle-class tastes—these are all examples of cultural resources, or cultural capital. If middle-class children have been practicing these behaviors, developing these attitudes, acquiring these tastes, and adopting these values for their entire lives, it can make it easier for them to "fit in" and excel in middle-class environments. On the other side, it can make the process more difficult for the working class and poor to climb the class ladder or fit into their new environments. Chapter 2 explores this cultural mismatch.

There are also numerous positive elements of working-class culture. Many people from this class think it is very important to establish less competitive relationships with siblings, develop more connections to extended family, enable children time to simply be kids with unstructured time, defer to adults, prioritize the group over individual ambition, maintain personal integrity, and communicate in a straightforward and direct manner. Indeed, these cultural resources can help poor and working-class people thrive in their communities. But these cultural norms do not carry over into college and the professional environment in the same way. We will explore these challenges in the next chapter, but wanting to help family while away at college can make it harder to focus on classes, and a sense of constraint with authority figures might lead a working-class student to avoid standing out. Being straightforward in a professional office might get you labeled a troublemaker, whereas other middle-class people are seeking to avoid conflict.

It is also important to remember that these cultural resources are based on tendencies and are not all-or-nothing, and they can change over time.[44] It is not that working-class people do not value socioeconomic achievement and self-actualization at all. In fact, a quarter of the working-class people in Lamont's study fully embraced middle-class values.[45] The dominant (middle-class) culture is something by which they too are shaped. But in general, working-class people are more likely to adhere to one set of cultural norms, values, attitudes, and tastes; middle-class people are more likely to adhere to another set. Just like the people in the studies cited above, readers may find that different cultural elements resonate with them but that they tend toward one group or the other.

So what does this mean for how we experience cultural conflicts? How might it shape our attitudes toward our roots and our means for doing well and living a meaningful life? As we continue to explore these tensions, we will also learn about the moments when these norms get flipped on their head. The people I spoke with had to become fluent in middle-class culture, but they also drew on their working-class cultural resources to be successful in their professional work.

2

Classism and Cultural Mismatches Faced by Upwardly Mobile Working-Class People

I asked April when she became aware of class differences for the first time, and she recounted a vivid example from her sixth-grade English class. April identified herself as a writer having "worked very hard" on a poem, copying it over and over in her "best printing." April proudly brought it to her teacher. Her teacher "looked at it, then she looked at me, and then she looked at it" and asked, "Can you stay after school?" April's "heart was jumping with joy." She believed the English teacher was "going to realize I'm a poet and she'll give me some help!" But when they met, the teacher asked her, "Who wrote this poem? April, you're a very nice little girl. Sometimes though we read somebody else's words and they mean so much to us that we take them. Who wrote this poem?" April told me that she was feeling "angry and humiliated." When April confirmed she wrote the poem and then pulled out her notebook to "show her my drafts," the teacher turned "bright red." The next words out of her mouth were, "I'm so sorry. I thought you took someone else's words." But then the teacher told April something she would never forget: "I know you went to Conger," which was the working-class elementary school. "And we don't expect work like this from students who come from Conger. So, you will have to work harder because we just know most of you are not as able."

In that moment, April said "class differences" hit her "right in the face. And it never ever left me." It became clear that teachers expected less of working-class students like her, as well as students of color. Those teachers often misunderstood students' behavior and abilities, just as April's teacher misinterpreted her writing for plagiarism. The consequences are often severe. April observed that poor and working-class students, and students of color, frequently received harsh penalties and often "got dismissed" from her school. But she saw that when something went wrong for the middle-class students, they "didn't get dismissed" but instead got second chances. Guided by their own middle-class culture, teachers and administrators treated students differently because of their class.

Working-class students often experience classism and cultural mismatches as they navigate schools and professional workplaces. These settings are dominated by middle-class culture so those from the middle-class will fit in more naturally into the norms and expectations placed on them by teachers, professors, and managers in charge of hiring and promotion. But working-class first-gen students like April often encounter *classism*. Classism refers to the myths and beliefs that "working-class cultures and people are inherently inferior."[1] It is the notion that poor and working-class people deserve to be at the bottom because of something wrong with them, such as not working hard enough or being incapable of good work.

Furthermore, upwardly mobile people socialized into working-class culture can experience a *cultural mismatch* between their upbringing and the demands placed upon them in schools and professional offices.[2] Not only do working-class students have to learn academic knowledge to succeed, but they must also learn middle-class culture—an invisible and unspoken set of cultural norms, rules, values, and behaviors. If they do graduate and enter professional occupations, cultural mismatches can continue to make it harder to fit in at work or get promoted. This chapter explores the classism and cultural mismatches that upwardly mobile working-class people face. The following chapters will then reveal how first-gen graduates who make it through can flip the script by leveraging their working-class cultural capital as strengths for the professional world.

Unequal Schools and the Hidden Curriculum

If you could have any one or two pieces of information to predict a child's academic success, what would it be? Decades of research show us that the best predictors of a child's academic performance are actually their parents' income and education.[3] Children from families higher on the class ladder will, on average, be awarded higher grades, attain higher degrees, obtain more stable jobs, and earn higher incomes.[4] Furthermore, the gap in academic achievement between high- and low-income families has actually increased over the last several decades.

There are many reasons explaining differences in educational outcomes. For starters, rich kids attend rich schools and poor kids attend poor schools. The United States is unique among wealthy countries in how it funds schools, with the majority of school funding coming from local property taxes. This funding structure means that if a neighborhood has big, expensive homes, the local schools will receive much more in school funding than poorer neighborhoods. On average, high-spending school districts spend two to three times more per pupil than low-spending districts.[5] But the extremes are staggering: The top 10 percent of school districts spend *ten times* more than the bottom 10 percent. Children of color fare worse at every level as well. As a result, wealthier (and whiter) school districts can attract better teachers with higher pay and better working conditions, afford better academic facilities and technology, stock better libraries, pay additional support staff, and offer more college-level courses. In contrast to this American funding model, nearly all other industrialized countries fund schools more evenly.

There is another set of cultural factors that affect educational inequalities, which relates more closely to this book's focus on class cultures. An important concept here is the *hidden curriculum*.[6] The hidden curriculum refers to the values, dispositions, attitudes, social expectations, and behavioral expectations that schools have for students but that are not usually communicated. In other words, teachers and administrators have certain rules for running classrooms and for rewarding and punishing student behaviors. Students are expected to know these cultural rules, expectations, and norms—which are not explicitly taught and which most closely align with middle-class (and white) culture. Teachers and administrators, who tend to come from white middle-class backgrounds, are often not even aware of their class-based cultural expectations. As a result, they inadvertently end up rewarding students with middle-class cultural capital, increasing the likelihood of their educational success. In contrast, there is a cultural mismatch for working-class students. Their behaviors are often misinterpreted, they do not get the attention they need, may become frustrated, and have a harder time succeeding in school.

There has been a tremendous amount of research on this cultural mismatch and the hidden curriculum in primary, secondary, and higher education. It shows how class-based culture significantly affects social mobility and our pathways through life. In this chapter, I will illustrate how class culture shapes these experiences with stories from my respondents and classic studies from the field.

The Cultural Norms and Values of Schools

When April and other working-class children attend their local school, they experience it differently than middle-class children. This is, in part, because cultural norms and values held by schools better match middle-class culture.[7]

The hidden curriculum, in which cultural values, dispositions, attitudes, and expectations are embedded, is well illustrated in a series of books by Shirley Heath.[8] Heath spent ten years living in and studying three communities in the Southeastern United States. First, there was a middle-class community of both Black and white "mainstream townspeople," which she referred to as "Laurenceville." Second, a rural Black working-class community was dubbed "Trackton." Finally, a rural white working-class community was called "Roadville." Heath observed children in and out of elementary school and saw very different patterns across them.

In the middle-class community of Laurenceville, parents socialized their children with a set of skills and behaviors that prepared them well for the norms of their schools. For example, both Black and white middle-class parents read to their children from very early ages—usually by six months old. Parents asked "what" questions about images in the books and encouraged their children to explore connections between images and real-world objects. As the children got older, parents added their own commentaries and encouraged their children to do the same. Parents taught their children to be comfortable with printed text, to ask questions frequently, to interact as conversation partners, and to elaborate their own responses. In preschool, children would engage with "listen-and-wait" book reading and storytelling. They learned social behaviors for when to listen and when it is "appropriate" to comment and discuss. These activities helped them transfer these skills to the school environment, where such behaviors would feel natural to them. These skills are also very consistent with the parenting of concerted cultivation, where parents actively cultivate their children's skills and advocate for their children, as found in Annette Lareau's research from the previous chapter.[9] As Barbara Jensen described it, "finding familiar language, teaching methods, and rules of interaction in school enables middle-class children to feel they belong there and that school is there to help them."[10]

In the Black working-class community of Trackton, interactions at home and between teachers and students were very different. Black children were regularly in the company of older children and adults, who did not dumb down their conversations or ask children to state the obvious. Instead, children learned to speak by proactively joining a conversation and speaking clearly and entertaining enough to get adults' attention. Young boys would often receive appreciative hoots when doing something entertaining and learned that jumping into a conversation was encouraged rather than simply "waiting their turn." Girls created complicated and constantly evolving rhymes. Through such interactions, boys and girls learned to read the nonverbal reactions and emotional tones of others, developing empathy and emotional intelligence. They learned complex verbal language, sometimes as a part of Black culture or their own invented language, but these forms of communication did not match the norms of elementary school environments.

In Trackton, when a teacher would announce "Story time!" Black and white middle-class children would immediately understand how to arrange and conduct themselves for listening and discussion periods. But Black working-class children did not understand the norms and had difficulty interpreting the periods of silence, not having the physical or emotional cues to read the situation. When children were playing with toys at school, the teacher would ask, "What do we do with things when we are done with them?" and children were expected to know to put them away and where they go. But among the Black working-class children, material scarcity and smaller housing meant children had fewer store-bought toys and a different relationship with them. There was a strong cultural value placed on caring and sharing, socializing them to place people over things. With far fewer toys and less space at home, they were not used to such instructions. The children often seemed confused by such commands, and when they did not comply in the way the teacher expected, this was interpreted as disobeying. A common complaint from teachers was that the children had poor manners, and the students were perceived as lacking intelligence, ambition, or cooperation. But such interpretations were through a middle-class white lens and missing an awareness of how class and racialized culture affected it.

The white working-class school in Roadville was most similar to the elementary school that April attended. At Roadville, children learned to defer to their elders and not talk back. They were raised to say things "right," or the way things had always been done. In contrast to the Black church in Trackton (which was full of creativity, spontaneity, and emotion), churchgoers were taught to literally follow the Bible. Taken together, these emphases promoted respect for others and a clear sense of right and wrong, but one that was more about absolute truths and black-and-white thinking. Early in elementary school, teachers interpreted such behavior as cooperative and able.

Over time, the behaviors that working-class Roadville children learned as normal increasingly diverged from the hidden cultural expectations of their teachers. Increasingly, teachers expected children to express creativity on assignments and elaborate on their responses. By the fifth grade, teachers asked fewer "what" questions about recalling information and more "what if" questions requiring more creativity. Their sense of a clear right answer was less appropriate as the curriculum became more complex. In Heath's study, teachers regularly expressed frustration that working-class students lacked imagination and initiative, often giving "minimal answers." But the children were doing what their culture socialized them for in finding the right answer and not talking back. Like April and her classmates, they encountered classism and were perceived as less capable or unintelligent. By the time the children reached high school, requiring more interpretive knowledge, they too would likely feel more out of place.

Teachers also reward children who ask for help and advocate for themselves, which further advantages middle-class students. This is well illustrated by a study from Jessica Calarco, who spent two years observing working-class and middle-class children in an elementary school classroom.[11] She recounts a time observing students working on a math problem when the teacher, Ms. Dunham, made her way around the room to check on students. She stopped next to the desk of Jesse, a white working-class student. Ms. Dunham sensed Jesse's frustration and asked Jesse if he was OK. Calarco noted "Jesse looked up sheepishly," pointed to a question, hesitated, and "then admitted quietly, 'I don't get this one.'" The teacher "gave Jesse a quick explanation," but Jesse still appeared confused. Ms. Dunham did not seem to notice and focused her attention on Ellen, a "tall, middle-class, white student" across the room. Ellen was "waving her hand in the air and calling out in a loud whisper, "Ms. Dunham! . . . What does number five mean?" When the teacher provided Ellen with the same brief explanation, Ellen asked, "Wait, but does that mean we're supposed to multiply?" This query prompted Ms. Dunham to help Ellen with a longer and more detailed response. The teacher stayed alongside Ellen as she worked through the problem, providing feedback and a big smile when Ellen completed it successfully. Meanwhile, Jesse continued to struggle, slumped in his chair, and eventually skipped the question.

In this case, Jesse and Ellen appeared nearly identical academically: They had similar standardized test scores and the same placement for math ability. But Jesse was reluctant to ask for help. As Calarco observed, the parents of working-class kids like Jesse teach their children "to take responsibility for their own success in school and to avoid burdening teachers with requests for support." Ellen, however, was quick to seek further help through follow-up questions. Like the middle-class families from Lareau's research, Ellen and other middle-class students are taught that it is "the teachers' job to help them succeed." As a result, she ultimately received more assistance from her teachers, with dramatically different outcomes. As Calarco describes it, she "regularly saw middle-class students overcome problems that stymied their working-class peers." Middle-class children are advantaged because their behavior is a better cultural match for the expectations of the school environment. As I will show in subsequent chapters, educators possessing working-class cultural capital are equipped with resources that can be used to help translate these expectations and better support working-class students in such circumstances.

Different Curriculums and Expectations

As illustrated by April's story that opened this chapter, class-based culture shapes expectations that teachers, administrators, and their schools have for students. For example, teachers systematically underestimate the capabilities of working-class students and students of color,[12] offer them lower-quality instructional learning opportunities,[13] and discipline them more harshly.[14] These expectations affect what students are taught, how they are taught it, and how their lack of understanding or behavior might be addressed. Jean Anyon's work, further illustrates these tensions when she studied the learning expectations and curriculum at five different public schools.[15] She observed second and fifth grades at two working-class schools, a middle-class school, an upper-middle-class school, and an upper-class school.

At working-class schools, fifth-grade curriculums focus on memorization and obedience. Teachers expect students to copy notes from a chalkboard; textbook questions have a single right answer; and the knowledge communicated is based on memorizing facts. There are very few "what if" questions. Teachers do not prompt students to provide interpretation or meaning, and facts are not applied to students' lives. There is little, if any, learning that challenges how students make sense of the world. If students do not follow instructions exactly, teachers punish them. In one instance, students were asked to make a grid in a specific way. A girl developed a more efficient way to make the grid, but the teacher scolded her and required her to do it over again without telling the student why she had to do it that certain way. Teachers appeared more focused on controlling the classroom, including rules prohibiting students from leaving their desks without permission and students being told to "shut up." When Anyon asked a second-grade teacher what was important knowledge for her students, the teacher explained that "we try to keep them busy." Many teachers and administrators talked negatively about the students, such as one teacher stating, "I hate to categorize them but they're *lazy*." When a new teacher expressed worry about her teaching, a principal told her, "Just do your best. If they learn to add and subtract, that's a bonus. If not, don't worry about it." As a result, Anyon observes that many students often exhibit resistance at school, develop behaviors to amuse themselves, and feel resentful toward teachers and the school.

Anyon's second school was a mostly middle-class school. Students again learn there is a single right answer, but they have to evaluate choices and reason through problems to arrive at the correct answer. Compared to the working-class schools, teachers are more likely to explain assignments and the steps for solving a problem. While students are also taught obedience, teachers express more concern for students understanding what they read. For example, a teacher stated, "I think that's more important than skills, although they're important, too. But if they don't understand what they read, they won't know anything." This understanding also extends to learning not just facts but abstract concepts that can be generalized to new scenarios. However, controversial topics such as workers' strikes are often avoided because teachers are concerned that parents would complain. Nonetheless, this curriculum makes students more interested in learning and in their grades, viewing school as important for going to college and obtaining a good job. As opposed to the resistance in the working-class school, students are left with more of a sense of possibility.

While this book focuses on the differences between working-class and middle-class cultures, the curriculums that Anyon found in the upper-middle-class and "executive elite" schools are even more telling. In upper-middle-class schools, academic work is more creative, enabling individual expression and permitting a range of options for completing assignments. Rather than memorizing facts, teachers encourage students to approach learning as discovery, making connections between ideas and applying concepts to their own lives. In the fifth grade, assignments include developing plays, writing editorials about issues taken up by the school board, and painting murals depicting "the division of labor in ancient societies." In the "executive elite" school, children in fifth grade are already learning to analyze complex ideas. Teachers place the highest expectations on them to work harder and produce more. In both schools, children can come and go as they please as long as they note it on the chalkboard. When students misbehave, the teacher reasons through what happened and often leaves it up to the students what they should do as a result. Students learn about racism and class conflict and are taught to care about social issues but internalize a deep sense of individualism. They are also trained that our system's class divisions and distribution of economic power are "natural." For example, students learned texts that argued "rule by the ignorant and easily swayed lower classes led to grave errors . . . when 'common men' became leaders of Athens: the rationality, direction, and sensible restraint . . . suddenly evaporated."

This sharp contrast in school experiences helps shine a light on additional dimensions of the hidden curriculum. Working-class children aren't only missing out on advanced skills because they are learning rote memorization of facts. In classrooms and schools where obedience is paramount, they are also implicitly learning about hierarchical authority and accepting their place at the bottom.[16] Teachers further instruct students to follow the rules, conform to standardized ways of doing things, and not push back. These dimensions prepare them not for college but for low-level jobs where they are expected to take orders from the boss. For those hoping for more, it deepens the cultural mismatch they will face in college and the professional world. In contrast, the higher up students go on the class ladder, the more teachers treat them as equals in the learning process, build their confidence, and prepare them for more advanced academic work, and the more students learn to take on leadership roles. In addition to learning higher-order skills, they internalize a drive to achieve and a sense of their natural place at the top of that hierarchy.

These divergent expectations and curriculums also send hidden messages about the social order and students' place within it. April's story at the beginning of this chapter about how her teacher misidentified her writing as plagiarism showed how these expectations can lead to dramatically different outcomes. I also interviewed Kinsley, who had a teacher tell her she "would never amount to anything" and that she "would end up living off the system."

Students can then internalize these classist messages in a "self-fulfilling prophecy," which affects their attitudes about their own future and place in the world.[17] No schools teach students about the existence of class cultures, let alone the positive dimensions of working-class culture. Instead, they learn to accept the existing class system, with its highly uneven distribution of economic resources, as natural. Meanwhile, students in more affluent schools learn to name classes and to understand some elements of class conflict. They also learn to internalize a sense that they will do great things and rightly climb into positions of power, to which they are entitled.

The curriculums that students learn send other cultural messages about how society should operate and what their role is within it. In addition to systems of class, numerous studies have documented how top-selling school textbooks distort history, encouraging students to adopt an uncritical and blindly patriotic perspective of the United States.[18] Similar studies have shown how the hidden curriculum reproduces dominant ideas about race, gender, and sexuality, and how these systems intersect.[19] As such, the hidden curriculum often teaches students to accept the world as it is, obscuring systems of oppression and reproducing inequality.

In summary, studies show that schools offer very different curriculums and have contrasting expectations for middle-class and working-class children, as well as for children from other marginalized backgrounds. Middle-class children whose behaviors, beliefs, and attitudes are more aligned with middle-class norms are more trusted by their teachers and pushed to excel. Teachers help children develop a belief in their own potential and reinforce their sense of entitlement as they internalize a feeling that they are poised to be at, or climb to, the top. The skills they are developing align well with skills that will be needed for college and professional life. In contrast, teachers expect much less of working-class children. Without an understanding of their behaviors and attitudes through a working-class lens, teachers mislabel student behaviors as rude or uncooperative and subsequently discriminate against working-class children. They focus more on discipline and offer a less intellectually challenging curriculum. Teachers' expectations make it more difficult for children to develop a sense of belonging or view themselves as able. The curriculum prepares them for less advanced work, encouraging acceptance of their natural place at the bottom of the hierarchy, and deepens the cultural mismatch they experience.

Higher Education

While poorly funded schools, the hidden curriculum, classist teachers, and cultural mismatches can turn some poor and working-class students away from education, many of them continue striving for college. But the hurdles these students face mean they have far lower college attendance rates than their middle-class peers. Recent statistics show that the percentage of high school graduates enrolled in college varies significantly by income.[20] It ranges from the lowest quartile (60 percent) to the second (66 percent), third (76 percent), and fourth quartile (84 percent). These gaps also reflect little change since 2000. In the middle class, higher education is simply expected, and students have fewer barriers to getting to college.

For working-class students who do seek to go to college, there is a new library of cultural knowledge that is needed for the journey. It begins with how to select and apply for college. It can help to know the many different types of colleges (e.g., community colleges, public four-year institutions, private and public liberal arts colleges, online colleges, for-profit colleges, and Ivy League colleges) and the opportunities associated with them. It helps to know how to complete the Free Application for Federal Student Aid (FAFSA) and how financial aid works. If you don't have people within your family who have gone to college or know how to differentiate educational institutions from one another, the process can be daunting. Most of the people in my study chose colleges based on their proximity to home to be closer to a support network and have cheaper travel costs. They often made choices based on perceived cost, not truly understanding how much financial aid is available or how it works. Middle-class families who have attended college, often attaining advanced degrees, are in a much better position to coach their children and other family members on this process and make it work for them.

College and the Hidden Curriculum

Even for those first-gen working-class students who do make it to college, they face another hidden curriculum. Institutions of higher education, including their professors and staff, have their own values, dispositions, attitudes, social expectations, and behavioral expectations for students. Students need additional cultural capital to navigate these settings and relationships effectively. Again, those who have been socialized into middle-class culture are at an advantage. Working-class first-generation students have a more difficult time translating their cultural skills to the new environment, which perpetuates this cultural mismatch.

Academic skills and strategies (e.g., time management and study skills) for being a successful student are sometimes part of the formal curriculum and made explicit, but they are often assumed. In her discussion of the hidden curriculum of higher education, Buffy Smith quoted an Asian-American working-class first-gen student as saying, "You can't just come [to college] and just think that you are going to do all of your homework . . . and think you are going to just be social, so you need to find the balance between both of those. And, most people never do [*laughter*], you are either one or the other and it's real hard."[21]

Similarly, many of my students from all backgrounds—but especially first-gen working-class students—struggle with time management. A significant class difference is that middle-class students have been more likely to have been raised to practice these skills at an earlier age. The practice of concerted cultivation and its hectic schedules put children in situations where they need to juggle more formal activities. Middle-class parents model strategies for time management and are more likely to explicitly coach their children on how to prioritize their time, strategies for selecting which tasks to focus on, and how to allocate time across academic and social activities. Relatedly, middle-class children are more likely to have learned effective study skills. Because they come from more demanding schools with higher-quality teachers, and with more academic support at home, they have often learned strategies for learning and demonstrating academic content.

In higher education, classes are often organized into discussion-style seminars, which have their own culture of engagement. The subject matter becomes increasingly complex with no single right answer, and in many disciplines, students are expected to reason their way through it in class discussions. Here again, middle-class students will have practiced verbal and reasoning skills more at home with their college-educated parents. In higher ed, students are increasingly expected to form their own views, even respectfully disagreeing with one another or the instructor.[22] For some working-class students, this type of disagreement can feel unnatural. Working-class students are more likely to defer to professors and other authority figures and perceive that challenging their professors would appear disrespectful. Working-class culture tends toward building agreement with the group, and it can clash with the more individualistically oriented culture of the college classroom.

Students will inevitably encounter difficulties in college. For working-class students, their understanding that things don't come easily can help give them the drive to work hard and be resilient. But this can be a double-edged sword because they are less likely to ask for help and therefore may not get support in responding to difficulty. Working-class students are more likely to be intimidated by authority figures like professors, believe that they are burdening others,[23] feel judged by others for asking for help, and expect that life will be hard and that they simply have to carry on and get by. By not asking for help, they may not acquire the institutional knowledge about which resources are available for support. This can lead to heightened stress and lower academic performance.[24] In contrast, middle-class students are more likely to expect that professors are there to help them, ask for support, and receive coaching from parents about how to pursue that support. When a student receives a low grade on an assignment or exam, middle-class students are more likely to have the confidence to discuss low grades with professors, understand the norms for doing so, and feel entitled to sometimes challenge a low grade.

Working-class students are also less likely to have the institutional knowledge to navigate the college environment. In one of my interviews, Sen. Nina Turner explained, "I didn't have a road map because nobody in my family had [gone] to college." Terms like "bursar," "registrar," and "expected family contribution" can feel like a foreign language. If a student cannot afford to pay their tuition bill, is struggling academically, or is seeking paid work on campus, they may have a difficult time navigating the various campus offices or knowing the correct questions to ask. It is no surprise then that first-gen students are less likely to use academic advising and academic support services. One study found that among first-year first-generation students, 55 percent used academic advising and 30 percent academic support, whereas among continuing-generation students, 72 percent used academic advising and 37 percent academic support.[25] Middle-class and continuing-generation students are also more likely to get such support from family members.

Not only are students expected to utilize those resources, but the hidden curriculum demands the development of networks that include professors, administrators, and peers. While it may be reasonable to expect that network building would come naturally to group-oriented working-class students, professional networks have distinctive qualities. They are laden with hierarchical relationships and unequal levels of authority—which are often avoided in working-class life. Some of my students perceive "networking" to be a dirty word, and it feels inauthentic to them. When working with these students, I discuss networking as an opportunity to meet people who have similar interests, which truly can be enjoyable. Kinsley, a fellow educator I interviewed, described needing "a network of caring professionals" to help lift up students. For those students who do develop closer relationships with their professors, administrators, and college staff, they will inevitably have more opportunities available to them. They are more likely to be offered research opportunities, learn about internships, receive strong letters of recommendation, and ultimately obtain the careers that they desire.

Imposter Syndrome and the Fear of Failure

Certain dispositions or attitudes, such as self-confidence, are also forms of cultural capital that contribute to student and professional success.[26] But as a college professor, I see so many students struggle—perhaps above all else—with a fear of failure. This impacts first-gen students more than their middle-class peers. When I interviewed Katie, who worked a variety of working-class jobs before attending college, she described her struggle with self-confidence:

> I think with my academic career at college, it was like a mental battle—the whole thing. Because number one, I don't think my self-esteem was such at the time where I felt confident in my abilities because never in my life had they

even been recognized as far as any type of academic success or intellectual achievements. It was almost like I expected failure around every turn. I studied like crazy because I thought I was going to fail. Every exam was do or die for me because I thought I was going to fail. I didn't want to go back. I didn't want to go back to working at the front desk of the hotel or taking personal ads. I really wanted to move forward.

Katie's "mental battle" was full of self-doubts and regularly questioning whether she was good enough. She was constantly on the edge emotionally.

Self-confidence is important because it can help motivate students and empower them to take action and follow through on their work. College and professional workplaces are often highly competitive and built on a middle-class norm of individual accomplishment.[27] Students who are fearful that they cannot meet expectations or perform at a certain level can become disengaged or have difficulty completing their work. When the fear drives them to work harder, as it did for Katie, they might adopt inefficient work habits. Hard work is necessary, but as the popular phrase goes, one should "work smarter, not harder." Without confidence, students may avoid asking for help and thus not know how to work smarter with better time management, effective study skills, and so on.

A lack of self-confidence can also lead to imposter syndrome, or a sense that one does not have a "right" to be in college or that they don't belong. Both middle-class and working-class students can experience imposter syndrome but in uneven ways. Because middle-class children are raised with a deeper sense of individuality, place greater value on accomplishment, and have their identity anchored in individual achievement, they can feel an especially strong pressure to perform at a high level. Students who have a strong support network and their identities tied to the group (as working-class students are more likely to do) may be less obsessed with demonstrating peak performance. However, working-class students' upbringing is more likely to equip them with a sense of constraint in professional settings like college. They are less likely to feel that they belong at college, have confidence in their abilities, or believe they are worthy of their professors' time and attention. On the whole, imposter feelings are more associated with first-gen working-class students. Studies show it can lead them to lower class engagement, lower attendance, poorer grades, and intentions to drop out.[28] A large body of research shows that all marginalized groups can experience imposter syndrome, such as women and people of color entering largely white and male-dominated fields—especially those in science, technology, engineering, and math (STEM).[29]

Not all of my interviewees experienced this lack of confidence, but at least eight of my respondents explicitly brought up imposter syndrome in their educational and professional experiences. One respondent noted needing to be "pushed" because "I don't think of myself as a writer." Others explained it as a constant feeling of "inadequacy," "insecurity," or "being insufficient." Some of them explained that this imposter syndrome contributed to a sense of isolation at college, feeling a lack of social belonging. First-gen students also often struggle with feeling a sense of belonging in the campus community and academics.[30] Without these forms of belonging, students are less likely to be engaged and do well in the classroom, persist, graduate, and be upwardly mobile toward better and more rewarding work.[31]

Financial Resources and Time Poverty

When working-class first-generation students face these cultural mismatches, it takes time and resources to understand the new norms, adapt to the new cultural environment, and build middle-class cultural capital. This is a double disadvantage because they require additional time to build new cultural capital while having less time available if they require paid work to sustain themselves. Consider Jacob's days as an engineering student: "I was getting up at like three o'clock in the morning to do homework. I'd go to class, go work two to three jobs, come home, do homework, maybe go to bed at two, get up at like three or four again, you know. And maybe catch up on the weekends." This lack of time increases stress dramatically. He recalled "times when I didn't have enough to eat or was worrying about my bills in engineering, and the stress that engineering has on its own is just terrible."

In a study comparing first-generation and continuing-generation students at selective colleges, Janel Benson and Elizabeth Lee found vastly different work experiences among students.[32] When asked if they had to work for pay to finance college, 47 percent of first-generation and 22 percent of continuing-generation students reported doing so. Among those who worked, first-generation students worked more hours than their peers.

Learning the hidden curriculum of higher education requires significant time developing relationships with professors and being coached and mentored by faculty, academic advisers, and college staff. It requires time to participate in additional experiences such as networking events. Sometimes, it requires financial resources to participate in opportunities such as educational travel or unpaid internships.[33] In addition to poor and working-class students having difficulty seeing the *hidden* curriculum, they also have fewer hours available—what researchers call *time poverty*—to spend on experiences that can help them learn it.

Continuing Cultural Mismatches in the Professional Office

While working-class first-generation students graduate at lower rates than their middle-class peers, many of them do make it through and into professional careers. But newly minted straddlers will find that the professional office is also built around middle-class norms, values, and ways of interacting. Accordingly, they will confront cultural clashes in the workplace and must learn the new norms to get by. Understanding the ongoing cultural mismatches between our upbringing and our new environments can help us see that it is not an individual problem and offer clues on how to navigate it effectively.

When I interviewed journalist Alfred Lubrano, he recounted a variety of cultural conflicts he experienced. Many examples were based on the fact that working-class people tend to be more direct in their communication styles. Alfred explained, "I've gotten into trouble by opening my mouth when I shouldn't have and speaking out when silence was the smart, middle-class alternative. Especially in the early days of my career. There was no such thing as an unexpressed thought. I believed it was more honest that way, more manly. If the boss is wrong, you tell him. You think the assignment is stupid or the editing bizarre? Just say it. That's what my father would have done. Growing up, blue-collar types have no reason not to speak their minds: there's nothing to lose when you're on the bottom."[34] But in the middle-class office, the boss expects something different and upwardly mobile straddlers now have something to lose. A direct and honest comment might be perceived as challenging a supervisor's authority and being confrontational. Speaking out can cost you a promotion or a job. Indeed, studies show that employees from working-class backgrounds do get promoted at lower rates than their similarly qualified peers.[35]

The office is a hierarchical space with varying levels of authority and that values a team orientation. Given that working-class people are more socialized to be group oriented, one might expect that this could easily translate into a team dynamic prized in the office. But the situations are different. In contrast to middle-class people, it is much less common for working-class people to socialize with those higher up the class ladder.[36] Our comfort with a group tends to be people of similar rank with whom we can speak openly, wearing our hearts on our sleeve, jumping in, and talking loudly. The expectation from middle-class colleagues, however, is to be deferential to supervisors, measured with our words, and calm in our tone. In some contexts, being direct and not mincing words with a supervisor can be perceived as combative or disrespectful.

Many straddlers struggle with the lack of directness from middle-class colleagues in their work environment. In an interview, John explained to me, "I'm much more comfortable in a place where we're having a direct conversation, and I would much rather somebody say, 'John, you just pissed me off when you said that and let's have an argument about it,' rather than you have to read between the lines of some passive-aggressive email about something you said." Similarly, straddlers might believe that self-censoring to avoid being direct feels like we are being fake or phony. We may feel resentful over agonizing how to say something the middle-class way when you could just say it directly to someone in the working class and know things will be OK.

There are also class-based conflicts around how people carry themselves in professional spaces. In several of my interviews, my respondents expressed anger and frustration at how their colleagues talked about working-class clients or students. For example, Samantha works at a university career center. She explains that her fellow career development professionals make classist comments about working-class students "all the time." They might make fun of how students present themselves for a mock interview or how they do not have appropriate words to discuss a work experience. Samantha believes those colleagues "may not realize that they're making fun of someone because of their class," viewing working-class students as a "charity case" and lacking empathy to support them. Leigh, a speech therapist, expressed a similar frustration to me: "It just makes me more and more angry . . . to see how spiteful people are and how damaging they are towards working-class people. The older I got, the more I see it and I can't let that go. I can't let that go. It's just wrong. It's just wrong to treat other human beings that way." Straddlers ultimately face difficult choices of if, when, and how they respond to such comments—in the culture of the middle-class office, challenging such comments in a direct way risks them being perceived as being confrontational or not a team player. If a straddler is also a woman or a person of color and they push back, they further risk being perceived through stereotypes, such as "bossy," "angry," or "aggressive."

Many straddlers describe these judgmental comments as part of class-based attitudes that people can develop. Alfred Lubrano quoted a fellow straddler who shared, "If a blue-collar person like me gets to the top, she asks, 'How did I get here?' If a white-collar person gets there, he's all puffed up with that sense of entitlement they have. Blue-collar people are more self-effacing. These others are self-centered and have high opinions of themselves. Any success I have, it just never crossed my mind that it's something I deserved. But these people with their superior attitudes all believe they did something special to get there."[37] Indeed, research shows that people from higher class backgrounds will be more likely to attribute their successes to individual traits, rather than contextual factors, such as the advantages afforded them through their upbringing or schooling.[38] Middle- and upper-class people feel a greater sense of control over their environment. They have grown up with greater opportunities and advantages in life. But they suffer from middle-class *solipsism*, or an individualistic orientation to the world that explains outcomes based on internal efforts and behaviors. It is a belief that because they have had such opportunities, others have had them as well. In the face of this, straddlers are left facing imposter syndrome and struggling with whether or not they belong or if they have to change themselves to fit in.

Working-class values can also make it more difficult to navigate one's career. In job interviews, applicants must be able to articulate why they are the right candidate for the job, and successful candidates will describe details of work and educational experiences that make them the right fit. Middle-class people's strong sense of individualism, competitiveness, and sense of entitlement can help them more comfortably share their positive qualities and elaborate on their accomplishments. But working-class first-gen students are more likely to have been socialized to defer to the group, not stand out, and to show modesty and not brag about themselves. As a result, they may give overly brief responses to interview questions or not present themselves as qualified as other candidates who will talk about their accomplishments at length. They might not project a sense of confidence. This sense of humility, valued in their own communities and in many settings, might not serve working-class first-gen graduates in climbing the professional ladder. It is not that this humility is a bad thing (it is very good!), but it represents a cultural mismatch from the norms of professional life and makes it harder for straddlers to navigate their new middle-class surroundings.

Professional networking and socializing with bosses present additional terrains for potential cultural clashes. Most people have a commonsense understanding that "it's not what you know, it's who you know." In other words, we understand that by forming the right relationships, we can learn about new job openings, acquire new information about our fields, and build connections that can lead to career opportunities. Those from the middle class have grown up socializing with people in organized settings with formal rules. They tend to be more comfortable interacting with authority figures and have been coached to proactively seek the help of others to get what they want. Alfred Lubrano explains that, for some straddlers, "it all smacks of phoniness and is antithetical to their blue-collar backgrounds, which emphasize honesty in human relations—'real' relationships."[39] The belief for some is that "networking is making friends with people because they can offer you something valuable. It's therefore not a real relationship, since you're using people." If networking also entails interacting mostly with people raised in middle-class backgrounds, then perhaps straddlers have fewer things in common with and different tastes from them. Straddlers again face a potential conflict between how they were socialized to relate to others and the new norms of the middle-class world. Not learning how to navigate these social dynamics can be costly for one's career.

The Costs of Classism and Cultural Mismatches

When working-class first-generation students enter college or the professional workplace, they often find themselves immersed in entirely new worlds. Because the institutions of social mobility—schools, colleges, and professional offices—are dominated by middle-class culture, upwardly mobile working-class people will encounter classism and cultural mismatches. They must learn the unwritten rules for how to speak, behave, and interact with new peers and colleagues.

In contrast to many of those from higher-class backgrounds, first-gen students and graduates can feel like they are constantly playing catch-up or that they don't belong. As they strive to fit in and do well, the costs can be high. They risk a heavy toll of alienation, shame, imposter syndrome, not feeling true to oneself, or broken ties with friends, family, and their community.[40]

But there are ways to flip the script. In the following section, I present stories of how straddlers draw upon their working-class culture as a strength. Using a more storytelling form, the next four chapters offer a new contribution to understanding the straddler experience and how our working-class roots can become an asset in our professional work. While first-gen graduates had to learn the rules of new cultural worlds, they also found that their working-class background equipped them with unique skills in their professional careers.

Part 2

The Hidden Strengths of Working-Class Cultural Capital

3
Cultural Empathy

Schools, colleges, and professional offices are dominated by middle-class culture. This puts people socialized into middle-class culture at an advantage because they've been socialized into the norms, values, and attitudes that will help them navigate those environments. When these cultural advantages are paired with the advantages that their economic resources and social networks bring, it helps to explain why so many middle-class children are so much more likely than working-class children to secure higher positions. And yet, many working-class folks do climb the economic ladder into middle-class lives. When I tried to understand how their working-class background affected their journey, these straddlers' responses revealed skills and attitudes that gave them strengths that are rarely acknowledged in popular or academic discourse.

I refer to the skills, cultural knowledge, and attitudes that emerged from my interviews as *working-class cultural capital* because they are rooted in the social conditions and cultural experience of their working-class origins.[1] They function as a set of cultural resources that gave my interviewees cultural assets in a variety of social settings. As a new perspective on the straddler experience, we can think of them as hidden strengths that help straddlers articulate their skills and feel pride in their working-class roots. Of course, these cultural resources do not negate the numerous disadvantages and barriers that these upwardly mobile straddlers have to overcome. Instead, these cultural traits coexist as a complex set of disadvantages and resources through which class, race, and other systems of inequality have shaped people's lives.

When I asked straddlers if they had positive aspects from their working-class background that they used in their professional careers, empathy emerged as one of the most commonly cited responses (in over half of the interviews—nineteen of thirty-seven). Straddlers felt that their experiences with hardship helped them to relate to what others go through, made them less likely to stereotype or judge others, and enabled them to be able to see the world from multiple perspectives. They sometimes also contrasted this with a lack of empathy found among wealthier colleagues, whose privileged lives might lack the experiences helping them to understand what others have gone through.[2] While everyone has the capacity for empathy, being an empathetic person is not a given.[3] It emerges from life experiences shaped by our social context and honed through reflection.

Empathy is understood by many researchers as a cultural skill that people acquire to emotionally and cognitively relate to others.[4] Respondents explained ways that they used their knowledge and diverse lived experiences to better understand and emotionally connect with colleagues, clients, and students.[5] As a cultural resource, this capacity for empathy also transcends class-based connections to apply to many other situations.[6]

As a form of cultural capital, empathy is a resource that can be exchanged and converted into other resources. For example, empathy can bring more social capital through better relationships with students, colleagues, and supervisors.[7] Empathy can help one build professional confidence and a "positive self-image."[8] In professional spaces dominated by middle-class tastes and social networks, where middle-class people possess more of a sense of entitlement and self-advocacy, straddlers can find strength in their empathy.

Relating to Hardship: Katrina

Despite a difficult childhood, Katrina credits her upbringing with giving her an empathetic perspective that has been an asset throughout her professional work. As a Black woman working in student affairs, it enabled her to connect with students, improve organizational policies, and help students pursue their own passions and careers.

Born in Kentucky, Katrina spent most of her childhood in South Central Los Angeles. She lived with her mother and brother, and the household survived with the help of food stamps, Section 8 housing vouchers, and a hardworking mother. As a certified nursing assistant (CNA) with a high school education, her mother assisted clients with everyday activities, such as dressing, eating, and bathing. But the field pays little and she never earned more than twelve dollars an hour. Katrina's father had a substance abuse disorder and was in and out of jail for several years. After several rounds of incarceration, her father went through rehab in a halfway house and got clean. He eventually earned a certification in heating and air, which landed him a steady job with decent pay. By the time Katrina was in middle school, her father contributed with child support, helping lift the family's income. But the social environment was very challenging, and her brother started getting involved in a gang. Given the threat of gang violence, Katrina's mother arranged for the children to move away with their father. In her senior year of high school, their father brought them back to Louisville, Kentucky.

After graduating high school, Katrina enrolled at a local community college. She finished her associate's degree and transferred to the University of Louisville. Along the way, a family member referred Katrina to the Black Achievers program at the local YMCA. The YMCA describes the program as "a multicultural effort to create equity in education as well as in the workplace by motivating African American/Black and other minority youth to develop and pursue high educational and career goals." It serves Black youth from diverse economic backgrounds. Katrina was interested in going into education, and through the program, she participated in field study projects. For example, her group went to orphanages to teach and develop plans for counseling and educational opportunities for students there. The program introduced her to a high school teacher and academic counselor who became her mentor. Because they have less guidance from family, research shows that "students from poor and working-class families benefit more from mentoring than students from middle- and upper-class families."[9]

With the help of her mentor, Katrina identified career goals and a pathway to graduate school. As Katrina recalled, "She basically mentored me on the route. That's why I knew, after finishing my bachelor's, what would be the direction—to go straight into a graduate program." Because of her experience in the field study, she already knew she needed to have a master's in counseling. Her understanding of that goal gave her a positive self-image and kept her "focused and driven." Katrina asked herself, "If I want to go more higher ed and get more of an administrative role, what do I need to do? I looked at those steps, and that's why I'm here now." Having a mentor helped provide Katrina with a way to map out her goals and achieve them. She was acquiring middle-class cultural capital, such as building confidence in organized settings, knowing how to navigate college, understanding career pathways, and advocating for herself in pursuing them. Katrina later completed her master's in school guidance counseling, worked for four years, and eventually enrolled in a PhD program (which she was working toward when I interviewed her).

In her professional career, Katrina worked as a substitute teacher, a counselor with a TRIO program, and as an academic counselor at a major university. TRIO programs are funded through the U.S. government and include "outreach and student services programs designed to identify and provide services for individuals from disadvantaged backgrounds," including low-income, first-generation college students, and individuals with disabilities. In her position with the TRIO program, she worked with low-income schools "teaching college preparatory programming for freshmen to senior classes" covering topics "from ACT prep to resiliency to just academic persistence . . . to be a better test-taker, how to study, and how to navigate what type of career path you might be interested in." While middle-class students are likely to be introduced to these opportunities and skills through their families and higher-quality schools, the program was essential for extending them to working-class students. For a similar project, she "mentored eight or nine young ladies in a Woman Up program where they help high school students to pursue higher education" and different career fields. Now as an academic counselor, Katrina focuses on student development, supporting students through their academic programs and helping them in career planning—she is giving back just as someone helped her.

When I asked Katrina if there were parts of her economic background that helped her do her work more effectively, she immediately responded:

> My sensitivity level and my knowledge from experience, I feel like helped me connect with all populations. I feel like through life experience and having that connection allows me to be more understanding. When I encounter students who have similar backgrounds or might have grown up in single-parent household or poor or have experienced family members that had drug abuse or alcoholism or gang-related activity that they've been around, I have that sense of understanding. I can have more words of encouragement because I've been through it. You can learn a lot of things from a book, but I think, through experience, I have a more keen understanding of that piece, and that's why I'm passionate about it.

Like Katrina, many of my respondents emphasized this sensitivity and understanding as the empathetic skills that gave them insight into others' lives. They had experiences that middle-class people were much less likely to have, and it equipped them with an ability to relate to and support other students who encountered these challenges. For Katrina, it helped her to understand the issues that poor and working-class students face in preparing for college, test taking, and planning for careers—to be a better TRIO counselor and academic counselor.

Empathy functions as a form of working-class cultural capital. We know that working-class children are more likely to grow up being intimidated by teachers, school administrators, and other authority figures.[10] When they face adversity in the classroom or in navigating a school or college, they are less likely to ask for help or advocate for themselves.[11] Teachers, staff, and administrators who have developed empathy because they've "been through it" can present themselves as less intimidating.[12] By sharing their own struggles as a student, they can make a connection that empowers students to ask for help without fear of looking dumb. Middle-class educators are more likely to interpret students' struggles as a result of lower academic abilities and have fewer bases upon which to build that connection.[13] In contrast, this empathy gives working-class professionals an asset in breaking through to students to help them build confidence, connect them with resources that students might not feel are available to "people like them," achieve academically, and find potential mentors.

Katrina also described how her empathy helped her design better policy and organizational practices. Colleges and universities across the country are facing enrollment challenges and a need to retain students to help them persist and graduate.[14] With poor and working-class students facing so many barriers regarding academic preparation, navigating the institution of higher education, and using its resources, Katrina knows that just having resources available is not sufficient. She described needing to expand her communications to marginalized students with more reminders, face-to-face contact, and accommodating their work and family schedules. Increasingly, colleges are focusing more on holistic advising, which considers a student's whole life and complexities beyond their academic performance.[15] Katrina's empathy helped inform her in redesigning advising and mentoring programs to better connect students to needed academic, social, and career resources. Educators from the middle class may take these experiences more for granted unless they are trained well about working-class students' experiences in their formal schooling. In other words, Katrina's working-class cultural capital enabled her to support more students to graduation.

As a Black woman, Katrina has additional life experiences that help her to empathize with students. She understands it is not only poor and working-class people but also people of color and women who are often socialized to see themselves as deficient. As noted in chapter 1, people from all marginalized backgrounds are less likely to feel entitled to certain resources. They often develop a sense of constraint in which they have less confidence in organized settings and do not aggressively pursue opportunities or actively advocate for themselves. Given what Katrina has had to overcome, she views her background simultaneously as an asset: It is "a strength in the sense of giving students of color and from all nationalities a mentor or a leadership role." As a mentor who is both a person of color and a woman, she both relates culturally and embodies "women's rights and opportunities and equality." For Katrina, her dual experiences are a "strength" because "being a woman, you have a lot of that [overshadowing] of male leadership, but coming from being [an] African American woman, you have even more of a double standard." She explains that these "adversities and struggles" make her a better mentor in the field of student affairs by helping her relate to an increasingly diverse student body and helping students make sense of the challenges they face. Just as Katrina had her mentors, students looked up to her and she models the tenacity, determination, and coping strategies for persevering.

While she lacked the advantages that many middle-class children have, Katrina also acquired middle-class cultural capital and climbed the class ladder. Without understanding the full context of Katrina's story, it could be easy to mislabel her success as an individualistic effort that reflects the American Dream. Indeed, Katrina is a hard-working and strong woman but could not have done this on her own. Her family needed government programs, such as food stamps and housing assistance, to help them survive. While her parents struggled, they did what they could to support her. She also found a mentor through the Black Achievers program who helped her to make sense of her experiences as a Black woman. Now, she leverages those experiences and her empathy—as a form of working-class cultural capital—to do better work as a student affairs professional. Working in a job she loves, Katrina continues lifting up others around her.

Managing the Callousness of Rich People: Amanda

When Amanda hid in an art museum as a child so that she could sleep there because she did not have a home to return to, she could not have had any idea she would end up working in an art museum as an adult. But the empathy she developed growing up working-class and as one of a few white kids in a Latine and Black neighborhood, along with her degree in marketing, would give her valuable skills that would help her as senior director of audience engagement. In our conversation, she sharply contrasted her empathy with some of her wealthy colleagues' and donors' callousness toward those less fortunate.

Amanda's upbringing was highly unstable. When she was three years old, her parents moved the family from Chicago to Los Angeles to work in Hollywood. For the first few years, they were living with another family that was helping cover the bills, but her parents' heroin addiction created conflicts. By the time Amanda was in the second grade, there "was a series of apartments and evictions and poor choices and arrests." Her father was an artist working on music videos and in the adult film industry, and her mother worked as a costumer on shows like *Three's Company* and *Facts of Life*. These gigs would bring in "random bursts of money." But outside of that, "there were weeks where I only ate at school," and she described her family as "pretty poor." But despite the drug use, her parents "always worked really hard."

When Amanda's parents had gigs, they worked very long hours. She described herself as a "very scrappy... latchkey kid" but sometimes without a home to which she could return. She was often at a library or buying "a single thing at McDonald's to kill as much time as you can." Because her dad was an artist and she was raised in a culture of museum-going, she also spent a lot of time in art museums. Kids got in free, so she would pretend to be part of another family to sneak in by herself. She would then sometimes sleep there at night, "but as soon as the sun comes up, you have to skedaddle before people come to work." Other nights, she would return to the set where her mom was working and sleep beside her in the dressing rooms.

Amanda reflected that "the weirdest thing of being from poverty is being really proud of those years. I was very independent." She learned to be a survivor, adding, "I know you're not supposed to steal car batteries out of cars." But outside of her babysitting jobs and odd jobs like working at the movie theater, she learned she could sell car batteries or hubcaps to local recyclers. That would enable her to "buy some eggs and a loaf of bread and using some powdered milk and just make French toast for a few days." When the options were between hunger or theft, her choice was easy.

Not everyone was lucky enough to survive her neighborhood growing up, especially if they were not straight or white. Amanda said, "I had seen my mom's gay friends come home completely face bashed in [by police]. I saw a cop shoot somebody in the back on Venice Beach once." When it wasn't the notorious LAPD beating or killing people, it was the AIDS epidemic, drugs, poverty, or cascading racial barriers. Amanda explained that "everybody from my LA neighborhood is dead. My mom's friends died—some of them died in jails, some of them have AIDS, or overdose, because some of them you can look up on IMDb" (Internet Movie Database). The only exceptions were the kids she remembers from a brief stint at a private school on a scholarship. She added that "the ones that didn't go to the gifted school, they're all dead." But for those at the private school, "their opportunities haven't stopped." For Amanda, "I don't think that's a coincidence.... [If I were not white] I don't think my white teachers would have assumed I had a normal background in situations that I stepped into." In contrast to her classmates of color, Amanda's white skin tone often got her the benefit of the doubt. When she made a "social class faux pas," people chalked it up to being "quaint or cute" rather than associating it with a lack of intelligence or ability.

Despite missing long stretches of school, Amanda showed great academic potential when she was in class. At a low-income school, "they had run out of gifted and talented education classes for me." But her timing was lucky because "I just sat in the back with the Apple II and just coded." She was fortunate to develop coding skills in the early 1990s when few people had that type of training. When her family moved to another school district, her school records were not transferred, which was "annoying" because she was then "put on a lower education track." She observed that "clearly lower education was also lower-income kids, and the gifted track was clearly the wealthier kids. That really upset me." Students were not given equal opportunities. This could have derailed her: "The kids on the lower track were doing drugs and threatening to kick my ass." But she kept at it.

Amanda explained that "when choosing colleges, I had no idea because my parents didn't go to college. They don't understand college. So, it was kind of funny.... I looked at only ones I had heard of on TV." She wound up at Marquette University. She never felt like she fit in with the more affluent student body there, so she transferred to the University of Illinois Urbana-Champaign and finished with a degree in marketing and an ability to code.

Amanda's early career had several twists and turns before returning to her roots. At age twenty-four, she made her way to California at the height of the first Internet boom. With her skills in coding and marketing, Amanda went to work for what would become some of the biggest tech firms. It was "raining money" and she rapidly became "worth $3.5 million on paper—on paper *only*." She had been unable to sell the early stock before it fell, and eventually, the terms of her divorce would cost her much of what she had been worth. She had enough money to comfortably start over, but not the millions that seemed so close. While working various corporate jobs, Amanda was also doing pro bono work: first in climate education, then at the Boys and Girls Club of Silicon Valley, and later running a kid's program for underserved youth in San Francisco. She was making good money, but "what felt good was the social work that we did." She saw a job ad for a director of audience engagement at an art museum in the Midwest that "was already doing a lot of the right things of broadening the lens of who's an artist, who is a collectible artist, who is worthy of display, so that when I saw the job listing, I was like, OK, I'm interested." With her love of art, skills in advertising, and her personal background, she was hired for her dream job.

In her current role, Amanda does "marketing, design, PR, as well as what we call audience cultivation or activation events which are trying to bring a less traditional atmosphere to the museum to get folks to the museum for the first time." She reflects on art and museums as a hierarchical space: "By its nature, the museum is a rather top-down, linear, elite organization.... It's all about how do we change the understanding of an art museum? How do we change the understanding of who belongs in an art museum, of how you can be in an art museum? My joke is there's no wrong way to art." While Amanda grew up visiting (and sometimes sleeping in) art museums, she understands that people from her home communities have the sense that "art is for rich people. It is a luxury." She believes that art can be something more, including for people who did not grow up rich.

Throughout my interview, Amanda referenced empathy as an essential tool for her work and was frustrated by the inability of many wealthy donors and colleagues to empathize with marginalized groups. She said that when you're thinking about trying to reach people from poor and working-class backgrounds, "I'm really advocating for empathy." Amanda explained, "The big lesson I don't know if I drive home enough is you can't ask people to come in from a different background, come into the museum and do the exact same thing that the people who are already here do." She noted examples such as these: "You think it's obvious that you can't touch the art or that you have to stand at arm's length," but "you have to communicate that." Similarly, "You think that people want to stare in quiet contemplation at the art when no one stares in quiet contemplation of anything these days." Instead, "both for our patrons and for our staff," you have "to tell everybody it's totally OK for somebody to slip their headphones in and listen to Spotify while they look at art. It's OK for somebody to just come here and make fun of art, to just come here and hang out."

Skills in cultural empathy become building blocks for many professional tasks and, as we will see in later chapters, for harnessing other forms of working-class cultural capital. For example, by empathizing with working-class and poor people, and people of color, Amanda better develops policies to welcome them into the museum. While nearly all art museums have certain free days, Amanda started aggressively promoting them and facilitating easier access from poor neighborhoods. She found companies to donate billboards in working-class and poor neighborhoods promoting free days and family access. Without convenient public transportation accessing the museum, Amanda works with donors to sponsor buses to bring children from low-income schools to the museum. Then "from there, how do we bring their parents back? So we give them family passes, which is, the kids have been on a field trip, had their first museum experience, so give them a pass to bring their whole family back and show them what they've seen. That's our best way of reaching families who have never been to a museum [and] who don't pay attention to our message."

Amanda draws upon her empathy and experience growing up as one of the few white people in a segregated neighborhood. She says, "The joke is even the signs [at the museum] are white. The people are white, the building is white, the walls are white, so there's a racial divide." When she is trying to promote the museum in Black and Brown neighborhoods, she understands that "you can't just show up when you have an African American artist on view and then be like, hey, come see this, or, hey, it's Day of the Dead, come down the museum and then not talk to you for another year." She adds, "There's a huge movement called decolonize the museum" and she views herself as a part of it.[16] Her experiences living with such diverse groups have helped her relate to—and cultivate—diverse audiences for the museum.

Amanda's empathy also helps improve programming to help new patrons feel welcome and enjoy the space. For example, they have a series, Art Museum After Dark, "which is a big dance party in the museum once a month that involves bars and non-curator-led art tours like a karaoke tour of the art . . . trying to lure people with a club scene into the museum but really tied to the arts so that possibly they'll come back." She and her staff found that "we'll get teens walking through, making fun of all the art. They feel like they're being really rebellious, and I'm like, I got those teens to look at art for three hours. That's better than high-end, rich, white dudes ever spent in the galleries." For Amanda, "that's kind of the goal is how do we shake some of the expectations of the art museum from my perspective, from the audience's point of view?" Her skills in empathy allowed her to adopt this perspective to invite them in and help them have an enjoyable experience engaging with the art.

However, Amanda explains that she gets pushback from people "all the time." People who "are entrenched in the museum industry" have a belief that parents "should teach their kids not to touch art" and other "proper behavior," to which she retorted, "Well, yeah, and money should rain from the sky. It's not going to happen." She has to choose her words carefully when explaining her new policies and programming: "I think the hardest thing is to say, where it's like, you have really good intentions, but you're actually 'othering' them in some way." For wealthy donors and curators, their good intentions might lead them to propose exhibits that address the experiences of marginalized communities. Amanda has to explain to them that "just because lots of Black men are incarcerated in [our state], doesn't mean a show about incarceration is for the Black community, or you can't just target Black people." That type of logic reduces people to a stereotype, but she is aware that "there is no one interest of poor people. There is no one interest of Black people. There is no one interest of the Latinx community. To treat somebody like a big lump, there's nuance in those audiences. I don't think it's out of intention" but rather a lack of understanding of their lives and cultures. To combat this, Amanda says,

> I will use terms like "poverty porn" to shame people, like, we're not just doing this little poverty porn show. I really have a problem with the whole, "we're going to put despair on display to bring in audiences." Because guess what? If you're living in despair, you don't want to see it. If you're not in despair, you're just a tourist, so how can you be joyful about somebody's community? You can be poor and be joyful and have strong family relationships and be really creative and be interesting. It is almost as bad to only see yourself in a museum when it is about despair as it is to not see yourself in a museum at all.

Amanda struggles with the lack of empathy and the callousness that she often sees in her profession and broader society. She told me that "there are some lovely people with money, don't get me wrong, but . . . even when they're trying to be generous, it's paternalistic. They [think they] know better. Because they're rich, they won, therefore, they [believe they] can dictate the mandates." One example she gave is this: "If it's talking to service workers, they're servants.

It's gross, and this like, 'Well, why don't they just buy new clothes?' 'Why don't they just pull themselves up?'—people who've never had to be evicted talking about freeloaders." Many of these wealthier patrons and donors have not had experiences with poor and working-class people and see them through stereotypical lenses. Her own lived experience gives her a different and more empathetic view.

I asked Amanda if she could change anything she wanted, what would it be, and she said, "I'd love to wave a magic wand about access and empathy." She added, "The callousness that rich people take towards poor people is really hard for me." Because of what she has seen, she quickly admits that "at the same time, as a stereotype, as a bias I have, and I'm aware of it, but I still don't like rich people." Amanda sees this empathy as a skill, something that is cultivated: "I'm working through it.... I'm trying because there are really generous, really wonderful people."[17] But the challenges in understanding one another do not have equally negative effects. Amanda notes, "I don't think poor people can understand what it's like to be rich, sure, but I think it's more toxic when it's the other way." Upper-middle-class people are in authoritative positions to determine who gets hired and who gets promoted. They shape workplace culture and government policy. So, when the wealthy look down upon working-class people and lack empathy toward them, the impacts can be disastrous. For Amanda and other interviewees, this makes it all the more important for straddlers to climb into these positions, maintain connections to their roots, use their empathy, and help others to understand people whose experiences are so different from their own.

Understanding Working-Class Experiences: Brianna

Of all the people who responded to my call for participants, there were more college professors than any other occupation. This fact is especially striking given how much first-gen students have to overcome to complete their PhD, and the working class is vastly underrepresented among college professors. College professors were especially eager to discuss their class journey and how it affects their work.[18] It became clear that empathy was an important cultural strength of these first-generation faculty too.

A common theme among the professors was the way they drew upon their personal knowledge of working-class life experiences to empathize with their students, help them to learn more effectively, empower them to be more successful students, and facilitate connections between their education and career goals. Given the benefits of helping students succeed in higher education, this form of working-class cultural capital is important for educating people for work and participating in our society, and of course, supporting first-gen students in realizing their dreams.

Brianna's journey went from a working-class kid to a professor receiving a prestigious award from the president of the United States. Brianna grew up in the only multiracial family in a homogenous white community in Michigan. Her white father was a Vietnam veteran and met her Chinese mother while serving overseas. He worked as a delivery truck driver for The Campbell's Company, and her mother worked at McDonald's. Brianna recalls that they never went hungry, but her parents fought constantly about money, and bill collectors called regularly. When Brianna needed the down payment for her braces, she had to work babysitting her neighbor's three children from 5 A.M. until 5 P.M. for an entire summer. Like many working-class families, her parents wanted her to be successful but were not involved in her schooling.[19] Her parents communicated, "If we ever have to meet any of your teachers, that means you're in trouble, and that's bad." Then there was the racism. Her two brothers got beat up for being Asian American, while she was often called "ugly" because of her race. They were all told to "go back" to where they came from.

Brianna always loved math and science and was especially interested in becoming a forensic scientist. Thanks to a variety of scholarships, she was able to attend the University of Michigan. She enrolled in calculus and science-heavy courses, excited to pursue her passion. But it didn't go well. In Brianna's words, "I took too heavy of a course load. . . . I did really badly, like *real bad*, and I didn't really have good advice." Like many low-income students, she was working too many hours.[20] Again, she lacked people in her life with college experience to guide her. Brianna barely eked by in her classes, painfully remembering, "I was not doing well, so there was a lot of panic that I had screwed everything up. . . . it was not a happy time."

Brianna enrolled in an Intro to Psychology course and performed better, earning a B+. But more importantly, she connected with her professor, who was a first-gen graduate and would become her most valued mentor. She took more courses with him and found friends along the way. Brianna was then in the right place to be introduced to new opportunities, and she participated in a special summer research program for first-gens and students of color. Her mentor won a grant helping children to learn science and offered her a paid research position. He also understood her other obligations: "He gave me all these affordances" with flexible scheduling and understanding grants "so I could work my other jobs and do the research with him." Her mentor did not operate on middle-class norms of independence, so he did not expect her to simply figure it all out with assumed skills in time management.[21] Rather, he had similar life experiences to her and was in a unique position to tailor the research position to the realities of her life as a working-class student. Brianna, who initially struggled in college without guidance or proper support despite her strong academic ability, had found a mentor who understood the effects of her class background and helped her to thrive.

Through the work with her mentor, Brianna learned about new academic subfields and career pathways she never knew existed. Her mentor was a developmental psychologist and introduced her to the related field of educational psychology. The field examines how people learn, including the effects of different teaching methods, emotions, and class and race. She was able to apply this to her lifelong passion for science. Brianna reflected, "I love the research and the learning, getting people excited about science, that intersection of the teaching and learning part, and I said... that's a job? That's a career?" She and her working-class family did not have other professionals in their social networks to expose them to such different careers, but her mentor and this opportunity helped her find her path.[22] Brianna added, "As I started to study the field, I realized how much I could contribute around class." She related it to her own class experiences, emphasizing how working-class parents "relate to school" and "how my parents never felt they could even enter a school building with any authority at all." Brianna recalled that "the only time my dad ever went to the school was to thank the teachers when we were seniors."

As Annette Lareau found in her research, working-class families tend to lack the educational and cultural capital for navigating schools as effectively as middle-class families.[23] Brianna's first-hand knowledge of working-class experiences—and those of people of color—gave her a deeper understanding of their role in learning and was supplemented by academic training. She could use her empathy to better support students and to train other faculty in their mentorship as well. But she maintains another working-class value: humility. "I can't claim to know everything on it." She added that the experiences of other people of color are "not my lived experience, but I definitely am a scholar of this area, and I'm a listener and an ally and an advocate." Working-class students may not have the advantages of middle-class cultural capital through their upbringing, but education and the right mentors can help students gain these skills, grow their middle-class cultural capital, and find ways to leverage their existing working-class cultural capital.

Brianna is now greatly energized by working with students at her liberal arts college. She quickly earned a strong reputation for her engaging teaching and is a nationally recognized scholar on mentoring, diversity, and career and identity development in adolescence and adulthood. Her work focuses on the persistence of first-generation college students, students of color, and women, particularly in science and technology. Her goal is "to understand how young people without easily identifiable role models and mentors in career domains manage to find the mentoring they need and sustain their desired possible selves, or who they hope to become in the future." Brianna draws upon her own working-class cultural capital and experiences, as well as her work as a scholar, to better assist and train other faculty in supporting marginalized students. She regularly offers lectures and workshops on these topics at the local, state, and national levels, converting her working-class cultural capital into greater social capital. Brianna was honored for her work when she went to the White House to receive the prestigious Presidential Early Career Award for Scientists and Engineers.

Brianna's understanding of working-class experiences also means she helps her students celebrate their accomplishments. She explained that "every year I have students who cannot afford to have their parents come for graduation." Brianna and her husband find financial support for parents to fly to their children's graduation. Given her cultural capital knowing working-class experiences, she understands students' role in an interdependent family and helps them to collectively celebrate.

My respondents repeatedly told me how they used their knowledge of working-class experiences to connect with first-generation students and design educational experiences that help them thrive. Mary Kate, a music educator who directed a college marching band, described working with students whose paid jobs interfered with rehearsals. While some directors have a policy of missing zero sessions, she willingly made an occasional exception: "I recognize that if you don't go to work, you can't pay to be here with us. Is the one rehearsal really worth the battle? You need to be able to pay for your school." Mary Kate also described herself as "more apt to take popular music more seriously, recognizing things like rock and roll and R&B and rap as secular music that is different but just as valuable." Music programs have historically privileged the "highbrow" musical tastes of the middle class, but working-class music from artists ranging from Bruce Springsteen to Tupac and Kendrick Lamar are just as legitimate means of learning music. Asserting these artists' songs as legitimate music helps level out the advantages of many middle-class children because of their socialization into classical music from an early age. Similarly, Ryan, a community college professor, reported being flexible on assignment deadlines and meetings with students. He understands that many working-class students have various obligations, such as family commitments, that must be balanced with their academics. In both of these cases, their own working-class experiences gave them knowledge about their students' lives that many middle-class educators lacked. This working-class cultural capital helped them to empathize with and better support their students' success.

Knowing working-class experiences can also shape the nature of assignments and how we teach. For example, we know that working-class people are more likely to be intimidated by authority figures, and as a result, are less likely to attend office hours or build relationships with their professors. So, I have developed assignments requiring students to visit with me during office hours and provide prompts for either getting to know their professor, or I require that we discuss a research proposal or other assignment. I also adopt a more informal teaching style in the classroom and use humor to help make myself more approachable. Other classroom techniques include using more active learning techniques and less lecture. Research has shown that lectures, as a teaching strategy, accommodate middle-class students, who are more likely to be socialized to sit for longer periods of time, take notes effectively, and are more individualistic in their learning. In contrast, active and collaborative learning is generally effective for all types of students but especially working-class first-generation students. Like my fellow educators, my working-class cultural capital better helps me support my students to be successful.

The Versatility of Cultural Empathy

In addition to the careers presented above, research shows that empathy is important in a wide range of occupational fields.[24] For example, medical professionals must have a good bedside manner that shows care and the ability to relate to one's patients.[25] In business, customer service professionals must understand the distress of their clients to resolve a problem.[26] Sales professionals can use empathy to make connections to potential clients.[27] Designers in digital technology, the arts, and the built environment require "cross-disciplinary skills" such as empathy to coordinate diverse groups and implement ideas into technical specifications.[28] Engineers require empathy to manage complex relationships with stakeholders,[29] often working across different cultures, languages, and virtual teams.[30] For example, one engineer I spoke with explained that his empathy allows him to better work with "project beneficiaries than some of my colleagues in Washington, who perhaps had been a lot less exposed to poverty or different classes, people from very different backgrounds."

The business publication *Forbes* even proclaimed that "empathy is the most important leadership skill according to research" and referred to empathy as a "must-have job skill."[31] Studies on empathy reveal that higher levels of empathy are correlated with greater productivity, innovation, life-work integration, positive work experiences, and employee retention.[32] Marginalized groups, such as women of color, "experience less burnout when they have more empathic senior leaders." Empathy also plays a role in career adaptability.[33]

Empathy is broadly understood to be a learned skill and disposition, but it is more likely to be acquired at an early age by certain social groups. In particular, women are socialized to have greater empathy than men, but it varies by context and men are similarly able to develop high empathetic skills.[34] Indeed, both the women and men I interviewed credited their working-class backgrounds as providing them with useful skills in empathy.

The stories throughout this chapter reveal how working-class life experiences, paired with reflection and awareness, helped straddlers to emotionally and cognitively relate to others and to see the world from multiple perspectives. Accordingly, it functions as a valuable form of working-class cultural capital. Empathy, as a cultural resource, can help working-class people excel in a variety of occupational fields and be upwardly mobile. Furthermore, as the stories throughout this chapter show, they can also be put to use to help lift up others from the working class and other marginalized groups.

4

Working-Class Norms, Language, and Communication

While professional workplaces are dominated by middle-class culture, there are moments in some professional contexts when following middle-class cultural norms can be a liability. In particular, middle-class behavioral norms can lead some professionals to misinterpret working-class people's behavior because they interpret it through their own lens. Middle-class manners of speech, such as indirectly stating one's position to avoid conflict, can lead to miscommunication. Assumptions that middle-class people make can impart unrealistic or misguided expectations for themselves and others. Projecting one's own middle-class tastes and preferences onto others might make it more difficult to form a connection.

The stories of my respondents reveal more ways that the usual script for cultural capital gets flipped on its head—when fluency in working-class norms, language, and communication make the difference in reaching a desired outcome. In these cases, working-class cultural capital can contribute to professional success. But because middle-class norms, meanings, and communication styles are taken for granted in professional contexts, these cultural dynamics largely go unnamed and unnoticed.

The need for such working-class cultural capital is not relevant for all professional settings, but middle-class cultural miscues can be especially consequential when professionals are interacting in working-class or mixed-class settings. In these contexts, working-class cultural capital is an asset for appropriately interpreting working-class language and cultural references, communicating with working-class people, and developing trust. The stories below demonstrate how following group-oriented working-class norms and using working-class communication patterns help straddlers build connections and community in middle-class spaces characterized by individualism and hierarchy. Their use of working-class language, interaction styles, and knowledge of working-class lives facilitate relationship-building, inclusiveness, and collaboration to meet professional goals.

Helping Connect Others and Build Community: Kinsley

As one type of professional workplace, schools are built around a middle-class culture that emphasizes individualism, independence, competitiveness, and the ability to express oneself and one's needs.[1] This can feel unwelcoming to working-class children socialized into a culture of interdependence, where they learn to orient themselves more toward others by relying on emotional connectedness to feel a sense of belonging.[2] Teachers who are unfamiliar with working-class culture might misinterpret children's tendency toward the group as a lack of ambition, mislabel their lack of self-advocacy as disengagement, or believe that their briefer self-expressions reflect low academic ability.[3] But teachers like Kinsley, who have working-class cultural capital of interdependence and connectedness, can better support working-class students to thrive in their classrooms.

Kinsley came from a white family in upstate New York, and summed up her childhood as "complicated." Her father was very abusive toward her mother and the kids. Kinsley and her three siblings often feared their father becoming violent, especially when he came home drunk or high. When they were still very young, the children all went to live on their grandparents' farm. She remembered her grandparents as very kind, but raising four children while trying to maintain a small farm was difficult for her elderly grandparents.

Kinsley described her class background as poor and recounted some of the painful memories in elementary school. Her family could not afford name-brand shoes or clothing (Jordache at the time), so she was often made fun of at school. She remembers riding the school bus and "kids picking on me" and calling her "Stinky Kinsley." Living in poverty can make you feel small, like you don't belong. Kinsley explained that her "dad was always in trouble with the law and ... we were dumped off on the grandparents" and did not "have a parent in our life." Her last name was Drummond and adults would respond, "Oh, you're a Drummond kid." She could hear the judgment in their voice, and it was clear that people around her had low expectations for Kinsley. In contrast to middle-class kids who are expected to go to college and view their world through a lens of possibility, poor children often internalize social messages that they are not smart enough or don't work hard enough to deserve better.[4] This can make it more difficult to believe they are worthy of the attention of adults and authority figures, to have motivation for school, or to envision a pathway to a more secure life.[5]

Because of the cost of college, she remembers her grandparents discouraging her from attending college: "When I was a teenager and I wanted to go to college out of high school, I remember my grandfather telling a family friend, 'Don't put that idea in our kids' heads because there [are] no resources for that.'" But that same family friend invited Kinsley to live with her to make college work financially. As Kinsley explained it, "There were people all through my life that have offered helping hands. I think that's the thing. It really does take a village." This kind of support from her community, an important working-class value, meant a lot to her.[6] She would put this value and orientation toward others into practice throughout her life.

Despite her grandfather's discouragement, Kinsley went straight to a for-profit technical school after graduating high school. But she had little guidance on the process. She ran into problems with financial aid and did not know how to resolve it or whom to ask. She attempted to transfer to a community college, and again, "there was some kind of glitch with the financial aid package" and she had to come up with an "unobtainable" amount of money. Kinsley explained the frustration that so many working-class first-gen students experience: "There was that panic in not knowing who to talk to or how to work it out. So it was like, 'No. That's done. That's done.'" Then Kinsley dropped out. These are common obstacles for working-class first-gen students, whose family members lack both the income to support them and the experiential knowledge of college to guide them through the process. If middle-class parents lacked the financial resources, they would have been more likely to confidently call the school for assistance or advocate for their child.[7] So, Kinsley thought that was the end of college for her, and she began an entry-level job as a bank teller and eventually married.

As a working adult, Kinsley and her husband got deeply involved in their local community. They volunteered at the local VFW, American Legion, 4-H (a youth development organization), and their church. Kinsley was even voted "Woman of the Year" in her local community. She told me that the core of life is "to be interconnected and to feel for others." Just as we saw in chapter 1, compared with middle-class people, working-class people are more group oriented than individually oriented.[8] For folks who value community so much, the award was a huge honor for her.

Kinsley worked for seventeen years as a bank teller, but it paid little, she felt it was a dead-end job, and she wanted to provide more for their three children. She started back at college part-time while keeping the teller job for her family's health benefits. Kinsley took an English class at a community college and found her passion, exclaiming, "I felt so alive!" She added, "At the same time, I was teaching Sunday school at our church. I really liked working with the kids." Customers at the bank were telling her, "You missed your calling. You should have been a teacher." With her newfound passion and the encouragement of others, she began pursuing a career in education and made a plan. This led to a few tough years being back in college as an adult learner. Kinsley remembers the "many nights that I stayed up all night long sitting at the computer, writing reports, writing essays, reading my homework, doing that kind of thing and never went to bed. My husband would give me a kiss. I'd be at the computer desk. And he'd wake up the next morning. I was still sitting at the computer desk. It was a crazy time." But she graduated with a 3.86 GPA and continued on to her master's, earning a 4.0.

After substitute teaching, Kinsley landed her dream job as an elementary school reading teacher. She finds great joy in helping her students learn: "There's those moments where you can see that glimpse of greatness and you're like, 'Yes! Yes! You're doing it! See, I knew you could do it!'" Kinsley views learning as a social process: "There is nothing more exciting than when all of a sudden somebody grasped a concept" that you're helping them learn; "they become excited. Then it's just contagious." But Kinsley also understands that children come to school with different home experiences that greatly affect the learning process. She explained that "the biggest thing is the background knowledge, their prior experiences." When Kinsley was a child, her home life was stressful, children picked on her relentlessly, and adults looked down on her. She knew how it could lead children to act up, so she could spot it in her own students.

Kinsley recalled some children from privileged families who have many opportunities, and they travel as a family every year for spring break. But "then we've got kids who they dread spring break coming and you'll see the [bad] behavior start because" their home life is so bad. She added that other teachers from middle-class backgrounds will act exasperated, saying, "I don't get it. Why are they acting up when we're getting ready to have a week off?" Kinsley knows that it is "because school is the best place for them" given their difficult home and family circumstances. She knows from personal experience what the research overwhelmingly documents: Adverse childhood experiences, which disproportionately affect poor and working-class children, affect their school behavior.[9] For those students who don't have families that can afford quality childcare or enriching experiences like travel, they may be placed in unsafe environments when school is not in session. Kinsley's working-class cultural capital enabled her to recognize the poor behavior for what it was and intervene to support her students' development and learning.

The middle-class norms of competition and a culture of independence can worsen the barriers that working-class children face in school.[10] Teachers can often attribute normal working-class culture or behaviors (e.g., interjecting comments spontaneously into conversation) as a sign of low ability or resistance. Like the teachers who could not understand why some children act out before spring break, they might perceive their bad behavior as disengagement or a lack of interest. Such interpretations might lead to disciplinary measures and a lack of trust between teachers and children. But Kinsley's cultural background and focus on the group, a part of working-class interdependence, helped her better interpret these cultural cues and build rapport with her poor and working-class students.

I asked Kinsley a hypothetical question: If you could have a magic wand and change any one thing to help your students, what would it be? Her response illustrated the group-orientation more common among the working-class:

> More than anything, I want our kids to have a sense of belonging, that their community loves them and they always feel included, that kind of thing. Personally, I don't care what your name is. I don't want anybody to ever have that stigma. I was so embarrassed for so much of my life about what my maiden name was. I actually couldn't wait to change it. But I don't want any of our students to ever feel like that. I want them to be proud of who they are. I want them to know that they're loved and they're included.

Kinsley's cultural focus on community is supported by academic research: A sense of belonging is very important for student motivation and learning.[11] In her approach as an elementary school teacher, Kinsley emphasizes the need for a sense of belonging above anything else. She feels that "people have become more egocentric," which can be a negative effect of the middle-class focus on the self, achievement, competition, and entitlement. She contrasts this with working-class values like community, interdependence, humility, and resilience.

As a teacher, Kinsley's group-oriented approach is a cultural resource to help her students succeed. She feels this approach made her a better teacher, recounting a painful memory: "On my own personal experience, when I was in sixth grade, I had one teacher tell me that I would never amount to anything and that I would end up living off the system. I remember being devastated." At the time, Kinsley shared the experience with another teacher, who asked her, "Do you believe them?" Kinsley recalls "just stopping in my tracks." When her teacher said, "So prove them wrong," this statement made a big impact on her, and she never forgot those words. Now Kinsley frequently draws upon her own experiences of struggling in school to connect with her students: "A lot of times, I will pull them [aside] one by one and I'm able to say, 'Hey, you know what? When I was a little kid, this happened to me. This is what helped me.'" Kinsley strives to create a connection with each of her students. Drawing on her working-class culture, she identifies shared experiences, interacts with familiar styles that invite agreement and build emotional connections, and speaks in ways that reflect shared meanings.[12] This is different from the individual-oriented culture and manners of speaking in the middle class. At the individual level, connecting to others and building community with group-based norms can help teachers with working-class cultural capital be more effective in their jobs.

At the institutional level, addressing the vastly unequal distribution of resources is needed to address inequalities more fully, but hiring more teachers and support staff with working-class cultural capital can help bring about positive change in our schools. It can be a way that teachers from working-class backgrounds can use our cultural resources to make a difference in students' lives and improve school performance.[13]

Enhancing Communication: Barbara

All people are socialized into normative ways of talking about themselves, sets of tastes, and ways of communicating that are a part of their culture.[14] Problems can arise when people assume that the way that they speak will be understood by others and that things they prefer are shared with others or are the "right" thing. And because professional workplaces and society more generally are dominated by middle-class culture, these middle-class assumptions are often invisible—they are believed to be universal and correct. But an understanding of working-class cultural assumptions can help straddlers and other professionals avoid projecting middle-class assumptions onto others and help them identify misunderstandings arising from them. These cultural skills became essential for Barbara Jensen as a therapist.

Barbara grew up in Minnesota, surrounded by a lot of extended family, with connections back to some of her Jewish family in Brooklyn, New York. "Everyone we knew was working-class," she explained. This included her father (a meat cutter) and mother (a telephone solicitor), both of whom dropped out of their senior year of high school. Barbara wrote about much of her life and work in a brilliant book, *Reading Classes: On Culture and Classism in America*. She is one of the founders of the Working Class Studies Association (WCSA), which is an interdisciplinary group of scholars and activists that focus on "working-class lives, cultures, politics, economics, and social movements."[15] I initially got to know her when I started attending WCSA conferences. But when I sat down to interview Barbara at her office in Minneapolis, I was especially interested in learning how she approaches her clinical therapy practice as a straddler.

For people who want to become a therapist, the first challenge in assisting working-class clients is that they are much less likely to enter therapy. There are several reasons for this trend. First, working-class people are less likely to seek out therapy. Tori, a social worker whom I interviewed, explains that seeking therapeutic help in working-class communities is "not the norm; it's taboo" and often "unwanted." She explains that "there could be a lot of shame in accepting services if you need them" or "admitting that there's any mental health issues." Middle-class people tend to view therapy as another tool for self-actualization and accept it as more normal.[16] Second, research shows that therapists themselves are less likely to accept working-class clients, with middle-class clients being three times more likely to get a callback to schedule an appointment.[17] Stereotypical assumptions that therapists have about working-class clients could be shaping their willingness to accept new patients from lower-class backgrounds. As a result, it is less common. But still, some working-class people find their way into therapy.

In therapeutic sessions, class cultures clearly impact the counseling dynamic, especially in mixed-class couples. Barbara described a typical example in which a middle-class husband said he wished his working-class wife talked more. But like other people raised in working-class culture, she was not raised to talk about herself. In Barbara's words, "She isn't about expounding and selling herself." The husband complained that "she doesn't share enough" and "that being close means you talk and you share." Coming from a family with a professional background, he was socialized to argue, debate, and express himself individualistically through language—and assumed that her tastes for interaction would be the same. With his wife's working-class background, "she feels really shut down when he wants to argue with her, and he doesn't realize that he needs to demonstrate that he's got her back." She seeks the group-oriented nature and loyalty more common in working-class homes.[18]

Barbara quickly points out that gender, ethnicity, and other factors can impact the counseling dynamic as well. For example, women are generally socialized to be more passive, and men to be more dominant. Barbara also compared the husband to the Jewish part of her family in New York, where "we argue with each other; nobody takes it personally." But counseling, which is a more psychologically and individualistically oriented field, often does not sufficiently train practitioners in these cultural dynamics. It is her working-class cultural capital—and her own research on the role of class in shaping counseling—that affords her deeper insights.

Barbara shared a second example of a mixed-class couple who had conflict around their social lives. The wife again was from the working class, and she said in a counseling session, "Why do we have to spend our Saturday night with your boss and his wife you know with the white wine set? That's not fun." Her husband, who comes from a middle-class family, responded, "Of course it's fun. You know we get to go to fancy places" where his boss pays the bills. But she preferred to "grab a burger and a beer" and to spend more time with her family. He complained that she wanted to spend so much time with family, but that is a core value in the working class, who spend much more time with extended families.[19]

The couple's marital conflict reflected both the different tastes they had developed and also their level of comfort across social hierarchies. Middle-class people are more likely to enjoy socializing across hierarchies, whereas working-class people tend to feel more uncomfortable in these settings. By understanding these class differences and the assumptions that the partners made of each other, Barbara was better able to help them see that there was not anything deficient about the two of them. Barbara's working-class cultural capital enabled her to identify the root causes affecting her clients' marriage to be able to work through them more effectively.

When counseling people from different class backgrounds, Barbara was also mindful of the assumptions built into the speech patterns of different clients. Through higher education, middle-class professionals learn to think and speak more abstractly using concepts.[20] In contrast, working-class people tend to think more concretely. It is not that working-class people are not intelligent or capable of abstract thought but they have not been socialized to speak differently, and concrete language feels more natural to them. Barbara explained, "There are working-class people who have a lot of wisdom and they're really bright," but they communicate "it with metaphor." Therapists and other professionals might assume different meanings to such divergent manners of speech, which can impede communication.[21]

The pitfalls of cultural assumptions in middle-class speech—and the value of understanding working-class speech patterns—are also well-illustrated in Betsy Leondar-Wright's study of class activists.[22] In her research, Leondar-Wright asked activists from different backgrounds about the goals of their group. Their responses revealed especially stark differences in the language used by working-class and middle-class activists. For example, when Leondar-Wright asked two different members of an antiwar group about their goals, they both responded that it was to end the war in Iraq, but then their answers diverged. The activist from a professional middle-class background elaborated that their goal was to build a "multiracial, multiclass, multiethnic peace movement for social and economic justice"—a highly abstract goal.[23] The working-class activist responded that they didn't "want to see the recruiters harassing the kids in the high school, which they do"—a very concrete goal. Other lifelong middle-class activists indicated goals such as "take action in solidarity with different struggles that are taking place internationally and locally," "end imperialism," and "educate about radical political issues and struggles."[24] They incorrectly assumed that others within their group perceived their group as having the same goal or that others would even understand the meaning of such goals.

In contrast to the abstract speech of activists from middle-class backgrounds, working-class activists "tended to make points with examples, metaphors, and especially analogies, typically starting with a phrase such as 'Say you and I were...'" One lifelong-working-class activist "used a metaphor to explain why she felt compelled to organize against extreme poverty: '[It] is like seeing kids on a railroad track, and when you push those kids off that railroad track, is that a choice or did you have to do that? I have to do that."[25] Some metaphors were typical cliches (e.g., "other fish to fry," "heavy foot on the gas"), but many were more vivid metaphors that working-class people "freshly coined," such as "I'm a pebble in their shoe." Despite—or because of—the simpler language, they often carried meaning that better resonated with a broader audience. Using this working-class language proved to be an asset for many class activists.

The use of metaphor—and its power—in working-class speech was referenced in other interviews as well. Journalist and author Alfred Lubrano told me that in his writing, sometimes he tries to be as "sophisticated" as he can, but that "some of the best quotes, some of the most pithy, most sophisticated, most worldly-wise things that were ever said to me were said to me by blue-collar people assessing a situation." He explained these quotes are "just by bits of experience and insight" that did not require "a lot of courses at a college." Working-class people "just understood." The abstract language of middle-class speech, such as references to "imperialism," can "occasionally [flatten] out a professional middle-class activist's speech into simplistic generalizations, unelaborated with examples"—which hinders communication.[26] The assumed meanings and overreliance on vague buzzwords might fail to resonate with one's audience. However, the concrete language and metaphors of working-class speech patterns are more direct and intuitive and have the potential to be more hard-hitting. They are another form of working-class cultural capital that can enhance communication.

Reclaiming Working-Class Norms and Heritage: Michael

When upwardly mobile straddlers continue with more college and advanced degrees, and we continue further into our professional careers, we can find ourselves talking, looking, and carrying ourselves more and more like people in the middle class. While this is very helpful for navigating much of professional life, there can be moments where it doesn't feel quite right—and where middle-class culture can actually lead us astray. Michael learned this the hard way. He came to find that consciously disregarding the norms and language of middle-class culture and reclaiming working-class norms could make him a better community organizer.

Michael was born in 1940 in Breathitt County, Kentucky, or as some call it, "bloody Breathitt."[27] His father was a coal miner and industrial worker but was murdered when Michael was only two years old. His mother raised Michael and his eight older brothers and sisters, barely making it on subsistence farming and his late father's small pension from having served in military combat. His family had been farming the land in those Kentucky hills for over two hundred years. Both parents had only an eighth-grade education. But his "parents didn't see themselves as poor and built into their children a sense of hope and that you can do better than [they] did." Michael believed this was "a precious asset that was part of the family heritage from both sides."

With prompting from his teachers and support from his principal, Michael would become the first of his family to graduate from college. While his family supported his decision to move away to college, the choice did carry some psychological costs.[28] Michael reiterated a common working-class value of the family. Often this can mean "family needs to come before saving money or becoming upwardly mobile, sending your kids to college or any of those upwardly mobile things. If somebody in the family needs something, you're gonna let them have it. Getting ahead was not part of the ethic." He was careful to note that isn't every working-class person's reality, as "there were certainly people who would kill their own mother to get ahead in our community." But the strain for Michael "was you had to pull apart from that warm and fuzzy family world, you know, going off to college is a pretty selfish kind of thing" because you're "leaving home and leaving the extended family." That choice was "one of the hurts of upward mobility."[29]

Relatedly, some people in his community were taught "don't give up your raising, so actually, the steps one would take to become upwardly mobile are actually penalized in the working-class community by the threat of rejection." He saw this with other children, such as one girl who moved away for a while and when she returned to Kentucky, "she dressed a little different and she walked a little and talked a little different, and I remember the sympathy I felt for her when I saw the other kids reject her." They despairingly called her "cityfied" and regularly ridiculed her. Fortunately for Michael, "My family never rejected me no matter how many years I spent in college," and he suspected "they probably felt that I was doing some stuff that they hadn't got to do."

After college, Michael became a community organizer. But "when I first started out as a community organizer, my education was in some ways a handicap," Michael told me. "The working-class families that I worked with in Walnut Hills would correct my vocabulary." In this case, "correcting" his vocabulary meant helping him talk more like a working-class person again:

> A group of African American women were feeding me sweet potato pie, and we were having a party after we had a victory with our block club. One of the women must've asked me why I was doing this kind of work and I said, "Well I just want to help people become more human." She said, "What do you mean? More human?" That came out of my seminary buddies and professors, that

kind of language. I realized you can't use all the language from this world, in that world. It kinda took me back. Where do I draw my vocabulary? Well, I need to use more of the vocabulary that I used to have before I went away and had all of these influences.

For Michael, the middle-class academic influences drew him further away from the people he wanted to be working with. He added, "What the Walnut Hills families did was make me reclaim my working-class heritage." He would come to "regain the treasure of life experiences that I had and that helped me work with inner-city families and rural families."

Michael's professional training sometimes put him at odds with working-class culture, and he had to learn when to reject middle-class cultural norms. As a community organizer, Michael had taken classes in social work, and "in social work you're taught not to share anything of your personal life with your clients." Despite social work training encouraging clear boundaries between your personal and professional lives, building relationships for community organizing often means that "people expect you to reveal some stuff about you."[30] He learned to walk a fine line by sharing details about himself. So, he "would eat with people, stuff that other social workers or community organizers wouldn't do." He said that the working-class families he worked with "know my kids by name and I know their kids by name." He added, "I realized this is a test; am I one of them or am I an outsider? I used judgment but I didn't go by the book."

Michael went further to explain the role of cultural norms beyond these class boundaries to think about other ethnic and racial boundaries. He recounted examples working in a variety of neighborhoods, including white Appalachian, Black Appalachian, racially diverse Appalachian, rural, and inner-city white and Black neighborhoods. Citing sociologist Herbert Gans, he noted that "there is an invisible cultural boundary that separates" the "hostile outside world" out there and the "person-oriented ethnic neighborhoods" that he was working in. "Most people trying to help these neighborhoods cross an invisible barrier without even knowing it. But if you cross it knowingly, it should affect your behavior," he added. Very early in his career, after the 1967 race riots, Michael was "assigned to visit the home of Black men who had been arrested for rioting, and they didn't want to talk to a 'white son of a b-tch.'" But as a white Appalachian entering poor Black neighborhoods of Cincinnati, he leaned into the person-centered orientation of his working-class culture. Michael said, "I made clear that I was interested in them" and "not as someone just brought in to change their lives." He consciously avoided judgmental and stereotypical language. As a result, despite all the justifiable race-based rage all around him at the time, he was able to continue helping to organize Black Appalachian communities without incident.

But person-centered cultural norms are not without their contradictions. For Michael, this meant that "I never did openly tell people I was gay; I didn't share that secret." This certainly was not true among all of the gay, bisexual, or trans people whom I interviewed—several of whom were open about their sexuality in their personal and professional lives. Indeed, Michael was among the oldest of my respondents and had grown up in a time when society was far less accepting of people on the LGBTQ+ spectrum. But there is also some research to suggest that working-class people can be less accepting of diverse gender and sexual identities.[31] While plenty of working-class people fully embrace such identities, they are also more likely to hold rigid moral values.[32] For Michael, his reluctance to share his sexual identity may also have been affected by his organizing affiliated with religious communities. Some of his career was with Catholic Social Services, and there had been a culture of "don't ask, don't tell" even though some of his colleagues were aware of it and fully accepting of him being gay.

By reclaiming working-class norms and communication styles, Michael built a career in community organizing and helped to empower poor and working-class people. He helped lead and run multiple community organizations and coalitions (e.g., Appalachian Committee of the Human Relations Commission, Urban Appalachian Council, Urban Appalachian Community Coalition, and Appalachian Identity Center), worked for nonprofit organizations, and consulted with nonprofits and churches. While he did move into the middle class, he chose not to "get above his raisin'" by maintaining his connections to his working-class community. Along the way, he fought for structural change that helped lift up others around him.

The Invisibility of Working-Class Culture

While it is true that middle-class cultural capital is needed for navigating professional environments, this chapter has documented ways in which it can also be insufficient or problematic. Middle-class norms, communication patterns, and expectations can also lead people to misinterpret working-class students' behavior, make it harder to build trust and forge relationships with poor and working-class clients, and incorrectly interpret verbal and nonverbal communication. When engaging with working-class people, an understanding of working-class values, language, preferences, and interactional norms can be an important cultural resource. In fact, this type of linguistic capital can be valuable for interacting within any particular community, such as communities of color.[33] In the cases presented here, working-class cultural capital made a significant difference in the desired outcome.

However, the dominance of middle-class culture and the simultaneous invisibility of working-class culture means that problematic prescriptions from middle-class culture can go undetected. Middle-class culture is largely taken for granted as the *correct* set of beliefs, and its associated norms are seen as the natural way guiding our behavior. Sociologists refer to such beliefs as *hegemonic* because these ideas are accepted as common sense and often not questioned.[34] We come to view and evaluate others' behaviors through this lens of middle-class culture, which further advantages those socialized into it from an early age. Because we largely remain ignorant of this cultural dynamic, it serves to reproduce social inequality. But those who have acquired working-class cultural capital—either through their upbringing or through other life experiences—are better positioned to name these cultural problems, connect with working-class people, and advocate for change.

This chapter explored only a few of the ways that an understanding of working-class norms, language, and communication led to better professional outcomes. But my interview data revealed a much broader set of occupational contexts where these cultural resources were important. As a nurse, Lisa is better able to diagnose working-class patients' ailments with a sensitivity to people's home environments and their tendency toward shorter responses. Success in her job requires building rapport and asking more questions to get important information, which was informed by her working-class cultural capital. As a judge, Suzanne better understands how to interpret working-class defendants' verbal and nonverbal communication in the courtroom to resolve disputes. As a politician and political organizer, Sen. Nina Turner knows how to craft a message that would resonate with her working-class constituents. Given the class structure of the United States, these circumstances are actually much more common than we might initially suspect. Naming this taken-for-granted cultural hegemony allows us to question the root systems of these inequalities and work to transform them.

The power of these cultural resources, furthermore, is amplified when straddlers can acquire both working-class *and* middle-class cultural capital. The next chapter presents stories in which the simultaneous possession of both forms of capital became essential across a variety of professional contexts. They became part of a multicultural skill set for both professional success and lifting up working-class people.

5
Translating, Code-Switching, Mediating, and Bridge-Building

Upwardly mobile first-generation graduates must learn middle-class culture that dominates professional settings. But as the last chapter shows, there are moments when middle-class culture leads us astray and working-class cultural capital is needed to reach a desired outcome. For navigating some situations, however, it is not enough to possess middle-class cultural capital or working-class cultural capital. Some instances demand having acquired both forms of capital.

In daily life, people interact across class lines in all sorts of situations—in schools, at the doctor's office, in the courtroom, at a job interview, or in government offices, just to name a few. We are often not conscious of these class lines existing, and yet, the effects can be dramatic. Important decisions can be made by professionals that affect if someone gets an appropriate medical treatment, or second chance that avoids punishment, or financial support that shields them from poverty, or if the best candidate gets hired for the job. Class culture is always there shaping how people make sense of what someone across that class line is saying, what is expected of them, or if they might work together effectively. For those people who possess both middle-class and working-class cultural capital, they can translate across the class divide, resolve potential conflicts, and facilitate shared understanding..

As straddlers climb the class ladder, they are uniquely immersed in both working-class and middle-class cultures that equip them with distinct multicultural skills. While it is essential that they acquire middle-class cultural capital to make it in their new professional contexts, those straddlers who maintain their working-class cultural capital have additional skills to offer. The stories below show how straddlers can develop unique capabilities for translating, code-switching, mediating, and bridge-building across class cultures. These skills become instrumental in decoding systems, developing organizational policies, resolving cultural conflicts, and building coalitions of seemingly disparate groups.

The Translation Work of Multicultural Navigators: Sydney

Like a majority of my respondents, Sydney had a more difficult time navigating college and searching for professional jobs than her middle-class counterparts. Without parents or other close adults who have attended college or obtained such jobs, working-class first-gen students have fewer models for how it works. Compared with middle-class students, we have fewer people to go to for advice.[1]

For those of us upwardly mobile straddlers who have successfully made it through college and are in professional jobs, we have a unique perspective on the process. In addition to better understanding the cultural context of working-class life, we have likely gained middle-class cultural capital in successfully navigating college and the labor market. Being conscious of these distinctive cultural contexts makes us excellent translators, or "multicultural navigators."[2] We have the resourcefulness to help decode systems,[3] communicate the norms and rules to others who haven't learned the appropriate language, and equip students with the skills to manage them successfully.[4]

Sydney had almost no family support in the college selection process. Her father worked as a bartender and construction worker, while her mother was an aide at the local library. They eventually earned their GEDs but never attended college. She was lucky that some of her middle-class friends were touring nearby colleges and she was invited to tag along. But when it came time for the application process and completing the Free Application for Federal Student Aid (FAFSA), Sydney bluntly stated, "I was on my own." She was in her mid-twenties when I interviewed her, just a couple of years after graduating college.

In college, Sydney learned to decode the hidden curriculum.[5] For example, while Sydney was attending school and working paid jobs, she started to learn she needed many skills and experiences that were not taught in the classroom. She especially came to understand the need for quality internships but that many of them were unpaid—and she needed paid work to afford college. At the same time, she observed that students from higher-class backgrounds could get "really prestigious internships or, heck, even internships internationally because their parents can foot the bill for it." These internships gave middle-class students career experiences and a leg up on the job market, further compounding the academic advantages they already had. Sydney came to realize that, by itself, "this bachelor's degree isn't going to get me" to a life with "more stability."

Sydney started to believe she was misled that a degree alone would help her climb the social ladder: "That's actually a lie. My parents believed it because that's what they saw happen with their friends.... But for my generation in particular, that's just not going to happen." Only then was she able to see that students like herself needed other types of support to translate their degree into a career—including on-the-job career experience and skills in resume writing, interviewing, and relating one's academic learning to a job. It was at that moment that Sydney found her passion: "So I realized I really want to be in the university setting, working with students." As she continued through college, Sydney gradually figured out the system and wanted to use her experiences to help others—especially working-class first-gen students—learn it more quickly and effectively.

Sydney now works at a career center at a major university. She works with students one-on-one and runs a variety of workshops. Her focus is on helping students select a major, learn about career pathways, identify their vocational interests, and apply for jobs. To be successful at supporting students in this process, she helps them feel comfortable accessing her office, develop relationships with their professors, identify appropriate language for resumes, and learn the norms of interviewing for white-collar jobs. Many students, but especially students from working-class and low-income backgrounds, are less likely to have learned these skills from family or to feel comfortable and confident in these tasks.[6] Sydney has a keen awareness of her own working-class culture, which she uses to relate to students and help them navigate college and office cultures. She has become a multicultural navigator helping students decode campus norms, the job search process, networking, and career-building by translating these systems in ways they can understand. Whereas middle-class students with college-educated parents learn many of these skills at home and are often coached by their parents, working-class students need to find new people who can help them understand college and how to navigate it.[7]

Resume writing is one area in which Sydney supports first-gen students. As noted in chapter 1, working-class people tend to communicate with a range of nonverbal cues and implied meanings and are usually raised with smaller vocabularies.[8] Resumes, which require explicit types of language more common among the middle class, represent another disadvantage working-class job seekers face. Sydney uses humor to introduce working-class students to this specific style of writing and speaking. She tells students, "When we're working on resumes in particular, I'll be like, 'You've just got to use those rich people words.'" By using plain language ("rich people words"), Sydney is direct and humorously refers to something that makes intuitive sense. She knows they are likely intimidated by just being in her office, so this style of humor can help them feel at ease and want to keep coming back. But she is careful in considering the students for which such language will resonate: "I always have to read my interaction with the students, see if it's appropriate, if they're going to think it's funny or get it."

Sydney is also mindful to help them select language that they can successfully use. She explained that "we do have a list of power verbs that we give students just to help them think through some language, but I do try to have them come up with it" so that it is language that they feel comfortable using. She explained that the language should be "representative of them," and knowing they are less comfortable interacting with authority figures, she wants them to "feel confident" using it in an interview. Her process seeks to explain the cultural expectations for writing resumes, which relies on a specific form of communication that is different from the communication styles more common among working-class communities. She tries to translate these norms ("power verbs") into humorous words ("rich people words") to which they can relate to help them build middle-class cultural capital. This language can be contrasted against the informal communication styles that they may be used to—not to devalue working-class cultural norms but to empower them to navigate multiple contexts.

As a white working-class woman, Sydney drew on her working-class cultural capital of empathy to relate to other disadvantaged groups and help them decode institutional processes in racial contexts as well. For example, she partnered with her university's office of diversity, equity, and inclusion (DEI) to better serve first-gen Latine students. She explained that in career services, advisers will see that students receive significant "pressures from outside people" in selecting a major. For example, "their friends are telling them to major in this or pursue this, or their mom is a nurse, so they should be a nurse." Career advisers often tell them to "wipe all of that out, don't listen to your parents, don't listen to your friends" so that they can find their own passions and strengths. However, encouraging students to be more independent when picking their major and disregarding their parents' wishes can be off-putting for some students: "With Latino students in particular, family is such a strong piece of their identity." She added that telling students not to listen to their parents "when they're choosing their major or their career choice is actually going to just completely shut them down." Instead, she has to be aware of additional (racial) cultural differences and how to support those students. In those instances, it might require helping them to have a conversation with their parents if they decide, "I don't want to be an engineer; this is truly what I want to do." Sydney knew that translating the culture of higher education for diverse working-class cultures required multiple dictionaries.

Our identity plays an important role, but not a totalizing role, in working with people across social groups. On the one hand, Sydney believes she has made first gens a priority and has worked with them more successfully than her middle-class colleagues because of her class experiences and working-class cultural capital. For example, she is better able to decode and explain effective resume writing to students socialized into working-class linguistic norms, understanding how their lack of confidence affects interactions with her office, how to grow their confidence for professional interviews, and so forth. She describes herself as being far more concerned than her co-workers with tailoring services to first gens and knowing how to communicate college expectations to them. Sydney also witnessed some of her more well-intentioned middle-class colleagues struggling sometimes to help first-gen students. It is not that middle-class people are incapable of supporting first-gen working-class students, but they have to be more active in seeking out opportunities to learn about working-class cultures and strategies for supporting them most effectively. Sydney's working-class cultural capital and class consciousness enabled her office to better assist students.

Similarly, Sydney does not have to be Latina to be supportive of students with that racial background. Working-class cultures vary significantly by race, among other factors. She reflected on her experiences as a white woman learning "about the intersections of how my experience has been different" because she has "white privilege [while] being first-gen." Like middle-class colleagues learning to better support working-class first-gen students, Sydney had to be aware that her whiteness gave her a specific view, and she sought out opportunities (learning from and working with her university's DEI office) to become a more effective multicultural navigator in supporting students of color.[9] She was aware of her own limitations but drew upon her experiences as a first-gen student to empathize with other forms of inequality. By partnering with colleagues in her university's DEI office, Sydney worked actively to broaden her multicultural navigational skills for working-class students from diverse backgrounds. Leveraging her working-class cultural capital has made her and her office more effective.

Code-Switching: Leigh

Growing up in East London, Leigh developed a thick accent that immediately shouted her working-class background to the world. She recalled walking through a crowded bar as an undergraduate where "the only way to get to get to the bar was to walk through these two women who were talking." Leigh squeezed between them and apologized on her way through: "Excuse me. I'm really sorry. I'm really sorry. Excuse me." As she walked past them, one of the women mocked her accent in an attempt to belittle her. Leigh explained, "I just took a step back" and made eye contact with her standing "the same height as me." As she recounted the story to me, Leigh held her thumb and forefinger inches apart, noting, "I was *this close* to her." Leigh retorted, "You got a problem?" The woman was terrified and shrunk back, hanging her head sheepishly. Leigh took pride in channeling her working-class background when she needed it, but she would also learn how to navigate middle-class culture. She would become a master at code-switching across class cultures.[10]

Code-switching refers to the process of adjusting behavior, style of speech, appearance, and other parts of one's self-presentation to fit into different social situations.[11] All people code-switch to some degree, such as when people speak differently around their friends than they might around their family or in the classroom. But code-switching is especially linked to people transitioning between social groups. For example, a Black student might use Black English among other African Americans but adopt a different interactional style among a predominantly white group.[12] We are often not aware of our code-switching, but a better understanding of the cultural codes—like class codes—that exist and how we use them can help straddlers be more strategic.

Despite the stigma of working-class accents in the UK, Leigh's background would ultimately prove to be an asset in her work as a speech therapist. Leigh's father dropped out of school at age fifteen and worked a manual factory job. Her mother was a retail clerk. During her entire upbringing, their family lived in council housing, which is housing provided by the British government. This was essential for providing them with a stable place to live because money was "tight." Her parents could not afford books, but her mother frequently took her and her younger brother to the library. "My family said education gives you choices," Leigh explained.

At age eighteen, Leigh began working as a bank clerk, which she described as a low-status working-class job. But she joined a labor union and was asked to serve as the union's health and safety representative. The collective agreement between the trade union and the bank afforded workers positions in setting rules and evaluating their implementation in the workplace. After receiving her training, Leigh conducted her first inspection with a "much more senior" office manager from a middle-class background. She recounted that "in an instant, I went from being least scumbag office junior to being this respected equal for that thirty minutes of inspection." It brought into focus how working-class people are so often looked down upon and treated with disrespect. She thought to herself, "I'm [a] working-class scumbag, but when I'm in the collective, you know you can't mess with me." It helped her develop a class consciousness and sparked her interest in a university degree in industrial relations, which she began when she was twenty-three.

After Leigh graduated with her bachelor's degree, she began a career working in services for the homeless and eventually earned a professional degree in speech and language therapy. When I interviewed her, Leigh was leading a nonprofit organization that she helped create. The organization focuses on providing clinical support in speech language and communication for people who are homeless. Leigh treats people with communication issues, addressing issues like how our speech sounds to other people, how clients' minds process what they are hearing, and how communication is affected by memory and attention. For example, Leigh found that people were misattributing speech problems to mental health issues or substance abuse in some of her clients, but she came to identify the cause as physical damage to the brain.

Leigh went further to say that, as an organization, "we are also very interested in making people aware of how powerful and influential language is and how it can be used to control and manipulate and judge people." One way through which this control and judgment occurs is the stereotyping of different accents, which is more prevalent in the UK. A recent report found that in the UK, accent is "arguably the primary signal" of one's class background.[13] Accents associated with industrial cities (e.g., Manchester, Liverpool, or Birmingham), working-class neighborhoods (e.g., Leigh's neighborhood of Essex in East London), or racial minorities (e.g., Afro-Caribbean or British Indians) are stereotyped and ranked lower socially. Accents referred to as "Queen's English" or "BBC English" are viewed most favorably, even though "less than 10 percent of the population [is] estimated to have this accent" and are "almost exclusively from higher socioeconomic backgrounds." Like Leigh conveyed in her story above, nearly half of university students (47 percent) and employees (46 percent) report being mocked or "singled out" for their accents. Beyond the personal pain, it can be a barrier to social mobility.

Leigh finds that people associate working-class accents with "stupidity, with coarseness, being offensive." As a result, her clients feel shame about their communication, accent, or vocabulary. They often tell her, "My accent, oh God, my English is terrible." She added, "That's class discrimination," and she strives to help them build confidence and deepen their communication skills. When she speaks with someone who has a working-class accent, she might convey that "it's beautiful. I can understand every word you say. Anybody from your area would understand every word you say." Leigh can use her working-class speech codes, and because she is saying it as an expert, "they heard it from a speech therapist now, so it must be clinically true." Leigh takes pride that she "can give people that confidence" because she has "those letters [after her name], that professional qualification, and I love using it in that way." She also signals to others that their organization will be a welcoming place to them, noting, "We're really clear on our website that we are run by working-class people. We identify as working-class." But through her education and life experiences, she has also learned middle-class codes and can switch in an instant.

Leigh's strategic code-switching accomplishes several important functions. She explained that when she is in "a formal context and I'm trying to achieve something," she will use "BBC English." Specifically, she adopts the more "formal accent" associated with that background and slows her rate of speech. Leigh "will deliberately choose" the jargon "that is technically or medically or legally a little bit more obscure" and specific to the "field they're used to using." It might include altering one's vocabulary, structuring sentences differently with more or fewer "I statements," changing the use of metaphor, or following different norms for who speaks when.[14] Leigh added, "My husband says I even changed the way I stand when I do it," with her "shoulders back." She might use this in a job interview or "when I want something" from a person she is interacting with, and "I don't think they're going to want to give it to me."

Leigh also code-switches when confronting stereotypes about working-class people and their speech. She lamented that "some people from middle-class or upper-class backgrounds think that their [style and accent are] the right and natural way to speak. They believe that "this is how we are as people, this is how we should behave, [these are] our views and our behavior, and our approaches [are] the best way for people." She explained that "society's not set up in a way to encourage people who aren't working class to think like that and to stop and question their own experience." So, she code-switches to speak to them in a way they respect that might challenge their stereotypes.

Straddlers' cultural capital of code-switching can help them better move between and connect with different groups. According to one researcher, "Code switching can make it easier to connect with others and build personal relationships when they see themselves in you and recognize shared traits."[15] Indeed, I saw this throughout my interviews, with people in diverse occupational fields using code-switching effectively in both their occupations and personal connections. For example, it was used by an international development expert to move between local farmers and global funding agencies, engineers working on projects in low-income communities who had to also speak the scientific language of their field, and therapists like Barbara trying to connect with working-class clients. This cultural resource is an asset for building one's social network and having legitimacy with distinct groups. It can become a powerful tool in both climbing the class ladder and lifting up the working-class community.

However, code-switching is a double-edged sword, and its burdens are not shared equally. Middle-class and white people are generally socialized into dominant ways of presenting themselves from an early age, so they more naturally fit into college environments and the professional workplace. Working-class people and those from other marginalized groups (e.g., people of color, immigrants, etc.) have no choice but to learn the cultural codes of the dominant group if they want to "fit in." These marginalized groups are required to invest more time and emotional energy into learning and practicing these cultural codes.[16] Learning to code-switch can be powerful, but it does come with a cost.

Mediating Class Conflicts: April

Working-class and poor people are socialized to develop a sense of constraint.[17] When interacting with people in positions of authority, especially in institutional settings, we often feel intimidated by people whose advanced degrees and status grant them power over us. This can lead to a variety of internal and external conflicts: Our nervousness may keep us preoccupied trying to understand a situation, we may be confused by the jargon or language that professionals use, we might feel too uncomfortable to ask questions, or miscommunication might arise from different understandings of a situation. So, when straddlers climb their way into these positions of authority, we might use our cultural capital to mediate class conflicts that arise. Like April, we can strategically reference our own experiences to connect with clients, develop trust, and better support both middle- and working-class people in resolving conflicts.

April's humble beginnings are something she will never forget and motivated her entire career trajectory. Her father was a machinist with a union wage but had not graduated high school because he "mouthed off" to a teacher who flunked him for it (that was the last class he needed to get his diploma). April's mother was a stay-at-home mom during her childhood, then became a bus driver for the local school system. April was an exceptionally bright child but was lucky to fare so well in her school that had such low expectations of its poor and working-class students (see April's story that opened chapter 2).

When it came time for college, April began at the prestigious University of Chicago. But she was not prepared for college, was "overwhelmed," and withdrew after one semester. She returned to her hometown in Ohio wanting to go into teaching. She spent a semester volunteering as a teacher's aide with a former English teacher who mentored her. When she was in high school, nearly all of her female classmates pursued traditional female occupations (e.g., nurses, teachers), and "no one talked to us about being doctors, lawyers." But April also "started attending all the school board and city council meetings." She was "fascinated" as she got to know a new young attorney on the council. April explained that "after a few months of sitting through council and board meetings and watching dynamics and who got to speak and who was voiceless, I thought, 'You know what? The only way to get in this system and make change is a law degree.'" She decided to go to law school. She bounced around between colleges and finished her law degree at Lewis & Clark College in Portland, Oregon.

As a working-class woman in law, it wasn't easy. In 2023, there were more women than men in law school, although women lag behind men in many upper-level law professions.[18] But when she was in law school back in the late 1970s, only 10 percent of law school graduates were women, and April explained that women "were not wanted" there. Some of her professors "verbally attacked female students and put them down." After starting her career in law in Oregon (representing Native American tribes) and California (for the Continuing Education of the Bar), April returned to Ohio again. As a practicing attorney, her experience with gender discrimination continued. She worked with male colleagues on cases, and clients often assumed she was the secretary. Male attorneys who represented the other side would appeal to her rather than her male colleagues to settle a case because as a woman, "they saw me as a weaker attorney."

April's law practice was focused on school law, zone and development law, and domestic relations. Domestic relations usually meant representing women in cases of domestic abuse, and almost all were low-income people for whom she provided deep discounts or free services. She explained that "divorce is economic disaster" because it usually results in a loss of an entire income and sometimes means going to zero income: "For me, it was a moral choice. How can I charge this woman X thousand dollars?" Many of them were dealing with custody battles and partners (usually husbands) who had higher incomes. Some clients even thanked her with baked goods. The income she earned from wealthier clients on zoning and development law, which she greatly enjoyed working on, subsidized her writing off bills for assisting low-income women and men on domestic relations cases.

April was very clear that she viewed courts as "white middle-class institutions." She added, "We talk to people as white middle-class institutions, and we expect you, the public, to understand us." When I interviewed April, she was working as a mediator with the county's juvenile court. In this role, April works with schools and students' families on attendance issues and with first-time juvenile offenders to divert them from the juvenile justice system. She explained that "as a mediator, one of the things you strive to do is equal the balance of power in a room." In addition to managing class inequalities, when you have "white school administrators [and an] African-American family," there is a clear "race imbalance" in court proceedings.[19]

In one case, April mediated between a middle school and a Black working-class girl who had gotten in a fight with and shoved a white classmate. The Black girl had been charged with assault, which is significantly more severe than the disorderly conduct charge usually applied in these types of cases. April read the police report and was confused about why the more severe charge was applied. Both the school and the girl's mother told April that this was very unusual behavior for the girl—she had never had detention or been called to the principal's office. During the mediation, April allowed the girl to speak first. The young girl was shaking and upset, quickly admitting she "shoved the other girl."

When April asked if something happened, the girl dropped her head low and said, "It's because of my skin color." Her classmate said very hurtful things so she "was tired of it" and pushed her. The girl had told this to the white school resource officer and the white police officer, but that never made it into the report. April paused and decoded the situation: "You're here for two reasons. One is because you shoved a girl at school. You're also here because you're Black." By acknowledging the racial dynamic and discrimination, April was able to better connect with the girl and help her family navigate an unjust situation and avoid the girl being drawn into the juvenile justice system. April sarcastically explained to me, "We're a nice community. And we don't talk about race in nice places, period."

With her working-class cultural capital and her middle-class knowledge of law, April mediated all kinds of class conflicts. She recounted working with one family on attendance issues. A white male teenage student had accumulated many late attendances and some absences, but "it turns out the reason he is often tardy is because of car issues." Knowing of the power imbalance in this middle-class context, she wanted to signal her understanding and build a connection to reach a better resolution. After hearing the family's explanation, she laid her pen down, leaned forward, and said, "I totally get that. Yeah. Car problems are hard. Let me tell you how I got here this morning." April explained that she drove a ten-year-old Ford Taurus, but "in the winter, the doors freeze shut. But what that means is the door will not latch until the car has warmed up." She and her husband "figured out two winters ago" that she "could bungee cord the door shut." It was a "bitter cold" January day when she had to use the bungee cord. After April told the story, the grandmother "smiles and she tells a similar story. 'Oh my God, the car, remember the car I had that we had to pull the window up and then you had to tape it up?'" They talked through how to address the student's tardies and absences, and the grandmother hugged April as they were leaving. Afterward, the assistant principal said, "I can't believe you told that story" because he thought April was "humiliating" herself. But April explained, "That was the fastest way to let them know I heard them." So rather than saying "Well, you need to do better," she modeled a proactive approach to addressing their car troubles with the school and inspired them to implement it by communicating her understanding. April completed a successful mediation not only because of her middle-class skills in law but also because she could strategically signal her working-class identity to connect with the family and build trust.

In addition to helping clients directly, April developed new school policies and court procedures for better addressing the power imbalance in school mediations. For example, she helped shift school mediations more toward an approach of restorative justice.[20] In contrast to more punitive approaches, restorative justice aims to help offenders understand the consequences of their actions, take accountability, and have an opportunity to redeem themselves. It aims to prevent further harm while involving victims in an active role in the process to help identify ways of repairing a situation. April also helped develop a mental health docket that steered people with mental illness toward supervised programs that were less punitive. The population is disproportionately low-income, and by addressing their needs regarding health care, housing, and employment, the county saw a dramatic drop in recidivism rates. Finally, she helped start a free legal clinic for people who had difficulty affording legal advice. By using her working-class cultural capital and middle-class legal skills in developing policy, April was able to move beyond helping individuals to make a bigger and longer-lasting impact to support the working class.

Bridging Classes: John

How does someone come from a third-generation coal-mining family, then become a climate scientist advocating for an end to coal and still make peace with his community? This was the dilemma facing John. But he would come to use both his working- and middle-class cultural capital and find his career niche. As a climate scientist focusing on worker transition, he actively bridges two class worlds.

John's grandfather was an Italian immigrant who settled in West Virginia to start a family and earn a living in the coal mines. He would crawl down into the mine and cut out coal with a pickax. Technology would evolve and by the time John's father began working in the mines, there were new extraction techniques. John's father was a longwall maintenance foreman. He explained that "the longwall is the machinery that's used to extract coal from an underground coal seam, so it's a very large. . . . It basically cuts the coal out of the seam and lowers it on the conveyor belts and then is shipped out of the mine on rail cars." His father fixed "everything when it broke down." As a third-generation coal miner, John's brother is a general laborer who runs the equipment that loads coal onto the cars that get the coal out of the mine. He is also the first family member of the United Mine Workers of America, the largest union in this sector.

The coal mines drew John's family members because they paid a decent wage, especially in unionized mines. But they took a toll on the family. The rhythms of family life revolved around a demanding work schedule: "Growing up, I remember being vividly aware of what shift Dad was on—primarily so that we didn't wake him up. Day shift meant that he left before we woke, and when he returned in the evening (after a stop at his favorite bar), we'd have a chance of seeing him in a good mood. Afternoon shift meant that he left while we were still at school and didn't get home until after we were asleep. Midnight shift was the worst. That's because we'd get to see him before he went to work. My dad usually left grumpy—or angry." When John was thirteen, the coal mines would also take his grandfather's life. He died of black lung, also known as "coal-mine dust lung disease" and the single largest threat to the health of coal miners.[21]

John had interests in science, astronomy, and the environment growing up. He studied physics, eventually earning his PhD. His research, working for NASA, was on distant planets. But after several years, he recalled that his "interests turned back to the environment—and to protecting *this* planet." He had a strong connection to West Virginia and remembers intensely feeling that "I want to give something back to this place that has given me so much." John told me, "I think it's actually not understandable to outsiders," but people from Appalachia "have a connection to place" that is uncommon in other regions.[22] Similarly, Michael (see chapter 4) said of Appalachia, "Growing up in the mountains involves a really intimate relationship with the mountains, the creeks, the sky, sun, snow, the elements, the birds, the snakes, the animals." He added that it is about "your relationship with your fellow human beings, the memories of the people, and just things that you don't get in modern, urban society." Michael gave an example of "someone who, like my mother, could just sit in a rocking chair without saying a word, and you could be in the same room with her [and] feel her presence but not have to use words. That's a spiritual thing." For many people, this is a core part of Appalachian working-class culture.

John switched careers to climate science and environmental policy in Washington, D.C. He asked himself, "If we need to reduce our dependence on fossil fuels in order to protect the climate, what's going to happen to a place like West Virginia, to people like my brother, who works in the mines?" John's brother found that "college wasn't for him. He tried working in just about every restaurant in our hometown," but it was never enough to live off. So, his brother eventually "found a job with good pay and good benefits: as a coal miner."

In John's middle-class world of climate science and policy, it was rare for his colleagues to have a deep understanding of the lives of workers left behind with necessary policy reforms. John felt that, as a result, the wonkish D.C. policy world "others" coal miners. He said, "To most people in [the] environmental community, coal miners are just other people that we don't have to really worry about or think about or figure out what to do with them." But, for John, "It's very personal":

> Imagine what it must be like for a coal miner to hear this message that what you're doing is bad for the planet. Think of it this way: It would be like someone walking into my office and saying, "John, the fact that you're a scientist is destroying the planet, and you have to do something else now." First, it would be really hard to hear that; I'm not a bad person any more than my brother is. And second, once I was over that news, I would just work on my resume and go get another job. [But] we're talking about communities where those other

opportunities either don't exist or don't pay nearly as well. . . . What's your answer to that, environmental community? We have no answer to that.

Because the environmental community lacks a real understanding of coal miners' lives or connections to their communities, John explains that they are "not seen as credible messengers in places like Appalachia." When coal miners are ignored (or made to feel shame) by the environmental community, it also makes sense that coal miners then often side with politicians and business executives who want to keep and expand coal production (and other environmentally destructive industries).[23] They are merely trying to provide for their families—an urgent need compared to what might feel like a distant problem.

John explained to me that he has "learned ways to leverage" his working-class roots in building bridges across class groups. He described it this way: "I have this other experience that nobody around me understands, and that allows me to speak with a different voice than most everybody else that I interact with professionally can. It also allows me to try to speak to people back home in a way that *they* can understand." If "you can speak both languages," John says, "you have value now because you're the person that can make the connections between these two worlds that can't communicate [with] each other." It's not only his ability to code-switch that is an "asset" but the ability to help one another understand the other's experiences and see that they have a common interest in solving a problem. It is his dual possession of both working-class and middle-class cultural capital that makes this possible.

Back home, John returns to his working-class style of speaking to bridge his two worlds. He allows his West Virginia accent to return, avoids jargon, and listens deeply to what people have to say. His husband picks up on the language shift every time. John even shared that his mother recently told him, "You're just so down to earth, and you're not condescending." The implication, however, is that many middle-class and wealthy people *are* condescending. Working-class people, especially those from Appalachia, are used to being looked down upon and being told how to think and what their interests are.[24] When issues like climate change come up, he wants to be "able to say things in a way that wouldn't make my brother angry." I asked him to elaborate: "I just mean that when you talk about these issues, having the understanding that you're talking about real people and real lives and so what does that mean for people? When you talk about these big overarching policies, what does it actually mean for kitchen table conversations?" John allows his brother and others from their community to tell their own stories in the way that they want to share.

For John, using his cultural capital to bridge classes is about developing political power to shape policies that improve the lives of working-class people *and* the environment. He works as a senior energy analyst at a major nonprofit organization whose focus is on advocacy: "We only fight for policies. We work towards improving people's lives through policy development, so we advocate at the legislature, state law, and federal level, but we do so in a way that respects what the science and what our analyses tell us is the truth." This is what oriented his professional career to the area of just transition. This field, also known as worker transition, is focused on institutionalizing the role of workers in the shift to a clean energy economy. Without this important work, the structural problems facing Appalachian coal miners cannot be addressed.

John isn't only concerned about the lives of working-class people but also sees them as potential allies in building a coalition for a greener and more prosperous future. He said that "most people who are coal miners don't do it because they love going down in the mines. If you said, 'I'll give you another job—it's not going to be just fast food'.... If you could find a job where hard work is valued and you could make the same amount of money, most people would be like, OK, I can see that. I can do that work." John knows there is dignity in coal mining: "I remain proud of my family's heritage and our part in keeping the lights on over the past century. And as we transition to cleaner forms of energy and away from coal, I bring that perspective to the table." The work that replaces coal mining must also be dignified, and very low-wage work with no health benefits that society looks down upon is often not experienced that way. This is the work of just transition—where the interests of the environmental movement and the labor movement intersect.[25]

In the D.C. policy world, John draws upon both his working-class cultural capital and middle-class cultural capital to play the role of bridge builder. He continuously serves as a voice for the working class in his nonprofit work and is sometimes called upon to do so for Congress. John recounted going to West Virginia to testify at a hearing on the repeal of the Clean Power Plan, which is a regulation that sets limits on greenhouse gas emissions from coal plants. While his professional credentials qualified him as an expert to speak on the issue, it was simultaneously his "cred" of being a working-class guy from coal country that got him there. He said, "I was asked to go for that reason. They probably wouldn't have sent anybody there if it hadn't been for my connection." Scholars such as Jack Metzgar have called for more similar "cross-class coalitions" to help one another understand the others' lives and work together to address collective problems.[26]

Of course, serving as a bridge doesn't always mean you will get a smooth ride. When he returned from the hearing to his nonprofit, he was asked how his testimony went. John said, "I think it went pretty well" and joked that "all I know is I'm not out of the will yet." But his middle-class colleagues didn't get it. "Nobody laughed. Nobody got the joke. Everybody just felt awkward. I'm like, 'Come on, guys. It was a joke. It's fine. Really, it's OK.' It was particularly funny because I told my mom that story later, [and] she goes, 'What's funny about that is you think there's going to be anything left.'"

The Transformative Potential of Multicultural Capital

For those of us who grow up working-class, we face significant challenges learning middle-class norms, language, speech patterns, dispositions, and expectations. But with the right opportunities, mentors, financial support, and often luck, we can gradually acquire middle-class cultural capital. As we move into the middle class, maintaining connections to our working-class roots can equip us with a unique multilingual or multicultural skill set.[27] The stories in this chapter reveal the ways that acquiring and deploying both cultural skill sets enable straddlers to help translate or decode middle-class norms for working-class people, code-switch between cultural worlds, understand and mediate class-based cultural conflicts, and bridge classes for promoting social change. These multicultural skills make it possible for straddlers to accomplish otherwise impossible goals.

The opportunity of this multicultural capital operates at different levels within vastly unequal systems of power. At the individual level, straddlers are able to support other poor and working-class people by addressing their immediate needs. For example, Sydney helped working-class students to decode higher education to pursue better opportunities; Leigh helped clients overcome their class shame and take pride in their class roots and abilities; and April helped juveniles reach better outcomes in the white middle-class institution of law. While no individual can eliminate the economic barriers working-class people face, my interviewees all did their part to level the playing field within their professional purview.

Their multicultural capital also enabled them to change the system itself. Leigh co-founded a nonprofit to add organizational capacity for addressing the speech therapy needs of working-class people; in addition to starting a free legal clinic, April developed new organizational policies to make court mediations and legal proceedings better serve the needs of poor and working-class clients; and John's work in bridge-building and policy development at the national level sought to alter the structure of jobs while promoting sustainable development. In other interviews, I spoke with Katherine, who is a lawyer representing labor unions in collective bargaining, and Sen. Nina Turner, who runs political campaigns to build an economic system that benefits everyone. These straddlers used their multicultural capital to create structural changes in how our economy functions so that all people have access to dignified work that can support them and their families. Working through social movements, politics, and policy formation, they have the potential to transform our economic and democratic systems. All of the straddlers here worked hard, not to rise from their class but *with* their class.

6

Working-Class Dispositions

Hard Work, Practicality,
Authenticity, Resilience,
and Ingenuity

An often-overlooked form of cultural capital is the "long-lasting dispositions of the mind and body" that help us accomplish a desired outcome.[1] Dispositions refer to internal ways of orienting ourselves to the world that shape our expectations, aspirations, values, and behaviors. We can think of them as attitudes or mindsets that are shaped by our social class and guide our actions and beliefs.[2] They are often described as embodied cultural capital because they are largely unconscious elements shaping how we hold our bodies, what our bodies project, or our ingrained habits of mind.[3]

There are numerous middle-class dispositions that function as cultural capital in achieving professional success. As described in chapter 1, a middle-class sense of entitlement is advantageous in having confidence in oneself, providing motivation for going after what a person wants, believing that they deserve what they seek, and advocating for themselves.[4] Research has also shown how middle-class children learn to internalize attentiveness in class and conscientiousness in the completion of assignments.[5] At elite schools, they are socialized to develop a sense of ease that translates into comfortable sociability and confidence.[6] These dispositions frequently win them favorability with teachers and supervisors, helping advance their standing among gatekeepers in educational and professional environments. Middle-class socialization also means instilling high aspirations and a positive sense of one's own academic abilities.[7] These attitudes imparted to middle-class children help give them the ambition and confidence to guide their behaviors toward professional success.

In contrast, working-class dispositions are often described as making it more difficult to climb the class ladder and navigate professional environments. For example, a working-class sense of constraint tends to make working-class children and adults feel intimidated by people in positions of authority.[8] They are less likely to ask for additional help from professionals, expect to receive special favors, or have the confidence to go after what they want. As a result, they get less attention from teachers and other professionals, and they receive fewer second chances when something goes wrong.[9] They often moderate their aspirations and expectations given the fewer economic opportunities that exist for them.[10]

While the working-class sense of constraint and moderated aspirations do make upward mobility more difficult, they are only part of the story of working-class dispositions. Alongside these disadvantages, there is also a set of positive dispositions that function as working-class cultural capital for economic success. The most common forms cited by my straddler respondents included hard work, practicality, resilience, ingenuity, and authenticity. As I show in the stories below, they function as powerful cultural resources when configured in specific ways and with effective action. Whereas the working-class cultural capital discussed in the previous two chapters apply more to working-class or mixed-class settings, these dispositions can be more universally applied. Working-class first-gen students and graduates can leverage these strengths to be successful in middle-class environments.

Hard Work and Practicality: Cody

Many straddlers I interviewed praised their working-class upbringing for instilling in them a work ethic that enabled them to break into new career fields, gain the respect of their colleagues, and perform better at their jobs. But when it is not channeled appropriately, not paired with support, or cannot be turned off, it can carry a heavy cost. Cody's story reveals the strength of working-class dispositions like hard work and practicality, as well as how to leverage them for educational and professional success.

Cody's parents had a small farm, but they sold the farm when Cody was five years old. His father went to work in a warehouse, loading and driving food delivery trucks. His mother was a stay-at-home mom who cared for him and his brother and sister. Their home was a "fixer-upper" with a "literal hole through the back of it" when they moved in. Cody learned an ethic of hard work from his father: "I remember growing up, and my dad worked hard, always worked hard. He would come home from work and usually work more on something else, like fixing a car, chopping wood." When Cody was only thirteen years old, he started working twelve-hour days shoveling manure. He enjoyed working on the farm and explained that "the value of hard work is a core part of my identity."

Across my interviews, hard work was mentioned as something my respondents valued receiving from their working-class upbringing.[11] For Cody, it was part of working-class masculine socialization, but both men and women from my study emphasized a strong work ethic.[12] It usually came from seeing their parents work very long hours, often in physically demanding jobs. A comparable level of physical labor is virtually nonexistent in middle-class jobs, but Cody saw it all around him. As a teenager working in the warehouse with his father, one of his co-workers had "just come back from surgery and was on leave. I was loading this truck up.... He was like, 'Hey, man, keep going to school. You got to get the hell out of here. Look at all these guys around you. Their bodies are breaking down. This is my third back surgery I'm coming off of.'" Cody remembered thinking, "Yeah, all these guys are busted up." The manual labor was taking its toll on nearly everyone around him.

Cody took his co-worker's advice and continued with college but struggled to find anything that interested him for a career. He said "around the end of my bachelor's degree," he was begging his way back into a number of classes and "got a little more serious. I was studying English literature." Cody became "really interested in critical theory, how we can look at literature and what it tells us about the time and about social change." He was intrigued by how authors "were challenging how we viewed our history." Then he began to think, "I don't just want to read about this and look at it in literature. I'd like to maybe do something a little more active in the area of social change." Through literature, he was learning about global poverty and colonialism and developed an interest in international development. He moved to Washington, D.C., to obtain a job and explore possible graduate schools. Cody found work in a bank and worked full-time while attending graduate school.

Getting started in a career in international development was very difficult, especially without any social connections in the field. He would use vacation days to volunteer for a nongovernmental organization (NGO) in Guatemala. He later traveled to Mongolia and "just knocked on doors until I got a job teaching English." Cody said he got his first career-oriented international development job in Colombia, "which paid about three hundred dollars a month. I was not independently wealthy. I was just living on little money and grinding it out, eating what was cheap." With this level of persistence, "then it starts to pick up, little by little, but, for me, that was years." He attributes this to his working-class roots, including his ethic of hard work, sacrifice, and expectations that it will take time. In contrast, he has had numerous people approach him saying that "my cousin or my nephew or my daughter really wants to work in this field, but it's hard to break in," so they ask him for advice. After these conversations, Cody concluded, "People from an upper-class background have a harder time with the sacrifice." They're used to being handed opportunities without having to "grind it out" over the years as Cody had.

Cody eventually landed a stable career position with Catholic Relief Services, an international NGO. At the time of our interview, he was managing business development programs in Kenya and Somalia. He seeks funding opportunities, works with staff to develop proposals, writes grants and designs projects, and then oversees the funded projects that can have hundred-million-dollar budgets. The dimensions of his work that he most enjoys reflect the group-oriented norms of working-class culture: "I really like the project design part, getting down to the stakeholder level and bringing people in to be a part of project design." He added, "I can take time to build collaborative processes that cost money to do. I like that because people sit around the table, and they look at you in the eye, and they know that you hear them. They see their voice reflected in the project that you're building."

Cody identified a second disposition—the practicality of his working-class roots—as especially helpful in being more effective in his work. He explained that "all the people around me who are working hard, I tend to appreciate. I never let a waiter put something down in front of me without saying thank you. I never let a cleaner go by without saying hello. I see a lot of people who take those people for granted, and I don't like that." Cody viewed this awareness as having a practical dimension in his work: "I think it makes me oddly useful" because there are things that "other people overlook" but that "we need to budget." He notes that "you're going to need someone to clean that, right? We're going to need someone to guard that. That guy is there, right? They're kind of like, 'Oh, yeah, I guess you're right.'" His awareness of the practical details helps him write grants, plan events, and build relationships across the organization more effectively.

Cody's practical approach is also an asset in managing large budgets and maximizing impact. While he oversees very large budgets, he is known for being frugal. He avoids travel that is not essential for his position, such as to Somalia, which would require additional security. Instead, he brings partners to Nairobi, allowing travel expenses to be done at a fraction of the cost. Cody noted that some of his colleagues from other backgrounds are more likely to spend money outsourcing labor, ordering more expensive meals, and jumping at opportunities for costly international travel. In contrast to middle-class entitlement, Cody's working-class roots taught him to appreciate the small things and allocate money for something only when absolutely necessary. Sometimes he is encouraged to spend more money, but Cody's practicality and his thriftiness allow him to maximize budgets and funnel more money into direct services.

Cody viewed the ethic of hard work, however, as a double-edged sword. He told me that "my dad was my hero as a kid." When his father and brother got him a job in the warehouse, he "wanted to make them proud." So, "I worked my ass off, and I got a hernia when I was nineteen years old. You're lifting 100-pound cases of beef and stacking them up, and I probably weighed 160 pounds." Some years later, his father had a stroke, and "his body was breaking down." Cody pondered, "I wonder how much of it is just socializing the working class to work themselves to death." While he credited his hard work ethic as helping him succeed and being a "core part of his identity," he saw that it also has its costs. He concluded that "working like a mule doesn't actually pay off in the end. It's kind of a paradox." Their working-class jobs demanded hard physical labor, but without the reward of high wages and a generous health care plan, it cannot be justified.

For upwardly mobile straddlers, the paradox is less about the physical toll of hard work and more about how to leverage the hard work. Just as I did, many first-gen working-class students whom I work with have internalized this hard work to mean that when things are difficult, you just buckle down and try harder. We are not aware of what we don't know, and we have been socialized not to ask for help, not to expect that teachers or other professionals will spend extra time answering our questions, or that we are not worthy of that time and attention. I have students work incredibly hard but still not get the results because they simply did not ask for help on how to develop effective study habits or meet with a professor to understand course content.[13] In contrast, middle-class students have been more socialized to ask for help and advocate for themselves, therefore getting that needed support. So, the way to leverage a hard work ethic is to ask for that support from teachers and professors, educational support staff, and other professionals. It is about not just working harder but also working smarter. Then the hard work can be directed in the most effective way possible and help working-class first-gen students to stand out.

Finally, several respondents raised the issue of not being able to turn it off. Cody put it this way: "I often feel guilty if I'm not working on something" or that he is "wasting" his time if he is not working. Another respondent, Katie, said, "I feel like I have to work, work, work." This sentiment really resonated with me as someone who has often found it hard to turn off my working mode. Having grown up feeling economically insecure with few opportunities (at least until I got my college degree), I felt like I had to take on every opportunity available to me and show that I could do it. I had this sense that any such opportunity could be my last, and I had to work extra hard to prove myself because I did not have the connections and experiences that others had. While my work ethic served me very well in many ways, I did this for so long that I still feel that way even as an accomplished professor. I found myself agreeing with Tori, who told me that she had to "unlearn" her approach to work "over the years because I realized how much some of that is unhealthy and is a way to just burn yourself out." While it is an important working-class disposition, hard work has to be accompanied by working in a smart way, asking for help, and learning a way to find balance in one's life.

Authenticity and the Bullshit Meter: Tori

"Even when I was younger, I always had this 'I want to help people' mentality," Tori told me. Like many working-class kids, she was raised on the value of helping others. Having grown up in a "blue-collar working-class" family, she was socialized into working-class norms, manners of speaking, and ways of carrying herself that would be particularly helpful in a career of direct service. Her experiences imparted a humility and authenticity that would help her to become a highly effective social worker.

Tori's parents held a variety of working-class jobs throughout her upbringing in western New York state. Her father fixed dairy farm equipment until most all the local dairy farms went bankrupt. He ran his own motorcycle mechanic business out of his garage for some time and eventually worked as head of maintenance at a school. Her mother babysat kids and worked as a teacher's aide before health issues prevented her from working. Tori explained that her family was "extremely frugal growing up," which included cutting coupons for hours every week, finding the best deals for different grocery stores, and buying in bulk. They did not go out to eat, and the rare vacation was to a nearby state park to stay at a cabin with an outhouse and no electricity or running water, but it made for many happy memories.

Compared to others whom Tori saw in their rural community, they had it good. For example, the school that her mother worked at served many children who lived in a residential facility associated with the school. One of the children was found abandoned in a house in "sub-zero temperatures in the middle of winter." Tori explained that "he had no place to live," and "my mom wanted to be able to give him a home and a family." So, her parents helped start a therapeutic foster care program in their community. Virtually all of the children in the program "had mental illness, a lot of emotional issues, had been traumatized, abused, neglected." Tori and her family saw that these children often did not have many professionals or other people who could understand what they had been through, and it shaped her career aspirations.

Like many working-class students, Tori worked paid jobs throughout her education to make ends meet. She babysat, pulled weeds, and waitressed at a run-down restaurant—whatever job she could get. When she was in college, she worked at a school, sometimes as a substitute teacher and other times as a custodian. One day she was running a classroom, and the next day she was cleaning it—and it revealed powerful class dynamics. In contrast to the teachers, "cleaners were largely ignored." With this dizzying alteration between having authority and then being looked down upon, she sometimes felt "a little bit of embarrassment as you're going in to like clean out their garbage and scrub their toilets." But she had family members who did this work, and it was just something she accepted as normal. As another respondent, Bob, put it, there is "no job that's beneath you. If you want to put food on the table and a roof over your head, you have to work."

Having seen children suffer from trauma, depression, and anxiety in the foster care program, Tori took courses in sociology and psychology as an undergraduate and went on to pursue a master's in social work (MSW). But college and graduate school were a culture shock. Despite the fact that working-class students often pursue professions in human services, most of the students in her programs were from middle-class backgrounds. The classmates whom she befriended were "shocked" at the paid jobs she took on because it was "out of their realm."

Tori was even more disturbed by how some of her middle-class peers reacted to a community-based research project in her MSW program in Washington, D.C. The instructor designed a project where students would go into a high-poverty, high-crime Black community and "interview community members about what do they want to change in their community." Tori was excited because it leaned into "organizing, activism, community grassroots stuff, social justice." As a white working-class woman, she knew the importance of listening to people about their experiences in their own words. But her more privileged classmates were not so thrilled. She recounted that "a lot of students got very upset about this. They didn't feel safe going into these communities." Students protested to university administrators to get the project shut down. Tori remembers thinking at the time, "You're training for social work in Washington, D.C., you think you're never going to talk to impoverished families or you're never going to work in a neighborhood that has crime? Like, are you kidding me?" She felt her classmates' reactions were "bougie" and "classist."

Despite the culture shock she faced in graduate school and professional life, Tori's working-class roots would be an asset to her throughout her social work career. Because of her upbringing, she was socialized into working-class norms and dispositions. She used working-class language and communication styles and deeply empathized with her clients. These behaviors and ways of interacting helped her carry herself with an authenticity to which her clients positively responded.

Research on authenticity frames it as being true to oneself and one's experiences.[14] Working-class culture places a high value on being authentic and has disdain for people who appear two-faced.[15] Tori explained that "I feel like blue-collar people have a better bullshit meter [laughs] than middle-class or rich people do." When middle-class people use highly verbose language, beat around the bush to try to minimize how bad something sounds, or put on a false front, working-class people's antennae go up. We might get annoyed, become distrustful of them, and try to avoid them. For Tori, this became an asset working with poor and working-class people in domestic violence, sexual assault, and foster care—people who have been abused and are often distrustful of people in positions of authority.[16]

As a social worker in the foster care system, Tori worked with children in the system, birth parents, and foster parents. Nearly all of her clients were poor or working-class. Her disposition of authenticity included a variety of behaviors, such as speaking with clients in a "down-to-earth" way and "not using bougie-ass language." This was especially the case with kids: "If the teenagers were comfortable with you, they'd call you out in a heartbeat if they thought you were bougie." In contrast, other more middle-class social workers "can be really good at tap dancing around the truth, tap dancing around being really direct." But working-class families need to hear you directly and trust that you're being sincere about the situation and your role within it: "If you're going to bullshit them or talk around them, holy shit, are they going to be upset about it; they're going to call you out on it, or they're just not going to work with you," Tori said. This often meant acknowledging to families that it was uncomfortable having her there and "just being able to call it for what it was." But "that's something that I don't see happening as readily with people who come from a middle-class background." A middle-class attitude of entitlement, sense of ease, abstract language, or indirect communication would be ineffective.

For Tori and other straddlers, being authentic also means that your attitude and how you carry yourself align with the lives of the people you are serving. In working with very poor families, she "would go into apartments run by slumlords that were falling apart, holes in the walls, filled with cockroaches. And I think a lot of my co-workers were pretty uncomfortable in those environments." She added that "cockroaches were a new thing to me being in a city from a country girl in the North; we didn't really have to deal with cockroaches." On one home visit, she and a middle-class colleague were sitting on the couch:

> I felt something crawling up my back, so I just reached my hand up my shirt and pulled out a cockroach and just flung it aside.... The other social worker looked at me, her eyes just about bugged out, her mouth fell open, and I just

nonchalantly kept talking to the family as if nothing happened. I didn't even like break in the conversation because . . . I didn't want to make the family feel bad. And this particular family, despite the fact that they live in one of the most disgusting apartment buildings in the city, every time I was there the mom was sweeping and tidying. She kept a clean house. She did the best she could with that shitty-ass building that she lived in.

Poor and working-class people often face difficulty finding safe and affordable housing. In many housing markets, such as the high-cost city of Washington, D.C., low-income renters often deal with slumlords who do not invest in their apartment buildings. Tori knew that her client did all that she could to keep her home clean and safe for her children, and it felt natural to her to carry herself in a way that conveyed normalcy and compassion. Her body and communication projected this type of authenticity, helping to build a strong rapport with her clients.

Part of Tori's work was providing therapy, and research shows that poor and working-class clients often seek authenticity in therapeutic relationships.[17] One study found that a majority of poor and working-class clients report being attuned to their therapist's class background by what they perceive around their therapist's "occupation cues, aspects of therapists' appearance and manner of dress, characteristics of therapists' office space, and therapists' vocabulary and demeanor."[18] A sense of authenticity is appreciated by working-class clients when their therapist is more casual, uses language they can understand, doesn't have a wall up around their own personal life, validates their class-based experiences, has compassionate responses, names class issues, and attends to class issues that are raised in therapy. While middle-class therapists can also be capable of these attitudes and behaviors, Tori believes that straddler therapists like herself are especially well positioned to offer personal anecdotes and build stronger rapport with their clients.

Another dimension of authenticity is being sincere about how one's experience might differ from another's.[19] Tori acknowledged, "I grew up in a completely white community, and I was working with a hundred-percent Black community" in D.C. foster care. This meant part of her experience was "very different," and she was not going to present herself as understanding all parts of her clients' lives. Furthermore, she was conscious of avoiding a "savior" mentality, knowing that her clients had their own strengths, skills, and knowledge. They were capable, caring, and hard-working people but lacked the opportunities that others had. She knew of a need for support and sought to help but did so from a place of empathy and humility, not superiority. Acknowledging such differences in a comfortable and authentic manner had the paradoxical effect of building trust and stronger relationships.

Resilience, Grit, and Ingenuity

If working-class first-gen students are praised for one thing above all else, it is their resilience or their grit.[20] The notion of grit has reached pop culture success, as evidenced by Angela Duckworth's *New York Times* bestseller, *Grit: The Power of Passion and Perseverance*.[21] But while much of the popular literature and psychological research frames this as a highly individualistic trait, and it is true that anyone can develop resilience and grit, my respondents often understood them as a strength of their working-class upbringing. Their stories revealed several different ways to understand how it functions as cultural capital.

In essence, resilience and grit are about perseverance.[22] In one interview, Matthew credited his resilience with earning him professional success: "I could have folded for having a single parent. I could have stopped working because my dad was in and out of jail or not present. I could have folded because [my] high school teacher told me I wouldn't do anything. I could have folded because I couldn't afford college. But I never gave up. I *never* gave up." Michael overcame much adversity to become a beloved elementary school teacher, adding, "Still to this day, I go in hours before school starts to be the best I can be." Katie described it as a "toughness," saying, "It takes a lot to deter me or to make me give up." She learned it from her father, who persevered through tough bouts of work: "He just did it. He didn't complain." She anchored it in her upbringing: "When you come from a working-class or blue-collar background, you know what work is, you can kind of put your head down, you can push through." Katie works with college students and believes her wealthy students wouldn't "survive a week in the life of a typical [working-class] student" because they haven't developed the ability to deal with such adversity. It is about sustaining one's hopes and dreams for the future in spite of such obstacles.[23]

One building block of persistence is an understanding or expectation that things will not always work out in your favor. Khalid described it this way: "When you've had to come up having less, I think you can take less for granted." Conversely, Amanda said, "If you've never had hardship, and a bad thing happens, that's the worst thing that's ever happened to you. You melt down." Working-class people don't assume that their parents will be able to pay for another summer camp, that they will earn the perfect grade, or that they will be selected for the internship or job that they applied for. Khalid continued, "When you haven't had certain advantages, I think maybe you're not quite as devastated when things don't go your way because you don't expect things to always go your way." Accordingly, it allows you to move on and try for the next round.

Another working-class element of resilience is the inventiveness one often develops to solve problems one encounters. Amanda, the director of audience engagement at a major art museum, explains there is a "sense of, you have to be frustrated in order to be creative." When people are forced to encounter difficulty and make do with little, they think of new ways to tackle a problem. In contrast, "if everything just happens" for you and you always "get what you asked for—if there are no limitations—then when you do encounter problem-solving in your life, you don't know what to do with it."

Sam described this disposition as a type of "ingenuity." She explained that when you grow up poor and have to survive on almost nothing, you have to find ways to make things work. Her parents "basically trained themselves" in new skills, like her father training himself to "be a mechanic and a plumber and an electrician." Her mother taught herself to "work in a garden and preserve food." This came, in part, "from their lived experience, but just the fact that they were very adaptable and very much able to find solutions to things when it seemed like that there was no clear solution present." Sydney translated this to her white-collar job: "If my office says they're not going to buy this certain kind of software, well, OK, then I'll do it some other way. My earth isn't shattered."

However, there is also a danger in how society currently frames resilience and grit for the working class and the upwardly mobile.[24] While it is true that many of my respondents credited their working-class roots as equipping them with resilience, grit, and ingenuity, these dispositions alone cannot be enough to overcome difficulty and achieve upward mobility. There is a tendency within popular culture and media to portray hard work and grit as the determining factors in people climbing their way out of difficult economic circumstances. But the structural barriers of class—including the vast educational inequalities, financial burdens of attending college, exposure to crime, threats to one's health, and cultural mismatches they face—are all very real. These must also be addressed to enable more working-class people to harness their resilience in doing well for themselves and their communities.

Like other dispositions, resilience can best function as a form of working-class cultural capital when it is leveraged with social and economic support. While working-class students and straddlers have often developed resilience, we can sometimes get overwhelmed with challenges that confront us, and there are limits to what resilience can accomplish. In particular, the resilient techniques for surviving working-class life do not always translate well to handling unfamiliar institutions. We need mentors to help make sense of what we encounter, how to navigate novel institutional challenges effectively, and how to channel our efforts successfully.[25] Our grit might help us to persevere through familial or social challenges at school, but sometimes even lacking small amounts of money can prevent us from registering for classes or persisting through to graduation. We might need financial assistance to pay our tuition balance or fix our car so we can make it to work. Most of all, we need university programming, organizational policies, and government support to institutionalize such assistance so that we do not expect working-class people to make it on grit alone.[26]

Don't Whine, but Fight

Working-class children learn a variety of attitudes and dispositions that can be leveraged as strengths for their educational and professional success. This chapter focuses on how hard work, practicality, authenticity, resilience, and ingenuity can help working-class people and first-gen students climb the class ladder. We can add that working-class people also learn the idea of sacrifice, and they often draw inspiration and motivation from their families.[27] They are more interdependent than independent, and like Tori, they are more likely to have a desire to help others. In contrast to middle-class people, they are less likely to see themselves as being above certain jobs—they will do what it takes to get the job done. Indeed, these are attributes that employers seek from workers and offer concrete ways that first-gen grads can make the case for themselves in job interviews.[28]

Of course, these dispositions do not negate the very real barriers that poor and working-class people face in doing well for themselves and their communities. They also coexist with restrictive dispositions, including a sense of constraint when interacting with people in positions of authority, like teachers, doctors, lawyers, and government representatives. Nonetheless, dispositions addressed throughout this chapter do function as cultural resources rooted in the life experiences of poor and working-class people. While middle and upper-class people can also develop these dispositions, my respondents and existing research show that the structural experiences of growing up poor and working-class help give rise to these cultural traits. These dispositions can function as powerful forms of cultural capital when they are channeled appropriately with the encouragement of mentors, other support networks, and programs designed to level the playing field.

Barbara, the straddler therapist, addresses the effect of these dispositions and encourages us to fight for changes. She appreciates "how little we whine" as working-class people, which is a result of not growing up with a sense of entitlement.[29] We understand things do not always go our way and appreciate the things that we have. But Barbara adds that this should not make us complacent— we should not accept these conditions as they are. There is so much stacked against poor and working-class people. She says, "We need to fight, *really fight*" to bring about necessary structural changes. To expect that working-class people can necessarily use their strengths to climb the class ladder would put blame on them if they didn't make it. Furthermore, if they do make it but only do well for themselves or those they personally know, then it would also leave that system intact. Instead, we must band together to make sure the poor or working-class person coming up behind us will not have to try making it on their work ethic and grit alone. This hard work, resilience, and ingenuity should also be directed toward uplifting others by making the system more fair and just. The next chapter reveals additional ways that straddlers are using their professional work to bring about these structural changes.

Part 3

Lessons Learned

7

Managing the Threats of Assimilation, Complicity, and Co-Optation

As straddlers move up the class ladder, we will inevitably change. The changes are not inherently good or bad, but without reflection on them, we may find ourselves experiencing unwanted changes. Instead, we should intentionally pause to ask ourselves, What parts of ourselves are we losing, and which of those parts do we want to hold onto? How do I want to relate to my roots? As I gain more security and comfort and pursue work that I enjoy, what type of relationship do I want with people from my working-class community? Who do I want to become? We cannot possibly anticipate all the changes we will undergo. But in navigating the changes, upwardly mobile people face at least three threats to our sense of self and relationship to the groups that we straddle.

One choice that straddlers face is how they will relate to working- and middle-class cultures and the possibility of assimilation. Many straddlers appreciate at least some parts of working-class culture, such as the norms of interaction, straightforward manners of speech, tastes, humility, and authenticity. For straddlers who want to hold on to any of these elements of working-class culture while becoming more integrated into middle-class culture, they must manage the threat of assimilation. The question here is about whether a straddler fully embraces middle-class culture, rejects the middle-class culture that they increasingly find themselves in, or strives to take the best of both worlds by finding some type of balance between the two.

Other challenges that straddlers may encounter are complicity and co-optation. For straddlers seeking to maintain a group orientation and working-class value in helping others, climbing the class ladder isn't just about doing well for themselves. For these straddlers, it is also about doing well for their working-class community—not rising from their class but with their class. As someone climbs the social ladder, the question is whether they strive for financial success and higher status purely for themselves—or if they view themselves as a part of a group that they seek to uplift. By disregarding how their professional work or systems from which they benefit are affecting others in the working class, straddlers risk becoming complicit or co-opted in perpetuating class injustice. This can bring them significant individual rewards but at a cost to their sense of community and helping others. These challenges raise questions that extend beyond culture and into the structural conditions that shape our communities.

This chapter presents how the threats of assimilation, complicity, and co-optation work and how straddlers have handled these threats. At its core, managing these threats requires ongoing reflection and working in solidarity with others from the working class, fellow straddlers, and our middle-class allies. Without such efforts, we can find ourselves perpetuating those same class inequalities and the devaluation of working-class culture that made life so difficult for us in the first place.

Assimilating, Resisting, or Balancing Middle-Class Culture

Assimilating into Middle-Class Culture

As straddlers climb the class ladder, one dilemma we encounter is how to relate to middle-class culture. If parts of working-class culture have any value and are worth holding on to, then the threat to manage here is assimilation. The process of class assimilation entails working-class people taking on more and more cultural characteristics of the middle class over time.[1] This is not a one-size-fits-all approach, the process can be very awkward, and it is unevenly experienced.[2] But in general it means straddlers steadily embracing middle-class values and speaking more and more like middle-class people regardless of whether they are around other working-class or middle-class people. They become less direct in their speech, raise their children more through the practices of concerted cultivation, develop a stronger sense of individual identity, talk more frequently about their accomplishments without a sense of humility, adopt more middle-class tastes, and so on.[3] Straddlers have many reasons for wanting to adopt middle-class culture, and assimilating into the middle class is not inherently a bad thing. But it can mean that we help perpetuate the devaluation of working-class culture, disconnecting us from our roots and maintaining the cultural mismatch for working-class people coming up behind us.

There are a number of factors that nudge upwardly mobile straddlers into assimilating further and further into middle-class culture. First, society teaches us to place greater value on middle-class norms and culture. We are socialized to see the ways that middle-class people speak, how they raise their children, and the things that they like as *the right way*. There are few situations or people who are likely to help us take pride in our working-class roots, and our socialization encourages us to adopt this strategy of assimilation above all others. Second, the pursuit of professional jobs and promotions—especially jobs that are highly specialized—often requires us to move geographically to acquire those jobs. This can mean that we move away from our family of origin or our associated network of friends, neighbors, and acquaintances. Those original networks might be our strongest connections to our working-class roots, and severing those ties can mean less and less time surrounded by working-class people and culture. Third, the more time that we spend in college, professional workplaces, and the social environments attached to these middle-class institutions, the more that we are drawn into middle-class culture. With greater exposure comes greater practice, and likely more and more comfort in that culture. As it becomes more ingrained, we may internalize a sense of that culture as more natural, right, or at least helpful for pursuing our professional goals. This also likely means less and less time with working-class people or being steeped in working-class culture. We might, unconsciously, become assimilated and lose our working-class culture.

While some straddlers may be unconscious that they are assimilating into middle-class life, others have internalized disdain for working-class culture and consciously seek to avoid it. They might actively adopt strategies to hasten their assimilation by distancing themselves from their poor or working-class roots. For example, Irv Peckham wrote about the feeling of being born into the "incorrect" class.[4] He stated, "I erased my incorrectness by infrequently going home. In time, I more or less forgot who my parents and siblings were." Because of the shame or deprivation forced on poor and working-class people, many people run as fast as they can from their class origins. A business executive explained that she regularly lies to other executives about her background. She stated, "I'm embarrassed by the blue-collar origin" of the town where she grew up. She was constantly comparing herself to colleagues who were making millions of dollars and placing their children in exclusive schools, adding, "I don't want to feel inferior.... I don't want them to know what my origins were."[5] Instead, some straddlers will actively emulate the tastes of the middle class, take classes to learn about abstract art and how to enjoy fine wines, and exclusively socialize in spaces where they will interact with others from wealthier middle-class or upper-class backgrounds. They largely celebrate the emphasis on the individual self and individual accomplishment, and they enjoy the constant competition and the luxuries, traveling, and opportunities that wealthier careers afford them.

Upwardly mobile assimilationists might also be more likely to end up in occupations where their working-class cultural capital is less of an asset. While their cultural empathy, hard work, practicality, and resilience may help them in any field, they may work in occupations that do not interact with working-class people or in mixed-class settings. They may seek out fields where they only engage with fellow professionals or elites, thereby only needing to master dominant cultural capital. Remaining fluent in working-class norms, language, communication styles, or the ability to translate, code-switch, and mediate between classes may be less relevant in their professional work. Class assimilationists don't seek to rise with their class but from their class.

The pressures of middle-class assimilation are further complicated for working-class people of color, particularly among immigrant groups. Because of the racial discrimination that Black, Latine, Indigenous, and Asian American people face, cultural assimilation can be a strategy to resist racist cultural stereotypes. From this perspective, maintaining one's ethnic or heritage culture is viewed as hindering social mobility.[6] They may choose, instead, to make a "straight line" to the white middle-class by shedding their racial, ethnic, and working-class culture to fit into the dominant culture.[7] This is done by continuously emulating successful middle-class white people to adopt their norms, values, customs, manners of speaking, and behaviors.[8] Similarly, they may internalize negative mainstream views of their own racial or ethnic group's culture. For example, upwardly mobile Black straddlers may look down on others who use Black English vernacular, or Latine children may refuse to speak Spanish with their parents at home. Doing so can be a strategy to avoid interpersonal racism that they might encounter, but it can have the unintended consequence of further devaluing non-dominant cultural capital.

Resisting Middle-Class Culture

Because upwardly mobile straddlers inevitably face cultural mismatches when they rise into the middle-class, some straddlers resist adopting the new culture. This book is filled with examples in which working-class people and straddlers are looked down upon for how they speak, their different tastes, or their lack of understanding of middle-class references. Given the shame and judgment that often accompany these cultural conflicts, some straddlers find ways to hold on to what they know and practices in which they are comfortable. They might move into professional middle-class jobs with higher incomes but stay largely within their working-class communities and culture. This strategy entails resisting dominant middle-class norms and culture, although it is probably the least common.

For these straddlers, the individualism, ambition, sharing (or bragging) about one's accomplishments, speaking indirectly and seemingly being two-faced, and sense of entitlement might be too off-putting to want to join the club. They might hate being in social settings with authority figures or trying to fit into the cultural tastes of the middle class and simply avoid it whenever possible. Straddler Barbara Jensen wrote about her brother in Minneapolis that resisted middle-class culture.[9] He worked his way up to postmaster of several post offices but used an "employee-involved" management style that drew upon the group norms of his working-class roots. Her brother "still plays rockabilly guitar and sings karaoke, [and] wears a cowboy hat." He maintains strong connections to extended family, an important element of working-class life. This allows him to opt out of many elements of middle-class culture, where the job largely remains a way to have a more comfortable life and support one's family rather than an end in itself. For some straddlers, it is the life they would rather live.

Balancing Working-Class and Middle-Class Cultures

A third strategy suggests that straddlers need not choose between working-class and middle-class culture. While it is a difficult task, it is possible to take the "best of both worlds" by balancing working-class and middle-class norms, attitudes, and tastes.[10] This is the choice taken by the vast majority of people whom I interviewed for this book, as well as myself. For upwardly mobile straddlers, this strategy of selective cultural integration or balancing cultures becomes a way that we can maintain connections to our roots while embracing the positive aspects of the class into which we have climbed.

Sociologist Karyn Lacy's concept of "strategic assimilation" is useful for understanding this third approach.[11] Lacy studied the Black middle class, finding that many Black people "with access to majority white colleges, workplaces, and neighborhoods continue to consciously retain their connections to the Black world as well."[12] She adds that "through their interactions in these Black spaces, middle-class Blacks construct and maintain Black racial identities." Her respondents used a range of strategies, including choosing to live and socialize in predominantly Black neighborhoods or to be active members of Black social organizations. While they assimilated and fit in when they were in predominantly white middle-class environments, they also consciously spent time in predominantly Black environments. This allowed them to continue practicing the cues of Black identity—such as using the norms of greeting someone, how to enunciate certain words, or what tastes they develop in films and pop culture. This type of code-switching reconnected them with other Black people "after spending the bulk of the day in the white world," gave them temporary respite "from ongoing discrimination," and helped them build and maintain Black racial identities.[13]

Some straddlers similarly adopt an approach of "strategic assimilation" to maintain connections to their working-class roots. To quote Jensen again, she stated, "I wanted middle class skills and knowledge, but I was afraid that if

I strayed too far, I would never again feel I belonged in my loving extended family."[14] Like the challenges confronting middle-class Black people wanting to maintain a Black identity, if we don't want to "stray too far" from the working class but also don't want to resist the appeals of middle-class culture entirely, we have to make conscious choices about how and where we live, work, and play. It is especially helpful to consider the values and purpose that guide some of those choices.

There is an additional hurdle for straddlers that Black people are less likely to encounter when striving to maintain their Black identity. Specifically, Blackness exists as a clear racial identity, with race being something that is explicitly talked about among Black people and other people of color. In contrast, working-class identity seldom exists outside of blue-collar trade unions and class does not function as strongly as an explicit topic of conversation among poor and working-class people. The notion of a working-class culture as something to celebrate and take pride in exists much less as a cultural narrative. Movements of marginalized people, such as the Black Power movement, the Chicano movement, or the gay pride movement have helped to nurture these identities and infuse them with pride.[15] The labor movement, while existing for centuries, has lost much of its power and has been less successful in developing a desirable working-class identity within the popular imagination. Interestingly, the celebration of working-class culture might be most prominent now in certain musical genres, especially hip-hop and country music.[16]

There is no single pathway for balancing class cultures and identities, but my respondents' stories reveal how people have accomplished this through their professional work. Specifically, these straddlers found careers in a wide range of occupational fields in which they worked with working-class and poor people. Maintaining these social ties reminded them of the comfort of letting their guard down and allowed them to continue using working-class communication styles and norms. It enabled them to bond over shared working-class tastes, feel a sense of security in seeing people help one another, and find refuge in the humility and lack of entitlement during social interactions. The social bonds that happened through their careers enabled them to remain connected to their working-class roots. They leveraged their working-class cultural capital. At the same time, straddlers embraced middle-class culture and its emphasis on self-actualization and the intellectual pleasure of debate, the opportunities that came through professional work, and using concerted cultivation with their children to create new opportunities.

This type of strategic assimilation or balanced cultural engagement can be achieved through social connections. It may most commonly be done through maintaining relationships with family and extended family. Some people choose to live in more working-class or mixed-class neighborhoods. Another strategy is to seek out social spaces with more working-class people.

Depending on one's upbringing and tastes, it can include hunting and fishing groups or bowling leagues. Personally, I have participated in and brought my students to the Mid-Ohio Workers Association in Columbus, Ohio. It is a community organizing group through which we work alongside poor and working-class people to administer a benefits program and advocate for policies affecting their lives. In addition to volunteering opportunities, we have chances to simply hang out at a cookout or community event.

Finally, taking the best of both the working-class and middle-class worlds requires reflection.[17] We have to ask ourselves, What are we losing when we integrate further into the middle class, and what do we want to hold on to? What do we appreciate about working-class culture, and how can we maintain that within ourselves and our children? While individual reflection and activities like journaling are important, we might achieve our greatest insights when discussing our experiences with other straddlers. You might seek out fellow straddlers in your family, friend groups, or at work. You could start a reading group to discuss books like this and share one another's cultural journey. It can start with very simple questions: Do you ever think about your class background? What class do you believe you belong to and why? Do you think working-class and middle-class people are different somehow? Does it drive you nuts when people have a sense of entitlement? A simple starting point can lead to very interesting conversations, especially when they are explored over time. They also provide opportunities to apply what you have learned in this book and explore the possibilities with others.

Avoiding Complicity in Perpetuating Injustice: David

In addition to the possibility of assimilating into middle-class culture, straddlers will also face a choice about their own role in resisting or perpetuating the system of class inequality. Guided by our group orientation, empathy, and value of helping others, the stories throughout this book reveal how straddlers actively resisted this social structure. They did not simply transcend their working-class roots to become a part of the system that made things difficult for them. Rather, they used their working-class cultural capital and newfound positions of power to open doors for first-gen students, to help people in poverty acquire needed resources, to build pride in their working-class roots, and to rewrite the rules for the benefit of all—in short, to uplift others around them.

A challenge facing straddlers here is that professional jobs are largely shaped by middle-class culture and encourage complicity in perpetuating that system and its dominant culture. Complicity might entail acquiring jobs that economically reward individual success at the expense of working-class communities, preserving rigid-status hierarchies that put working-class people on guard and make it harder to participate in all areas of life. It means continuing working-class people's dependence on institutions rather than empowering their participation within them, and emphasizing middle-class values of socioeconomic achievement over working-class values like integrity, authenticity, and humility. Complicity means allowing the continued devaluation of working-class culture while upholding the status quo. Rather than resisting the system that makes working-class people's lives more difficult, complicity is about becoming a part of that system, thus perpetuating it—even if it is done unintentionally.

To illustrate the threat of complicity, I return to my interview narratives. David's story conveys his conscious effort to use his career for the common good and avoid work that made him complicit in perpetuating the inequalities that shaped his own life. David was born into a working-class family in Glasgow, Scotland. His parents were divorced and his mother worked "full-time, plus two side jobs" to support the family. When David was approximately ten years old, and with his mother was working so much, she arranged for people to look after him and his siblings. But the people tending to them were "maybe twenty-five, twenty-eight, chain smokers, alcoholics" living in dilapidated housing. He wanted out: "I just really didn't feel like I belonged. I wanted to really escape all of that. I just felt deeply uncomfortable. I wanted to get far away from those people."

School was a refuge for David, and he excelled academically. His favorite subject in high school was geography, and he became particularly interested in water access. He told his teachers, "I want to go into geography. I want to do stuff that helps reduce poverty around the world." His math teacher was also his guidance counselor, and "she knew my capabilities" as well as his ambitions. He had internalized a middle-class emphasis on status and socioeconomic achievement, wanting to "transcend the working class to become middle class." So, she advised him that "geography is not going to get you the prestige and the great career you deserve. You need to do engineering."

David "got the feeling she would think geography is for losers." He learned that civil engineering also deals with water resources, so he "reluctantly" switched to engineering. He added, "I was a little bit sad about it. I was sold on the myth of prestige and career and stuff." In his mind, he reconciled it this way: "I'm going to be a really good engineer and help the world a lot with this technical skill set that I can use in the developing world." He was still focused on fighting global poverty.

David completed a top-ranked engineering program in Scotland. He landed a job at Engineers Without Borders, a nonprofit organization that links engineers to infrastructure projects that address poverty and promote sustainable development. He worked with communities in Ecuador to build gravity-based water supply systems. It was a "very formative" period and inspired him to return to grad school for sustainable development at

Cambridge University. That led to a position at the World Bank helping communities adapt to climate change. One project was building a "five-kilometer sea wall off the coast of Senegal to protect its coasts and these vulnerable fishing populations where sea level rise and storm surges are causing erosion and flooding and loss of livelihood." He later assisted communities in Nicaragua and Honduras to build water supply infrastructures that are more resilient in periods of droughts and floods.

However, during these projects, David became "quite cynical" about using engineering and technology alone to address poverty. When he was building water systems in Ecuador, members of the community expressed so much frustration at mining companies in the area: "These are beautiful areas of Ecuador in the cloud forest, pristine nature, but you have Canadian mining firms going in there and doing opencast mining for gold and silver, chopping off tops of mountains." The chemicals used to extract the gold and silver would release toxins into the ecosystem that would find their way into local water systems. While he saw positive impacts of his work for Ecuadorian villages or people on the coast of Senegal, he felt like they were "very, very, very small" in comparison to other projects that were worsening the poverty and exploitation of those same communities. These programs kept working-class people dependent on institutions like the World Bank, and their built-in status hierarchies prevented professionals from seeing their working-class clients as equal partners.

Given David's motivation for prestige and climbing the class ladder, he could have been quite satisfied with a high-paying and prestigious position at the World Bank. He developed ample middle-class cultural capital and was able to "pass as a middle-class professional." At the World Bank, he acquired "the highest level of power and influence I've had in my career and probably ever will." He accomplished much of what he thought he wanted, even "transcending" much of his working-class background.

While David could blend right into a prestigious global institution like the World Bank, he felt like the majority of their projects were exacerbating the problems he wanted to fix, and he was tacitly participating in it. Despite the World Bank's stated mission to "end poverty and boost prosperity for the poorest people," he saw it as a "destructive" force because of its model of development.[18] Its top-down strategy prevented the organization from empowering the working-class people they were impacting. He became disillusioned when his work was counteracted by the work of others, sometimes even by the World Bank itself or the governments with which it partnered. He saw "well-meaning people who are fighting for fairer futures for their communities. I've seen them be captured by elite interests in Chile, and in Ecuador," and in the United States. David observed that decisions about high-level government policies or World Bank programming were ultimately responsible for building an unfair set of rules. While such decisions made room for smaller-scale projects that did good, their positive effects were dwarfed by decisions made by the wealthy elite to benefit themselves. He felt that not addressing this bigger root cause made him complicit within the broader system.

Ultimately, David concluded engineering didn't allow him to make the changes he felt were necessary. He left engineering and returned to graduate school for urban studies and planning to be able to effect broader policies "in the corridors of power." Drawing upon his original love of geography, he became interested in "how different social movements contest water rights" and the use of "water governance to try and seek a fairer, more equitable access to water." He described it as a shift from "water engineering" to "water politics or water justice." David added, "If I had a magic wand, I would get big money out of politics. . . . My pessimism or my cynicism has not killed my hopes for a better world, but they certainly won't be through engineering and technology alone that that's achieved, but rather through political and social movements." He added, "I have optimism" that engineers and social scientists can work together to make a bigger impact because they "have a blend of technical knowledge, expertise, and a good understanding of how institutions, rules, and political systems work."

Assessing complicity can be very tricky. As David noted, it requires that we have a big-picture understanding of how systems work and our role within those systems. For example, consider those of us who work in higher education and support first-gen students in developing middle-class cultural capital so that we can "level the playing field" and help those students compete with their peers. If we only focus programming on helping them to develop middle-class cultural capital, which naturally distances them from their working-class family and friends, and we do not support them in understanding that transition or developing an awareness of the strengths of working-class culture, we might be contributing to the devaluation of working-class culture.[19] These unintended effects could make us complicit in perpetuating a system that frames middle-class culture as the right way of being, encouraging us to look down on our working-class roots and the people who come from there. Such a perspective might frame it as something to escape and rise from rather than something to preserve and balance.

To avoid complicity, we need continuous reflection about the role of our work and how we live our lives, including their possible unintended consequences. You might ask yourself questions like, If I am striving for financial success, in what ways does that come at the expense of the well-being of others? If I have been successful, did I receive help, support, or mentoring that some others didn't receive, so should I seek to uplift them as well? If my work does strive to uplift others, does the planning and execution of that work rely exclusively on middle-class professionals, or does it defy status hierarchies to invite meaningful participation from the communities we seek to impact? Do I want to help poor and working-class people climb the ladder, or do I want to make it so that the important work done by poor and working-class people is fairly compensated, thus raising the floor for everyone? What are the unintended consequences of my work? It's never a perfect harmony, but we have to strive to align our lives with what we value from our working-class culture along with other values that we hold.

The concept of "bougie" offers an interesting analogy here. If bougie has generally been used to criticize a person of color climbing the ladder to achieve individual financial success at the expense of racial solidarity, what might it mean to be bougie from a class perspective? From the perspective of working-class culture, might straddlers who pursue only something for themselves be betraying their friends and community in the working class? If a straddler wants to avoid being bougie, how might they uplift not only themselves but the entire working class?

Changing the System Without Being Co-Opted: Sen. Nina Turner

The straddlers throughout this book have sought to lift up members of the working class through their professional work. But in the process of trying to improve conditions for workers and striving to make a fairer world, there is the threat of becoming co-opted. Co-optation occurs when "those in authority who are being challenged may try to bring the challengers into the system as participants but without granting equal influence or substantive power, or significant policy changes."[20] It is the process by which people in power seek to neutralize change-makers and prevent them from altering the status quo. Sen. Nina Turner talked with me about the need for straddlers pushing for change in all areas of life and how to prevent them from getting co-opted.

Turner grew up in a Black working-class community in Cleveland as the eldest of seven children. She started working at age fourteen to support her family and remembers the "shame" she felt from being on public assistance throughout their upbringing. She saw people around her work so hard but continue to struggle, observing that "you, by and large, cannot necessarily work your way out of poverty." Using a common form of working-class speech, she provided a metaphor: "It is like being in a barrel with oil on the sides of the wall of the barrel and you're saying I'm trying to get myself out. Every time you climb up you might get a step higher but you're slipping back down. That's systemic failure."[21]

After a very rocky start to college, Turner stumbled into a political career. As she put it, "Politics wasn't a conscious decision—politics chose *me*." As an undergraduate at Cleveland State University, she got to work with Cleveland councilwoman Fanny Louis. Turner said that work "really opened my eyes to how important it is to register people to vote and believe that people could change the trajectory of their lives through the power of the vote." Louis represented a poor community, which given the history of segregation and racism, was also predominantly Black. Turner added, "Under her wings, that really opened my eyes to grassroots politics, grassroots work: getting close with the people, hearing from the people. And that changed my life too." They had an ethic for lifting up others around them: "We believed that our education gave us the responsibility to help people in our community even though economically we didn't have any money." She was proud of her working-class roots, but maintaining connections to her working-class culture wasn't enough for her. She wanted to spend her career changing that system and mobilizing others to the cause.

Turner overcame numerous hurdles to eventually serve on Cleveland's City Council, as an Ohio state senator, leader of multiple grassroots organizations, and cochair of Sen. Bernie Sanders' national campaign for U.S. president. Throughout her political career, Turner has sought to build movements to support social democratic policies and fight corporate power in politics. Regardless of one's political beliefs, social democratic policies like those found in Denmark, Sweden, Norway, Finland, and Iceland are most objectively associated with facilitating social mobility.[22] Turner has fought for legislation expanding health care, passing a living wage, improving collective bargaining rights, and criminal justice reform—all associated with making a fairer economy that enables anyone to succeed regardless of their class or racial background. As I was writing this book, Turner launched a new organization, We Are Somebody, "fighting for working-class solidarity." We Are Somebody is "a capacity building organization for the working class" whose "programming addresses immediate needs of working families while shining a spotlight on national and global disparities."[23]

Turner draws upon her working-class cultural capital to be an effective advocate for the poor and working class. She explained, "I want nobody elected who ain't gone through nothing. I want to know you had a foreclosure, or you had to sleep in your car, or you know what it's like to miss a meal, or you had bills stacked up to here, and you didn't know how you're going to make it." In other words, she uses her working-class cultural capital—knowledge of working-class people's lived experiences—to represent the "overwhelming majority of the people" who "are either the poor, the working poor, or the barely middle class." It has given her purpose and clarity in her goals.

Having people like Turner in such positions matters because it can help us to tell our own stories that shape our collective understanding. She leveraged her working-class communication style with another metaphor: "If the hunter always tells the story, then the lion's story is never told. That's why we need working-class people in that room so that working-class people can tell their own story. We can theorize about it but you need somebody with some practical experience like I lived this and I know. And, to me, it's the marriage of the lived experience with the theory that is what produces great public policy."

Because of the importance of having people like us—working-class people and first-gen graduates, women, and people of color—in such positions, Turner says we have to be everywhere. She prefaced her comment by saying, "This is probably considered blasphemy" for some people in progressive politics, but "I think progressives need to be everywhere—even in the [corporate] boardroom." For some time, she even ran her own small business as a consulting company "helping corporations and nonprofits see what they could do better." Turner explained, "I think the movement does itself a disservice if, in fact, we don't attempt to be in every room whether it's a faith-based room, a corporate room, a nonprofit room, and also electoral politics." She believes in an insider-outsider strategy where people work on the outside through social movements to put pressure on established organizations to do right by their workers and working-class people. But there have to be people on the inside of these corporations, nonprofits, and governments who have also developed middle-class cultural capital to effectively shape these institutions.

However, when people and movements do gain sufficient momentum to make change, people who benefit from the existing system might seek to co-opt them. A company may co-opt influential critics or labor rights groups by inviting them to join its board of directors, thereby gaining their insights while potentially reducing their opposition. It could similarly co-opt local community leaders and organizations by engaging in community development and social programs to turn potential adversaries into allies. Politicians whose policies benefit the rich could co-opt popular songs and musicians speaking to working-class life to try to win over working-class voters—such as right-wing politicians using Bruce Springsteen's music at their rallies.[24] Marketers might try employing straddlers to help design branding campaigns evoking images of hard work and authenticity to appeal to working-class consumers while orienting people toward stylized consumption and away from structural inequalities and hardship. Powerful people could tap into ambitious straddlers' working-class cultural capital like an understanding of working-class norms and empathy to improve their bottom line at the expense of workers.[25] Poor and working-class people who have had so little security and stability in their lives may get lavished with praise and resources, feeling like they are making a difference by having a seat at the table. But co-opting them is an effort to neutralize or demobilize efforts at change. David, the engineer from the previous section, put it this way: For people who work in government or in the private sector, "if they're idealistic, they'll quickly get captured by elite interests."

As Turner explained that straddlers and progressives should be willing to engage with these insider strategies, I was reminded of an Audre Lorde quote: "The master's tools will never dismantle the master's house."[26] It refers to the idea that the tools that oppressors use to keep people down will never be sufficient on their own to dismantle a system of injustice. In the case of corporations, their legal existence is based on the idea of extracting as much profit as possible—especially by driving down wages and other costs of labor. As a tool of capitalist production, corporations may not be a vehicle to bring about meaningful change to improve the position of workers.

I asked Turner about this Audre Lorde quote, to which she responded, "I'm not using the master's tools because I'm going in as a master myself that I'm bringing the working-class perspective into the room." By "master," she did not mean that she is seeking to exploit and control others, but rather that the working class, when working collectively, is the master of their own future and has the power to change things. An organized working class and coalitions of working and middle-class people promoting social democratic policies can change how the system works.[27] Turner added, "I'm not walking in this room as an equal; we got to infiltrate. So, we need an inside game and an outside game."

Turner gave the example of creating a green economy with good working-class jobs that are also environmentally sustainable. With the right kind of public policy, companies can see that "there is a profit to be made from doing good. Those two things are not mutually exclusive." In such a system, if you pay workers "a living wage then they're better employees, they will produce better, their whole environment is better because they can support themselves and/or their families." Such an insider strategy can *only* work when there is pressure from the outside, helping to alter the incentive structures that guide corporate decision-making—and straddlers hold a unique perspective to get it done.

But still, Turner acknowledged that "sometimes people can be co-opted" by the system. The key is to maintain a critical consciousness of how the system works and what we are trying to accomplish. She continued, "The goal going in there ain't to get seduced." In other words, if we enter politics, the corporate office, or any work seeking to achieve high status, maximize our salaries, or become accepted into an elite group, then we are going in to get seduced. We will be chasing the material rewards as they are defined within a capitalist system that put us, as poor and working-class people, in a position of shame and struggle in the first place. We will be assimilating into a higher class while accepting the interests of the rich as our working-class and straddler interests. As we accumulate material possessions and value socioeconomic achievement over working-class values, then we start to defend what we have, and we don't want to lose it.

Instead, Turner says that we must "do the seducing." We must have a clarity of purpose for our work and how to work with others—even others who see the world differently from us—to achieve it. We have "to try [our] best to meet people where they are without selling out [our] soul. That's sometimes hard; you got to know the audience and what motivates that audience." If others in the system are motivated by profit and status, then we must get them to see their goals as our goals, such as by aligning the common good with the corporate good. She argues that we must show them that "ultimately what is good for everyday people is good for corporate America. What is good for the planet is good for corporate America."

At the end of the day, bringing about these changes without becoming co-opted is about organizing, consciousness, and strategy. At an individual level, it requires being intentional about the kinds of changes we want to see and understanding the challenges and opportunities for bringing about those changes. The reflective prompts suggested above—and done in conversation with fellow straddlers, those in the working class, and our middle-class allies—can help us to build the critical consciousness for this work. But to truly change the conditions that give rise to these problems in the first place will require building coalitions and movements to create new public policy and change these systems themselves.

Reclaiming Pride and Solidarity with Our Working-Class Roots

As people move up the class ladder, we will undergo inevitable changes that we cannot fully anticipate. During this upward climb, we will be bombarded with messages encouraging us to look down on working-class culture—we will be taught to see middle-class culture as the right way of being and to adopt interests that preserve middle-class advantages. We must take responsibility for our role in this process to become the people whom we seek to become.

We can empower ourselves through ongoing reflection—both individually and within our communities—about our place in all of this. If we appreciate humility and sincerity, if we value people for who they are and not purely for what they have accomplished, if we believe using language that everyday people can understand helps us connect with others, if we respect people who call it like it is rather than being two-faced, or if we treasure any other parts of our working-class origins then we should take pride in our working-class roots. It gives us many strengths in our professional work and in our lives. Let's use that cultural knowledge to build group solidarity while enjoying the benefits of a middle-class life as well. Surely, our connections to friends and family in the working class can be complicated—and they may not all be worth preserving—but the ones that are worth hanging on to can help us maintain what we value about working-class culture. We can also lean on those connections when the seductions of materialism and status creep in. This does not mean that we must reject all middle-class culture—indeed self-actualization, opportunities for intellectual fulfillment, and material security are among the worthwhile goals of a middle-class life. But by taking the best of both worlds, we need not assimilate into a system that looks down on where we came from.

Our professional middle-class positions also afford us greater power within society, and we will be confronted with choices about what to do with that power. Our newly acquired middle-class cultural capital will enable us to better navigate institutions, more effectively participate in political life, shape how our organizations operate, and have our views taken seriously by others. Our new social and professional networks will connect us to others who have more influence. We can use our working-class cultural capital and middle-class cultural capital to benefit ourselves, perhaps reaping significant rewards by helping to further enrich those at the top. But this risks making us complicit with the system that made things so challenging for us in the first place. Alternatively, if we believe that system to be unjust, we can strive to use our work and our resources to improve the lives of those around us. We can leverage our understanding of the system to promote structural changes that benefit those coming up behind us as well as those who remain in the working class doing the less glamorous but necessary work of society. The next and final chapter provides more specific examples for bringing these lessons to our professional work and workplaces.

8

Applying the Lessons to First-Gen Students, Working Straddlers, and Our Workplaces

How can we apply the findings from this research to our own lives and organizations? I have argued that working-class culture and middle-class culture socialize us into different attitudes, dispositions, behaviors, manners of speaking, senses of self and belonging, values, tastes, and ways we spend our time. The institutions of upward mobility—specifically schooling, college, and the professional workplace—are dominated by middle-class culture. People are expected to interact in the way that middle-class people do, and the rules are designed around middle-class norms. This type of professional culture makes it easier for middle-class people to fit in and ultimately attain economic success. Along the way, it is common for people to look down on working-class culture, assuming it to be an incorrect way of being. But there are moments when that gets flipped on its head and working-class culture is an asset. As you have read this book, you may have reflected on how the stories and analyses presented apply to your own life. In this chapter, I conclude with some additional lessons for individuals and the organizations in which we study and work.

If we are most concerned with making a fairer society and leveling the playing field, the way to have the greatest impact is to address the structural inequalities that lead to such vastly different opportunities and cultures in the first place. Because research is clear that social democratic policies promote the highest degree of mobility, they offer a model for addressing these structural barriers. To cite a few examples, effective policies would include equalizing educational spending, providing universal access to college, expanding the social safety net to support people when they fall on hard times, reducing poverty, and providing better access to health care. We would create incentives to integrate neighborhoods racially and economically and take steps toward reducing the enormous racial wealth gap. Like Sen. Nina Turner, we can and should participate in social and political movements to bring about those changes. But here I will focus on other steps we can take in our individual lives, social groups, and organizations.

The first lesson is that it is never too late (or too early) to more deeply reflect on how social class has impacted your life in unexpected ways. This may seem to be too obvious of a point to make, but the taboo nature of discussing class in American culture makes it worth emphasizing. If you were socialized in the United States, then the dominant message most of us receive is that class does not meaningfully impact our lives. But even if we understand that to be naive, have you ever deeply reflected on how your class might affect how you hold your body, how you feel when talking with someone of a high status, or what you decided to do for your career? How much of your difficulties and anxieties in life have you blamed on yourself, when in fact they may be shaped by your economic circumstances and how you were socialized into a different culture than is dominant in schools and professional workplaces? How much do your behaviors and feelings change as you alternate between more working-class and middle-class environments? Let's be honest that it can sometimes be painful and require us to confront things we sometimes wish to avoid, but it will be worth it in the end. Let's start to normalize naming and talking about class.

For people moving up the class ladder, reflection means thinking about what we are losing, what we have gained, and how we present ourselves to different groups. Philosopher Jennifer Morton refers to the latter dimension as "clear-eyed code switching."[1] She argues that "we need to take responsibility for the self who inhabits the various spaces in which we live by being clear about what we're up to when we are codeswitching." There may be parts of our working-class upbringing that we wish to leave behind permanently or temporarily, but we must "be reflective about what we are sacrificing and why." Without reflection, our behaviors and beliefs will likely conform to the prevailing middle-class culture, pulled by our circumstances. We may find ourselves not recognizing or not feeling comfortable with what parts of ourselves emerge. When we are reflective about how we adapt to a situation, we can be more strategic. For example, if we are silent when we disagree with something, reflection might lead us to speak up, or we may see it to be in service of our broader goals and accept the need for such a sacrifice. By being reflective and honest with ourselves about the parts of our background that are core to our sense of self, we empower ourselves to live the life we want to live as well as build and preserve the relationships we seek. A "clear-eyed" approach to navigating these conflicts permits us to navigate such dynamics with more fluidity.

A second lesson is to find your people. As you enter new environments, like college or the white-collar office, seek out your fellow first-gen students and straddlers. While we experience our class backgrounds differently, we will undoubtedly find comforting similarities and can explore the effects of class together. The people throughout these pages found close friends and insightful mentors when they opened themselves to the possibilities. Lean into the working-class culture of interdependence in which we orient ourselves toward others. Have the courage to allow yourself to be vulnerable by sharing a difficult story. While this will most often mean opening up to people who share our background, don't assume that others have not developed working-class cultural capital. Michael told me that one of the most influential people in his life was from the middle class but helped him reclaim his working-class Appalachian roots. Turner told me she was shocked when she learned her African American studies professor was a white woman, but she turned out to be one of her most trusted mentors. Seek out others who can help you explore your complex class roots that have further been shaped by region, race, ethnicity, gender, sexuality, rurality, or nation. Humans are hardwired to need social connections.[2] We cannot do it alone.

Third, there is tremendous power in articulating the story of your own class journey.[3] As John told me, "People are not persuaded by charts and figures and numbers. They're persuaded by stories and by people who they perceive to share their values and perspective." Stories are a universal element of all cultures and are among the most powerful modes of communication. Telling our narratives can help us make sense of the challenges we have encountered, what we value about our upbringing, how it has shaped who we are, and where we are heading. At the personal level, a story can motivate us by giving us purpose for what we are building toward, including our personal goals and our dreams for our families, communities, and society. Like the stories in this book, our class story can highlight to others who we are. For employers, our class story can make the case for overcoming adversity and what we have to offer, including how our background has instilled in us dispositions like hard work or other working-class cultural capital.[4] By building an authentic story, it will help give you pride, purpose, and joy. Tools also exist to help build your story.[5] Practice telling it over and over to different types of people.

Beyond these broader considerations, my respondents and I offer reflections for people at particular points along your journey or within your organizations. In the sections below, I present recommendations for first-gen students, working straddlers, universities, and other organizations.

Advice for First-Gen Students

Every one of the straddlers I interviewed was a working-class student who was the first in their family to navigate college, acquire middle-class cultural capital, and transition that education into a professional career. I asked each of them, having made it through college, what advice they would give to first-gen students in college now. In addition to the idea of finding a community of people that you can relate to, there were two very strong themes that stood out in their responses.

First, my respondents overwhelmingly wanted to encourage first-gen students to ask for help when they need it and accept help when it is offered. They recognized in themselves difficulty asking for help as a student, believing that they had to "suck it up and try harder." For those of us who grew up working-class, we likely developed a sense of constraint when interacting with people in positions of authority.[6] We don't feel entitled to demand much time from professors and college staff, erroneously believing that we are burdening them with our questions. We are often intimidated by their status, finding ourselves distracted by worrying about how we come across to them and if they will think our questions are not good. As a result, first-gen students may either avoid interactions with their professors and educational support staff or ask far fewer questions. Katrina, a Black straddler who works in college advising, explains that certain cultures, including students of color, have a harder time asking for help. She wants first-gen students to understand "that this is new for you, so don't feel like you have to have all the answers." Chris, a university chaplain, emphasized that "asking for help is not a sign of weakness." Furthermore, asking for help is what middle-class students are socialized to do. They grow up with a sense that educators are there to support their development and to help them advocate for themselves in getting that assistance, which helps them get where they want to get. The students who are more proactive in asking for help will get ahead faster.

Second, my respondents got very emotional about wanting to help first-gen students develop more confidence. Sage is in workforce development at a large university and told me that first-gen students can internalize messages "that they're incapable." She added, "They don't feel that they have permission to do what they want to do or to work for what they want to achieve." One respondent after another wished for first-gen students to see themselves as capable— having something to contribute and deserving to have a shot at success. Of course, hearing someone tell you to "have confidence" does not simply translate into believing in oneself. Most of all, building confidence means finding a community of supportive people to help you recognize your strengths, set and pursue attainable goals, know that you cannot do everything perfectly, and continue to grow when things don't go flawlessly. Hopefully the stories in this book help students to identify how a working-class background equips them with many strengths and that the challenges they face are related to an unequal class system for which they should not blame themselves. Discussing these class dynamics with others is beneficial for growing confidence in themselves.

My respondents offered a variety of other suggestions for first-gen students as well. Several respondents urged students to have the courage to get out of their comfort zone and try something new. You never know where it might lead! Marie encourages students to pursue international travel, saying, "Until you've been away and seen the world, your world is so small." Echoing an argument I often make to students,[7] she said, "I just feel like it would change us as humans, and it would change the world if everybody could open their eyes to the rest of the world."[8] Bella, a professor of medical anthropology, said, "Nowadays, anybody that I'm mentoring, I always say, just say yes. Don't say no. Try it. Maybe you'll like it. If you do it for a semester or a couple of months and you don't like it, you could just stop, but you never know until you try it."

Another challenge working-class students face is navigating financial well-being and understanding debt. Advice regarding debt can be oversimplistically summed up: Some debt is OK, but too much debt can limit your freedom in the future. Like many first-gen students, I was terrified of any debt because my family never had extra money, and I wondered how I could ever pay it off.[9] I missed out on some experiences like studying abroad because I did not want to take out any loans, and I ended up regretting that. Having said that, if someone takes out excessive loans, future decisions will end up revolving around maximizing income to pay off those loans, and it will limit what they can do for their career and their life. There is no way to put a specific number on how much debt is too much without considering one's circumstances, so this should be discussed with your trusted mentors—especially mentors who themselves have known living with so little.

Finally, don't set your expectations on what you have been socialized to see as the "normal" path through college and to a career. Ava said, "It's especially typical for first-generation and lower-income students to have a seven-year path to a degree, to change institutions multiple times. To live in a van for a bit. To use emergency housing or a food bank. These aren't abnormal, and in fact, what really is abnormal is the fact that these stories don't get told." Personally, I changed my major three times before landing in my career field, and changing majors is very common in college. But if you expect that your path will follow a straight line and it does not work out that way, you may feel stressed or unfairly blame yourself. Middle-class parents who have been to college are more likely to have these types of conversations with their children, so the rest of us have to learn these realities a different way. Expect to try out different majors and career fields and be open to new opportunities to explore!

Reflections for Working Straddlers

During the course of writing this book, I spoke with so many straddler friends and colleagues about navigating upward mobility. Perhaps more than anything else, the topic that got the most attention was this: Is it *truly* possible to straddle classes without feeling in constant conflict?

My respondents had different opinions on whether it is possible to balance our working-class and middle-class parts of ourselves. On the one hand, John told me, "I don't feel at home in any place that I've lived, not truly." He describes himself as a "border person," adding, "I don't feel at home when I go home, and I don't feel fully at home in my professional life. I don't truly feel like I fit in anywhere." In his book *Limbo*, Alfred Lubrano similarly wrote that the duality of straddling classes leads to a "never-ending struggle with identity."[10] On the other hand, Ashley felt much more comfortable with the dual parts of herself as she progressed in her career. She said, "It took me a long time to realize that I could hold multiple identities." As the assistant director of a student success center, Ashley is both "a working-class Appalachian girl" and "a part of the academy and engaged in scholarly research and intellectual conversations." She views the positive and negative sides of both of these parts of her life, and when possible, she chooses to opt out of many of the negatives—like avoiding the elitism that can exist in higher education or ignoring an occasional working-class family's comments when they disparage college. For Ashley, reaching that understanding and learning how to live with it has "definitely been a big part of my development as a human being and as a professional."

During the course of this research, it occurred to me that maybe asking whether or not we are doomed to be in constant conflict is the wrong question. Perhaps it is impossible to expect the uneasiness to disappear entirely. Could it be that the conflict from straddling is actually what illuminates the respective cultural worlds and makes it a rich experience? If so, then the better question might be how do we embrace the inner conflict to learn about ourselves? How might we navigate the movement between cultural worlds, not to eliminate the tension but to use it to illuminate our own desires for ourselves and our communities?

For instance, John, who never feels at home in the two worlds, found wisdom in straddling. He said that it's "something that I've come to grips with or have learned to accept, just in terms of self-awareness and understanding." He likened it to being gay: "I'm the only person in my family who's gay, and that's never been an issue for my family, which is really amazing and significant, but it's a difference." While "there's no one in my family that can relate to my experience," he found pride in his gay identity when in community with his gay and straight-allied friends. Ashley told me, "I think as I grow older it's easier to navigate that complex intersectionality of my own identity." As she moves between class worlds now, she experiences it as a fairly fluid movement, and when conflict arises, she channels it into better questions to understand herself.

Another issue that came up frequently was the question of burnout and how working-class culture could even make it easier for employers to take advantage of us. Much of this has to do with our work ethic and our socialization to believe that anyone can make it with hard work. Tori described that, as working-class people, you "beat yourself up working so much," such as when you feel like "you can't call in sick when you're really sick," and that we can become "workaholics." When you combine this with insecurity about our financial futures, a real or perceived scarcity of opportunities, insecurity about our own abilities, or awareness of discrimination that we experience because of our class, race, gender, or sexuality, it can drive us to unhealthy approaches toward work. While an incredible drive can serve us professionally, as it did for Cody in chapter 6, it can be very difficult to unlearn. Employers, who are incentivized to extract as much labor and effort from their workers as possible, can use this to further exploit us by leaning on us to work long hours, be available all hours of the day, or take on less desirable tasks.

For straddlers struggling with burnout and demanding bosses, again reflection and social support are key. Understanding our working-class upbringing, including its likely financial insecurity and habits of mind, can help us to understand how we have developed such attitudes toward work. These experiences are not the result of individual shortcomings but rather economic inequalities that have shaped our cultural experience. While plenty of advice guides exist for managing burnout, one of the things I have found most helpful is leaning into my support networks. For example, when I am asked to take on another task at work, I politely tell the person requesting it that I will get back to them. Then I can consult with friends and colleagues (many of whom are fellow straddlers conscious of these challenges) to talk through whether I should take on a particular project. Their removal from the situation and their knowledge of me give them an objectivity that I might not achieve on my own. It is part of the art of boundary-setting, or learning when and how to say no. It is not a cure-all but it is another tool in the tool kit.

While this upward mobility is often accompanied by financial improvement, moving into the professional middle class is no longer a guarantee of financial stability and success. This is especially true for younger straddlers who are much more likely to have taken on college debt as the cost of college has risen. Precarious employment, including part-time and temporary work, has become increasingly common among white-collar jobs.[11] Furthermore, the dramatic rise in housing costs has increased financial precarity and made homeownership much harder. For some, significant debt levels limit one's career and life choices, especially needing to pursue jobs that maximize income. Pursuing jobs that are driven by one's passions often requires a safety net that privileges middle-class people.[12] As artificial intelligence alters how jobs are designed, this problem will likely continue to worsen. For straddlers, this might mean taking on jobs that are much less desirable in order to be able to pay off higher loans or cover daily expenses. Many of my respondents lamented that fewer working-class jobs pay a living wage for their family members, but this is increasingly impacting white-collar jobs as well. Again, solving these issues cannot be done individually and will require creative policy solutions, as well as diverse political coalitions to bring them about.

Finally, how does your work align with the world you envision? There is much about our jobs that is out of our control, but if you value a world where our class background does not affect our chances in life, what ways—even small ways—can you contribute to that in your own professional work? While some jobs are much more structured for this than others, straddlers can search for ways to support poor and working-class people in much of the work that we do. Think about the tremendous range of occupations represented in my interviews in which people perceived themselves as lifting up workers: climate scientists, college enrollment managers, business development specialists, journalists, therapists, engineers, community organizers, administrative assistants, career services personnel, nonprofit managers, international development officers, teachers and professors, lawyers, judges, chaplains, social workers, case managers, small-business owners, school guidance counselors, college advisers, diversity and inclusion directors, band directors, marketing specialists, speech pathologists, nurses, police officers, paramedics, medical anthropologists, policy analysts, politicians, labor relations specialists, and more. Even if these jobs were not explicitly focused on serving poor and working-class populations, my respondents identified ways in which they supported people from these communities in their roles and used their class background to do so effectively.

Recommendations for Higher Education

The expanded programming for first-gen students that colleges and universities have undertaken has had a lopsided focus. It is certainly a good thing that higher education has become more aware of first-gen students and the challenges they face in adjusting to college life and expectations. However, this programming often exclusively views working-class first-gen students through a deficit lens. Students assumed to be lacking in middle-class cultural capital are provided resources and programming oriented toward equipping them with the cultural capital needed for educational and professional success. There is virtually no attention paid to the value of their working-class cultural capital, the impact of social mobility on students' sense of self and social relationships, or providing faculty and staff with professional development in helping understand their class roots and how to assist first-gen students through this process.

To best support first-gen students, colleges and universities should be mindful of developing programming in all these areas.

Because college and professional workplaces are dominated by middle-class culture, it is necessary to acquire the cultural skills to effectively navigate these environments. There is a need for programming designed to help students learn the hidden curriculum of college, use appropriate language and formatting for a resume, build time-management skills, cultivate relationships with professors, develop comfort in professional networking, and build other forms of cultural capital. Workshops on these topics tailored for first-gen students can help them adjust to college and acquire the skills to navigate unfamiliar institutions.[13] Research shows that framing messages with a growth mindset has especially high effects for improving student academic performance and accessing academic resources.[14] While helping colleges fulfill their goals of improving student learning and persistence through graduation, programming must be student-centric. It should be designed with student experiences in mind to help them understand the context of their experience while equipping them with academic skills that they can transition into fulfilling careers and building meaningful lives.

But as I have shown throughout this book, working-class first-gen students have their own strengths and a rich culture, which they bring to their college experience. When we ignore these assets and focus exclusively on what they are lacking—especially without providing context for the class inequalities that give rise to these cultural differences—there can be several unintended consequences. For starters, students might experience college as a culture shock and be more likely to interpret this lack of understanding as personal shortcomings or failures. They must be given opportunities to understand why their experiences differ from those of other students, put them in context, and identify what strengths they bring with them.[15]

In her book *Polished: College, Class, and the Burdens of Social Mobility*, sociologist Melissa Osborne shows how colleges' efforts to promote upward mobility can be a difficult, even traumatic, experience for first-gen students. She argues that students who "buy in" to the demands and expectations of middle-class culture will inevitably experience changes in beliefs, habits, tastes, and identities. The college experience is indeed designed to produce these changes. But students and their parents often cannot anticipate the ways this will change them. The experience can lead to a crisis of identity and tension with family and friends back home. To cope with this process, "many students are forced to rethink their choices" around college "and must develop strategies for maintaining their upward mobility trajectories without being seen as a 'sellout' by concerned friends and families."[16] Osborne adds that "for some students, this double bind becomes too difficult to manage without adequate support—leading to difficult choices that can result in exiting school or cutting ties to home."

I fully agree with Osborne that colleges must then create programming and resources to support first-gen students through the process of social mobility as they manage their evolving identities. Most importantly, this means providing one-on-one work to assist students in understanding the cultural mismatch of college, how they are changing through the process of their education, and how it relates to their developing sense of self and orientation toward others. An important program through which this work can begin is a precollege summer bridge program, which should be paired with ongoing peer mentoring. Bridge programs should be designed for both academic skills and social experiences that create student bonding among a first-gen student cohort. They should introduce them to academic norms and expectations and help them build connections with a range of faculty. Universities can offer academic courses that integrate material on first-gen student experiences and help to further build community. For example, I have taught several first-gen student sections of our first-year seminar. In addition to introducing students to campus resources, it helps equip them with language and knowledge to make sense of their experiences at college and how to adjust to the new expectations they are facing. Additional programming can include workshops on specific topics related to first-gen experiences, one-on-one college advising, and expanded mental health services. All of this must be paired with robust financial support.

My research adds to these recommendations by showing the power of working-class cultural capital and suggests new directions for first-gen programming. As part of the programming to support first-gen students in their transition, they can be encouraged to identify the strengths that they already bring to college.[17] Through workshops or academic coursework on first-gen student experiences, students can reflect on class cultures and how they have been socialized into various elements of working- and middle-class cultures. Students can be prompted to identify their strengths, including their support networks, which can help them to be successful students. Research has shown that when first-gen and working-class students reframe their identity as a way to help them succeed, it increases their academic performance and grades.[18] Another study shows that when students from lower socioeconomic backgrounds are asked to reflect on background-specific strengths they have, their academic persistence and self-esteem increase, and they are more likely to see themselves as an asset to their school and society.[19] Relatedly, an experimental study with first-gen students in a biology course found that a values affirmation intervention "narrowed the achievement gap between first-generation and continuing-generation students for course grades by 50% and increased retention in a critical gateway course by 20%."[20]

Of course, some of the working-class culture does not immediately translate to formalized institutions like colleges. Students can be further encouraged to reflect on how they can direct or channel their behaviors and dispositions to the new environment. For example, the interdependence of working-class culture is oriented toward others but not in a way of asking for help—especially from people in positions of authority. Students can be encouraged to think about their values of helping others and how they might redirect this in a way that they begin to develop comfort with seeking and accepting support for themselves.

Faculty and staff will benefit from professional development on class cultures, using workshops to relate them to more effective pedagogy and advising. Due in part to the taboo nature of class in America, this is rarely a part of existing diversity, equity, and inclusion (DEI) training. Workshops, minicourses, or speaker series can help faculty reflect on their own class backgrounds and the culture of higher education. These can enable faculty and staff to see their own assumptions shaping classroom dynamics, course design, and interactions with students. Similar professional development opportunities can assist staff in identifying how class cultures affect the work of their office, what jargon or norms they assume students understand, and how to make their offices a welcoming environment for first-gen students. Showing concrete examples of working-class cultural capital can assist faculty and staff in seeing the strengths that working-class first-gen students bring to the campus, facilitate pride in being a first-gen graduate, recognize the value of class diversity, and facilitate more open conversation. Straddler faculty and staff can be encouraged to share their personal experiences supporting students. These can help colleagues see the strengths that their coworkers bring to supporting students and how to help students see their own cultural assets.

Trainings of this type are also wonderful opportunities to build community and a sense of belonging among faculty and staff. On my own liberal arts college campus at Ohio Wesleyan University, my straddler colleagues routinely engage me in conversations about their own class journeys. I cherish these moments of connection and pride and appreciate how the discussions help us better support our students. Lifelong middle-class colleagues also often express enjoyment in opportunities to expand their repertoire for promoting DEI and personal satisfaction in the conversations that it facilitates with their colleagues as well. Of course, we should expect resistance from occasional colleagues who cling to the misleading idea that all students should be treated the same or believe we are sacrificing academic "rigor" by prioritizing support in helping students who have not yet mastered the hidden curriculum. When colleagues become resistant to dialogue about these dynamics, sometimes we have to be willing to work around them. Having buy-in from campus leadership who value this work will also help these conversations to flourish. Personally, my experience is that the vast majority of faculty and staff do welcome such conversations and meaningfully engage in this work.

Recommendations for Other Organizations

For those outside of higher education, there is a wide range of organizations in which class cultures and stereotypes are almost certainly impacting the type of work that we do. For example, hiring managers discriminate against people from working-class backgrounds by viewing them as deficient,[21] and class-based cultural conflicts abound in professional workplaces.[22] The unspoken dynamics of class cultures can have unintended consequences for building a positive organizational culture, prevent capable professionals from fulfilling their potential, make it difficult to retain qualified employees, and get in the way of organizational missions. At the individual level, this results in professionals from working-class backgrounds on average getting paid less for doing the same type of work with the same qualifications, having a harder time getting promoted, and generally facing more challenges in achieving professional success.[23]

In her book on class cultures in social movement organizations, Betsy Leondar-Wright recommends one necessary "first step: talk openly about class. Share class life stories, without pretense and without any shame or blame about the hidden hardships and privileges that are revealed."[24] While this might be easier to begin among the social activist and non-profit groups she studied, the recommendation could certainly be extended to other types of organizations as well. As she puts it, this is a necessary but not sufficient first step, but it can pave the way for starting to inspect other organizational processes, policies, and experiences.

Enormous potential is lost when hiring discrimination leads to less hiring of people from working-class backgrounds. Experimental studies, called audit studies, examine how employers discriminate against stigmatized groups in the labor market. In these studies, fake applications are sent to real job postings to see how often people get callbacks from employers. To study the effects of class, applications are matched on all qualifications except whether or not their materials indicated they were first-gen.[25] In one part of an illustrative study, researchers found that people who indicated they were first-gen were less likely to get a callback from employers than applicants who were not first-gen. Researchers conclude this is because first-gen students are "often viewed through the lens of deficits. As a consequence, they were often denied opportunities to gain entry into organizations."[26] In the second part of the study, the researchers found that when they "nudged decision makers to adopt a strengths-based lens, they became more receptive to hiring first-gen applicants." This underscores the power of working-class cultural capital and discussing its strengths within organizations. Straddlers are in a unique position to make an impact on their organizations to reduce discrimination against other first-gen graduates. Audit studies have shown how people of color, women, and other stigmatized groups are similarly discriminated against in the labor market as well.

The reality is that upwardly mobile working-class people have much to contribute to their workplaces, and some large firms and organizations are starting to recognize this. The most significant example is the global consulting firm KPMG. In the largest study of its kind, KPMG in the UK studied twenty-five thousand employees over a ten-year period to examine progression between ranks and how it was affected by people's backgrounds. It required the company to systematically ask about people's economic backgrounds and normalize employees sharing their class origins and stories. This was enabled by leadership making it a part of their mission to track and improve social mobility within the organization. The data revealed a powerful relationship—that class background was a more significant factor than race, gender, sexuality, or disability in affecting whether and how long it took people to be promoted within the organization. On average, it took people from poorer backgrounds 19 percent longer to progress through the company. Furthermore, these factors intersected with other parts of identity, with working-class women and working-class people of color being most negatively affected.

Similar to my findings within this book, KPMG UK views upwardly mobile straddlers as having strengths within the workplace. But when straddlers are discriminated against in hiring or not promoted through the company quickly enough, the company misses out. Its report states, "We recognise that there isn't just a moral imperative for championing greater diversity on all fronts."[27] It adds that the unique contributions of people from working-class backgrounds make the "business case" for economic diversity "just as clear." For example, KPMG UK identified wanting to "build a stronger culture at our firm," for which working-class culture is especially well suited. Straddlers can emphasize their empathy, progroup norms, authenticity, and orientation toward others rather than placing attention on oneself, which each contributes to helping the firm's desire for a strong organizational culture. KPMG UK's diversity initiatives also seek employees who bring with them "fresh thinking" and "different perspectives." To complement the strengths of middle-class culture, working-class cultural perspectives offer more practical approaches, ingenuity in solving problems, translating and bridging across different cultural contexts, direct communication, and impactful use of metaphors. KPMG UK has reoriented promotion guidelines with a "greater focus on an individual's overall potential, while considering academic results in the context in which they were achieved," which recognizes the unique demands that first-gen students face in college. Such an approach also helps KPMG UK to identify working-class dispositions like resilience and persistence.

Once they began discussing the role of economic background, tracking it in their data, and making it a priority, KPMG UK began to see small gains. For example, over a four-year period, they increased the percentage of their managers from low socioeconomic backgrounds and decreased the progression gap in promotions (from 22 percent to 19 percent). The improvement was modest, but the company saw this as part of a longer-term strategy: "While this may suggest some progress is being made following the initial implementation of our Social Mobility Action Plan, we also know we have much more to do." This includes eliminating pay gaps based on people's social backgrounds and analyzing the "firm's approach to work allocation" by conducting "extensive analysis to measure access to top opportunities for our historically underrepresented groups, including measuring sentiment from our colleagues on equal access to work opportunities."

While KPMG UK uses some different language than I have used in this book, its focus on the unique contributions of people from working-class backgrounds suggests there may be more opportunities to discuss class cultures at a much wider range of organizations than we might expect. We may have to use our code-switching skills to translate the strengths of working-class culture to particular contexts, but straddlers can begin to articulate the value of their own class background. For straddlers and our allies in such organizations, you might begin by discussing the ways that class cultures affect employee recruitment or promotion. Referring to specific examples and using storytelling will aid communication. Relating examples from this book to your particular organizational context might be an effective approach. When buy-in is achieved among leadership, organizational audits like those done by KPMG UK could be a way to systematically evaluate and promote change across an organization. Straddlers can also start to form employee networks to share their experiences, support one another, and strategize on improving organizational culture.

Lifting as We Climb

For upwardly mobile straddlers, there is much to be gained by acquiring middle-class cultural capital and transitioning into professional life. But there are also many positive elements we risk losing from our working-class roots as well. While we may wish to leave behind some of these elements, careful reflection about our class roots can help us hold on to those we value and use them as an asset in our upward journey. This book has outlined many strengths of working-class culture with various lessons for how we might make sense of who we are and how we can use those strengths at different stages of our journey. There can be tremendous reward in exploring these with our fellow first-gen students, straddlers, and others in solidarity with us. Together, we can uncover these hidden forces, develop pride in our class journeys, and lift up others as we climb.

Appendix

Research Methodology

The Project

The social sciences, and especially sociology, have produced excellent research examining the advantages that middle-class children have over working-class and poor children in attaining professional positions. These advantages are multifaceted, but cultural sociologists and educational researchers have contributed to this understanding by focusing on cultural capital, the cultural mismatch between schools and working-class children, and cultural differences in hiring and the workplace. This body of research, as discussed in chapters 1 and 2, reveals that institutions for upward mobility, specifically schools, colleges, and professional workplaces, are dominated by middle-class culture and cultural capital. For upwardly mobile working-class students, this means they must acquire middle-class cultural capital to be successful. While some researchers are careful to point out the positive elements of working-class culture, they tend to emphasize these cultural traits are not helpful in navigating college and securing professional positions. For the most part, both public conversation and the vast majority of academic scholarship view working-class culture and first-generation students through a *deficit lens*. In other words, their culture is a failure of the working class—a resistance to striving, an inability to speak a certain way, and a stubbornness for not trying to "fit in." Seemingly, it is something to be overcome by gaining middle-class cultural capital and assimilating into the middle class, thereby leaving behind their culture and community.

But there is an untold story about straddlers and the role of their working-class roots in their professional careers. Specifically, I was finding that in my classroom discussions and conversations with friends and colleagues, there are ways that we valued our working-class roots. So, I was curious to know, for those upwardly mobile straddlers, those first-generation graduates who maintained connections to their working-class roots in their work, how and why did they do it? What did they value about their working-class roots? Did they believe those qualities of their working-class roots helped them in their upward journey and in their professional work? If so, how and in what ways did they use them to be more effective in their careers? If there were parts that they simultaneously wanted to leave behind, what were they? How were these working-class experiences further shaped by race, gender, sexuality, region, or age?

To start answering those questions, I designed a research project in which I could speak with upwardly mobile straddlers across a wide range of occupations. In addition to wanting to capture the diverse ways that straddlers drew upon their working-class roots and seeking patterns across fields, I also wanted to write a book that addressed a broad array of occupational fields in which any first-generation student or straddler could imagine themselves working. I set out to design my research project, obtained IRB approval from my university, and began collecting my data.

The Sample

My research design required that I speak with straddlers across a wide range of occupational fields who reflect the broader diversity (e.g., across race, gender, sexuality, region, and age) within the working class. The most significant challenge to constructing this sample was to recruit respondents across a wide range of careers. So, I drafted a call for participants, in which I described my criteria:

> I am seeking participants for a research study on first-generation college graduates (i.e. people whose parents do not have a 4-year college degree). Specifically, I am interviewing first-generation college graduates who are from working-class backgrounds and now work in professional/white-collar occupations that serve working-class or poor communities in some way. I am especially interested to speak with first-gen grads from a variety of backgrounds (i.e. across race, gender, sexuality, national origin, etc.) and occupations. From social workers to community organizers; from artists to policy analysts addressing poverty; from engineers working on infrastructure projects in poor communities to doctors and nurses working in low-income neighborhoods, I want to learn from and share your stories!

The call for participants added brief details about me and the book project. When relevant, it was tailored to a more specific audience from which I was trying to recruit, including several organizations outlined below.

I reached out to individuals and organizations to share the call for participants on a variety of list serves, social media, and organizational websites. I began with several general calls to invite participants from a wide array of fields. These included the social media pages associated with The Sociological Cinema (a website I cocreated and coedited); the Working Class Studies Association; and the Appalachian Studies Association. I asked people in my personal contacts if they could share it with social media accounts associated with their occupational fields, which got it posted to pages for social workers, K–12 teachers, international development officers, and artists. I was especially interested in identifying communities of people working in occupations in which I had been unable to recruit participants and which I thought might be more open to sharing my call with their members. This led me to share my call for participants with organizations and associations like Engineering, Social Justice and Peace; the Social Enterprise Alliance; the National Association of County and City Health Officials (NACCHO); Research Action Design (RAD), Hack the Hood, and Americans for the Arts. Many interviews came because people saw the call and referred me to people they thought would be a good fit. Sometimes a respondent referred me to another likely participant through snowball sampling. In a few cases, I reached out to specific individuals because they were more public figures working in occupational areas to which I was hoping to expand. These included the authors Alfred Lubrano (journalist) and Barbara Jensen (therapist), and Sen. Nina Turner—all of whom generously agreed to an interview.

When potential interviewees expressed interest, I confirmed that they fit my target demographic before scheduling an interview. Specifically, I asked them about their parents' education levels (screening out anyone who had a parent with a bachelor's degree or higher), their parents' occupations (screening out anyone whose parents did not work in jobs that would be defined as working-class or poor), and their own education and occupation (confirming that they held at least a bachelor's degree and worked a professional occupation). There were a handful of people whom I had to turn away, including some who expressed disappointment, but it enabled me to ensure that all respondents were working-class first-generation graduates who could speak about the straddler experience.

As I recruited participants, I had three primary criteria driving my total number of participants. First, I continued recruiting participants until I was no longer hearing new themes regarding working-class values and cultural capital. In other words, I reached a point of "theoretical saturation" at which point respondents did not introduce new concepts relevant to my exploration of working-class cultural capital. Second, I needed adequate diversity in my sample to explore the ways that race, gender, sexuality, region, and so on, affected different working-class experiences. Third, my research design required that I obtain a sufficiently broad range of occupations to examine how working-class cultural capital worked across different fields and for which readers might imagine themselves leveraging their own working-class backgrounds in their work.

In total, I interviewed thirty-seven respondents. This included twenty-two women, fourteen men, and one respondent who identified as agender; they were between the ages of twenty-four and seventy-nine (average age 45.7 years); seven identified on the LGBTQ spectrum; seven identified as people of color; and respondents represented all regions across the United States (except one was a British woman in London). Furthermore, they represented a wide range of occupational fields. To ensure I reached this breadth, I tracked my respondents into the following occupational groupings: Sixteen worked in education, student support, or educational administration; sixteen worked in human services and the arts; and nine worked in STEM, business, and health care (the numbers total more than thirty-seven because a handful of people spanned multiple fields during their careers). All respondents were given the choice of using their real name or a pseudonym.

The Interviews

My thirty-seven in-depth interviews were semistructured. The interview questions covered a wide range of topics, which always started with an open-ended question upon which I probed if necessary. For example, early in the interview I asked, "How would you describe your class background growing up?" and then I asked what label they might use to describe it, why they might use that label, and to describe their parents' occupations, type of house they grew up in, and their parents' education levels. In terms of their background, I also asked about their educational experiences, how they selected a college and a major, and if they found mentors along the way. I asked when they became aware of class differences and about their interactions with members of other classes. I spent time probing the elements of their working-class upbringing they valued or viewed as negative aspects of working-class life. A considerable portion of each interview was spent on their current and former occupations, including any work responsibilities that relate to working-class populations, motivations for doing the work, how their background shapes that work, and goals they have for people in those fields. I also asked open-ended questions ("What are the important parts of your identity?") about how else they might describe their identity and probed whether they believed that their race, gender, and so on, further affected their experiences.

Nearly all (thirty-three) of the interviews were conducted between 2018 and 2019. When outlining my book and developing my argument, I realized I needed some additional occupational fields represented, and eventually, I interviewed an additional four people in 2022. The interviews ranged in length from 70 to 153 minutes, with an average length of 103.8 minutes. I was able to conduct fourteen interviews in person, while the remaining twenty-three interviews were conducted over the phone or video chat. In-person interviews were arranged locally in Ohio or when I was able to travel to the respondents' locations (including Minnesota, Wisconsin, Kentucky, Pennsylvania, and Washington, D.C.).

The Analysis

My interview data provided rich descriptions of straddlers' upward journeys, including their class origins, educational trajectory, work experiences, and how their upward journey might have been affected by other parts of their social background. The bulk of my data coding was open coding and included me identifying values/qualities (positive, negative, or ambiguous) of their working-class upbringing and the themes that they highlighted when talking about how their working-class backgrounds helped prepare them or made them better at specific work tasks. The codes were respectively grouped into working-class values and working-class cultural capital. I created two other code groups, including one for class trajectory in which I identified key moments (e.g., moments when they developed class consciousness, how they got into their career field, if they returned to school after a delay, etc.) that helped me understand key life experiences shaping their class trajectory. My final code grouping was a focused category on intersectional experiences, identifying how race, gender, sexuality, age, region, religion, and disability affected their experiences. The codes were organized and tabulated in Atlas.ti, a qualitative data analysis software.

Although my sample size is not large enough to be statistically generalizable or to examine broad patterns across other forms of diversity, the descriptive data did reveal fascinating ways that respondents leveraged their working-class roots in their professional work. It permitted me to identify discrete examples of working-class cultural capital and observe these forms of cultural capital operating across different occupational fields. It also enabled me to create the typology of working-class cultural capital as presented in chapters 3–6. Furthermore, it allowed me to explore ways in which these experiences were further shaped by other forms of diversity and inequality.

Acknowledgments

Projects like this are not possible without the support of numerous people, and I was especially fortunate to benefit from the generosity of so many friends and colleagues. While I acknowledge many of these individuals below, my circle of support extends far beyond those named.

First and foremost, I want to thank my thirty-seven interview respondents whose stories are at the center of this entire book. My participants were so generous with their time and opened up about both the wonderful and difficult moments of their class journeys. I am deeply grateful for their kindness and inspiration.

Second, thank you to the team at Rutgers University Press for investing in this project from start to finish. Acquisitions editor Peter Mickulas was very patient with all my questions, highly responsive, and helped guide me through the entire process. Series editor Lisa Nunn offered critical feedback early on in the process and greatly deserved the "you were right" email she received as I restructured the organization of the book. Thank you to my reviewers for their constructive comments on the entire manuscript. Their insights have been tremendously valuable in bringing this book to fruition.

My class journey hasn't made me rich financially, but my large circle of friends has enriched my life beyond my wildest expectations. Several of those friends have spent long periods of time with me as we processed our own class journeys, helping me think through my project, and giving me valuable feedback on drafts along the way. This includes my amazing wife, Tia Shields Dean, and my friends Clayt Maring, Steve Yahn, Jeremy Richardson, Brad Pulcini, Alper Yalcinkaya, Valerie Chepp, and Terry Chang. Those numerous conversations have brought us closer together and helped me realize I could indeed write this book. In addition to speaking with me about her own straddler experiences, Barbara Jensen gave me terrific advice and encouragement as I worked through my book proposal. I also appreciate the ongoing conversations and support from Lester Andrist, Ashley Biser, Nihal Celik, Nancy Comorau, Vanessa Hildebrand, Jeff Nilan, Sally Leber, and Shari Stone-Mediatore. Finally, thanks to my lifelong working-class friends who help me remain grounded in my working-class roots, from which I find great joy and while they may not know it, also make a project like this possible. Here I would especially like to raise a glass to Jay Scheffel and Shane Andrews for the many fun times we have had together.

I also want to thank the Working-Class Studies Association, which has been the most welcoming professional association that I have ever been a part of. In particular, Betsy Leondar-Wright and Jack Metzgar were very kind to invite me to participate in their inaugural webinar and provided feedback on my chapter drafts. Betsy was so generous with her time to talk with me about her inspiring work with Class Action and how to maximize the impact of the research. I have greatly enjoyed hearing about people's class journeys at WCSA meetings, where I also presented and received comments on early versions of this work.

The seeds for this project and the theoretical framing and qualitative skills to undertake this were firmly planted in my graduate school training at the University of Maryland, where I benefited from several mentors. In many ways, it all began with Annette Lareau's course, Family and Class, in which I was introduced to her own work on class and cultural capital and other research that shaped this project. I also have Annette's courses to thank for my qualitative methodology skills used throughout this research. The scholarly work of another mentor, Patricia Hill Collins, was foundational in guiding my intersectional analysis of class experiences as they are further shaped by race, gender, sexuality, region, and nation. Her mentoring, including consultation during this project, has pushed me to excel as a scholar and served as an excellent model of public sociology.

I have also had the great pleasure of working with so many hard-working and amazing first-gen students who will go on to do highly impactful work, and who have also contributed to this project. Student contributions began with a reading group on first-gen students and working-class culture, which included Emily Luti, Dylan Hays, and Claudia Kelly. Dylan, Claudia, and fellow student Mallorie Watts would later help me with transcribing some of my interviews. Claudia, Mallorie, and Scottie Hughes would also be part of our first-ever first-gen international travel group to Denmark, which was one of the most rewarding professional experiences of my entire career. As I was finishing this book, first-gen students Amarilys Torres-Nunez, Journey Armstrong, and Paiton Walker gave me feedback on different elements of the book. Finally, thanks to the numerous students in the several first-gen sections of our first-year seminar, my Senior Capstone course, and Social Inequality course. The students are too many to name, but they helped me think through the challenges and strengths we have as first-gen students, and students in the latter courses piloted drafts of my book chapters to help me improve them.

Finally, thank you to Ohio Wesleyan University for supporting me with a special scholarly leave and sabbaticals that were essential for the data collection and writing of this manuscript. They also supported me financially with interview transcription and funding to present early versions of this work at professional conferences. Also, thank you to provost Karlyn Crowley for serving as a thought partner, for her ongoing encouragement, and for helping me think bigger about the possible applications of the work.

Notes

Introduction

1. Tønnessen et al. 2016.
2. Lubrano 2004.
3. Wright 2000.
4. Bourdieu 1986.
5. While there is no universally agreed-upon term, I use the term Latine here to refer to anyone of Latino, Latina, Latine, or Latinx identity. Some readers and respondents will prefer Latino or Latinx to refer to the community broadly. I use Latine as one of the gender-neutral and inclusive options, although I always strive to use and respect the terms of self-identity preferred by my respondents. For commentaries on the nuances and trade-offs between these terms, refer to Miranda et al. 2023; and Soto-Luna 2023.
6. Bonilla-Silva 2021.
7. Patillo 2013.
8. The U.S. Census Bureau created its official measure in 1963. It was calculated by determining the cost of a minimal food diet and tripling that cost to approximate other basics. The measure is adjusted by family size and inflation.
9. Darling-Hammond et al. 2010.
10. Gilbert 2021.
11. Chetty 2014.
12. Herrnstein and Murray 1994.
13. Glenn 2020.
14. The most famous study in this area is this, but many recent studies confirm similar findings: Bertrand and Mullainathan 2004.
15. See two interactive articles: Badger et al. 2018a; and Badger et al. 2018b.
16. World Economic Forum 2020.
17. Knudsen et al. 2023; Bureau of Labor Statistics 2024.
18. Lareau 2011.
19. Davis and Rizk 2018.
20. Lubrano 2004, 5.
21. Bourdieu 1986.

22 Lubrano 2004, 5.
23 Lamont 2000; Sayer 2011; Halewood 2022.
24 Collins and Bilge 2020; Nguyen and Nguyen 2018.
25 Bourdieu 1986.
26 Cartier 2012.
27 Crew 2024; Luczaj 2023; Stiles 2017.
28 Marks et al. 2023; Carter 2005; Yosso 2005.

Chapter 1   The Differences Between Working-Class and Middle-Class Cultures

1   Cocks 1983.
2   Lareau 2011; Davis and Rizk 2018.
3   Milne and Aurini 2015.
4   Deroche 2014.
5   Lareau and Muñoz 2012.
6   Calarco 2011.
7   Cheadle and Amato 2010.
8   Manning 2019.
9   Mukherjee and Barn 2021.
10 Warner and Milkie 2013.
11 McCoy et al. 2012.
12 Kisida et al. 2014.
13 Jack 2015.
14 Bernstein 1962.
15 Bernstein 1971.
16 Stephens et al. 2011.
17 Meltzer 1978; see p. 101 of Jensen 2013.
18 Leondar-Wright 2014.
19 Jensen 2013.
20 Bourdieu 1986.
21 Holt 1977.
22 Halle 1993; Biswas 2012; Warde 2006; Maciel 2017; Sherman 2017; Leondar-Wright 2014.
23 Sherman 2017.
24 Holt 1997.
25 Leondar-Wright 2014.
26 Holt 1997.
27 Leondar-Wright 2014.
28 Peterson and Kern 1996.
29 Markus 2010.
30 Carter 2005.
31 Obermiller and Maloney 2016; Taylor 2008; Yu 2016.
32 Brown 2006.
33 Ruffins 1994.
34 Sayer 2011; Halewood 2022; De Keere 2020.
35 Williams 2012.
36 Lamont 1992; Lamont 2000.
37 Sherman 2017.

38. Lamont 1992.
39. Kusserow 2012; Illouz 2008.
40. Newman and Skocpol 2023.
41. Williams 2012.
42. Ridgeway and Fisk 2012; Rivera 2012.
43. Bourdieu 1986.
44. Markus and Hamedani 2007.
45. Lamont 2000.

Chapter 2   Classism and Cultural Mismatches Faced by Upwardly Mobile Working-Class People

1. Jensen 2013.
2. Goudeau et al. 2025.
3. Reardon 2011; Sirin 2005.
4. Torche 2011; Walpole 2003.
5. Darling-Hammond 2010.
6. The term "hidden curriculum" was coined by Phillip Jackson in his book *Life in Classrooms*. Henry Giroux (48–60) distinguished four different approaches to the hidden curriculum, which is also covered in a helpful review by Margolis et al. (2001). The four approaches are traditional, liberal, radical, and dialectical, and my approach is closest to the dialectical critique. See Giroux and Purpel 1983.
7. Stephens et al. 2012a; Stephens et al. 2012b; Stephens et al. 2012; Wren 1999.
8. Heath 1983/1996; Heath 2012.
9. Lareau 2011.
10. Jensen 2013, 86.
11. Calarco 2018.
12. Ready and Wright 2011; Kozlowski 2015.
13. Oakes 2005.
14. Morris 2005.
15. Anyon 1980; Anyon 1981.
16. Stephens et al. 2012.
17. Jussim and Harber 2005.
18. Most famously is Loewen 2007.
19. Riddell 1992; Watson 2005; Carter 2005.
20. Statistica 2022.
21. Smith 2015.
22. Stephens et al. 2012.
23. Chang et al. 2020.
24. Stephens et al. 2012.
25. Center for First-Generation Student Success, n.d.
26. Rutherford 2011.
27. Smith 2015.
28. Canning et al. 2020.
29. Collins et al. 2020.
30. Nunn 2021.
31. Zumbrunn et al. 2014; McCabe 2016.
32. Benson and Lee 2020.
33. Dean and Kelly 2020.

34 See p. 31 in Lubrano 2004.
35 KPMG UK 2022.
36 Jensen 2013.
37 Lubrano 2004, 150.
38 Kraus et al. 2012.
39 Lubrano 2004, 144.
40 Morton 2019; Osborne 2024.

Chapter 3   Cultural Empathy

1   Bourdieu 1986.
2   Kraus et al. 2010.
3   Goldstein and Michaels 2021.
4   Cuff et al. 2016.
5   Richards and Camuso 2015.
6   Cottingham 2016.
7   Zembylas 2007.
8   Song 2018.
9   Reynolds and Parrish 2018.
10 Lareau 2011.
11 Calarco 2018.
12 King et al. 2017.
13 Heath 2012.
14 Schuette 2023.
15 Zeng et al. 2022.
16 Macdonald 2022.
17 Goldstein and Winner 2012.
18 See also Dews and Law 1995; Reilly 2022.
19 Lareau 2011.
20 Soria et al. 2014.
21 Stephens et al. 2012.
22 Lin 1999.
23 Lareau 2011.
24 Tatarlar et al. 2016.
25 Riess 2017; Decety 2020.
26 Booth 2015.
27 Dawson et al. 1992.
28 Tracy and Baaki 2022.
29 Walther et al. 2017.
30 Sheppard et al. 2003.
31 Brower 2021.
32 Van Bommel 2021.
33 Bilgili and Kara 2019.
34 Löffler and Greitemeyer 2023; Strauss 2004.

Chapter 4   Working-Class Norms, Language, and Communication

1   Anyon 1980; Anyon 1981.
2   Pendergast et al. 2018, 138.

3   Heath 1983/1996.
4   Weinger 1998.
5   Covington 1992.
6   Lamont 2000.
7   Lareau 2011.
8   Stephens et al. 2011; Jensen 2013.
9   McCarty 2016.
10 Sommet et al. 2015.
11 Nunn 2021.
12 Stephens et al. 2011.
13 Lampert et al. 2016.
14 Bourdieu 1986.
15 Working Class Studies Association. n.d.
16 Illouz 2008.
17 Kugelmass 2016.
18 Lubrano 2004.
19 Lareau 2011.
20 Meltzer 1978; see Jensen 2013, 101.
21 McEvoy et al. 2021.
22 Leondar-Wright 2014.
23 Leondar-Wright 2014, 156.
24 Leondar-Wright 2014, 156.
25 Leondar-Wright 2014, 157.
26 Leondar-Wright 2014, 157.
27 Wagner et al. 2013.
28 Morton 2019; Osborne 2024.
29 Morton 2019.
30 Cooper 2012.
31 Lamont 2000.
32 Williams 2012.
33 Yosso 2005.
34 Gramsci 2011.

Chapter 5   Translating, Code-Switching, Mediating, and Bridge-Building

1   Glass 2023.
2   Carter 2005.
3   Hurst 2010.
4   Yosso 2005; Crew 2024.
5   Margolis et al. 2001; Smith 2015.
6   Lareau 2011.
7   Hagler 2023.
8   Jensen 2013.
9   Researchers who study working-class culture in schools have successfully taught middle-class teachers and administrators about working-class culture to better support students. One example is Shirley Brice Heath, http://shirleybriceheath.net/.
10 Morton 2019.
11 Morton 2014.

12 McCluney et al. 2021.
13 Levon et al. 2022.
14 Lareau 2011; Bernstein 1971; Jensen 2013; Heath 2012.
15 Durkee and Mangan 2023.
16 McCluney et al. 2021.
17 Lareau 2011.
18 Pisarcik 2024.
19 Willis 2020.
20 Latimer et al. 2005.
21 Smith 2020.
22 Schumann and Fletcher 2016.
23 Dieterich-Ward 2017.
24 Scerri 2019.
25 Abraham 2017.
26 Metzgar 2021.
27 Yosso 2005.

Chapter 6   Working-Class Dispositions

1 Bourdieu 1997; for a theoretical overview of dispositions as cultural capital and habitus, see Edgerton and Roberts 2014.
2 Lahire 2003.
3 Bourdieu 1997.
4 Lareau 2011.
5 Farkas et al. 1990.
6 Khan 2021.
7 Stockfelt 2016; Hart 2016.
8 Lareau 2011.
9 Calarco 2018.
10 Hart 2016.
11 Kundu et al. 2024.
12 Simpson et al. 2016.
13 Chang et al. 2020.
14 Vannini and Franzese 2008.
15 Lamont 2000.
16 Lareau 2011.
17 Appio 2013.
18 Appio 2013, 115.
19 Jones et al. 2012.
20 Stuber 2011; O'Shea and Janine 2019; Ceballo et al. 2014.
21 Duckworth 2016.
22 Credé et al. 2017.
23 Yosso 2005; Crew 2024.
24 Slater 2022; Goward 2021.
25 Azmitia et al. 2018.
26 Covington 1992.
27 Kundu et al. 2024.
28 National Association of Colleges and Employers 2024.
29 Laureau 2011.

Chapter 7 Managing the Threats of Assimilation, Complicity, and Co-Optation

1. Gordon 2005.
2. Portes and Zhou 1993.
3. Lareau 2011.
4. Peckham 1995 (quoted in Jensen 2013, 167).
5. Lubrano 2004.
6. Massey and Sanchez R. 2010.
7. Portes and Zhou 2003.
8. Telles and Ortiz 2008.
9. Jensen 2013.
10. Tatum and Browne 2019.
11. Lacy 2004.
12. Lacy 2004, 910.
13. Lacy 2004, 925–926.
14. Jensen 2013, 54.
15. Ogbar 2019; Munoz 2007; Bernstein 1997.
16. Hodgman 2013; Fox 2004.
17. Morton 2019.
18. For some critiques of the World Bank and its model of development, see Goldman 2005; and Toussaint 2023.
19. Osborne 2024.
20. Coy 2022.
21. Jensen 2013; Leondar-Wright 2014.
22. World Economic Forum 2020.
23. We Are Somebody, n.d.
24. Terry 2020.
25. Lobb 2017.
26. Lorde 1984.
27. Metzgar 2021.

Chapter 8 Applying the Lessons to First-Gen Students, Working Straddlers, and Our Workplaces

1. Morton 2019, 95–97.
2. Wilkinson and Pickett 2011.
3. Van Galen 2020.
4. Belmi et al. 2024.
5. Van Galen 2020.
6. Lareau 2011.
7. Dean and Kelly 2020.
8. Dean and Kelly 2020.
9. Somers et al. 2004.
10. Lubrano 2004.
11. Snyder 2022.
12. Cech 2021.
13. Stephens et al. 2024.
14. Canning et al. 2024.

15 Bauer et al. 2025.
16 Osborne 2024, 168.
17 Bauer et al. 2025.
18 Bauer et al. 2025.
19 Hernandez et al. 2021.
20 Harackiewicz et al. 2014.
21 Sharps and Anderson 2021; Belmi et al. 2024.
22 Lubrano 2004; Leondar-Wright 2014.
23 Laurison and Friedman 2024; KPMG UK 2022.
24 Leondar-Wright 2014, 232.
25 Belmi et al. 2024.
26 Belmi et al. 2024, 667.
27 KPMG UK 2022, 14.

References

Abraham, Judson. 2017. "Just Transitions for the Miners: Labor Environmentalism in the Ruhr and Appalachian Coalfields." *New Political Science* 39 (2): 218–240. https://doi.org/10.1080/07393148.2017.1301313.

Anyon, Jean. 1980. "Social Class and the Hidden Curriculum of Work." *Journal of Education* 162 (2): 67–92.

Anyon, Jean. 1981. "Social Class and School Knowledge." *Curriculum Inquiry* 11 (1): 1–42. https://doi.org/10.2307/1179509.

Anyon, Jean. 1997. *Ghetto Schooling: A Political Economy of Urban Educational Reform.* New York: Teachers College Press.

Appio, Lauren. 2013. "Poor and Working-Class Clients' Social Class-Related Experiences in Therapy." PhD diss., Columbia University (Proquest 3596823).

Azmitia, Margarita, Grace Sumabat-Estrada, Yeram Cheong, and Rebecca Covarrubias. 2018. "'Dropping Out Is Not an Option': How Educationally Resilient First-Generation Students See the Future." *New Directions for Child and Adolescent Development* 2018 (160): 89–100. https://doi.org/10.1002/cad.20240.

Badger, Emily, Claire Cain Miller, Adam Pearce, and Kevin Quealy. 2018a. "Extensive Data Shows Punishing Reach of Racism for Black Boys." *New York Times*, March 19, 2018. https://www.nytimes.com/interactive/2018/03/19/upshot/race-class-white-and-black-men.html.

Badger, Emily, Claire Cain Miller, Adam Pearce, and Kevin Quealy. 2018b. "Income Mobility Charts for Girls, Asian-Americans and Other Groups. Or Make Your Own." *New York Times*, March 27, 2018. https://www.nytimes.com/interactive/2018/03/27/upshot/make-your-own-mobility-animation.html.

Bauer, Christina, Gregory Walton, Veronika Job, and Nicole Stephens. 2025. "The Strengths of People in Low-SES Positions: An Identity-Reframing Intervention Improves Low-SES Students' Achievement over One Semester." *Social Psychological and Personality Science* 16 (1): 45–55. https://osf.io/preprints/psyarxiv/54jsk.

Belmi, Peter, Kelly Raz, Margaret Neale, and Melissa Thomas-Hunt. 2024. "The Consequences of Revealing First-Generational Status." *Organization Science* 35 (2): 667–697. https://doi.org/10.1287/orsc.2023.1682.

Benson, Janel, and Elizabeth Lee. 2020. *Geographies of Campus Inequality: Mapping the Diverse Experiences of First-Generation Students.* New York: Oxford University Press.

Bernstein, Basil. 1962. "Linguistic Codes, Hesitation Phenomena, and Intelligence." *Languages and Speech* 5: 31–46. https://doi.org/10.1177/002383096200500104.

Bernstein, Basil. 1971. *Class, Codes. and Control*. Vol. 1. Theoretical Studies Towards a Sociology of Language. New York: Routledge.

Bernstein, Mary. 1997. "Celebration and Suppression: The Strategic Uses of Identity by the Lesbian and Gay Movement." *American Journal of Sociology* 103 (3): 531–565. https://doi.org/10.1086/231250.

Bertrand, Marianne, and Sendhil Mullainathan. 2004. "Are Emily and Greg More Employable Than Lakisha and Jamal? A Field Experiment on Labor Market Discrimination." *American Economic Review* 94 (4): 991–1013. https://doi.org/10.1257/0002828042002561.

Bilgili, Habibe, and Ahmet Kara. 2019. "Does Basic Empathy Predict Counselors' Career Adaptability." *International Journal of Science and Research* 9 (10): 1411–1416. https://doi.org/10.21275/SR201020193329.

Biswas, P. 2012. "Social Sutra: Yoga, Identity, and Health in New York's Changing Neighborhoods." *Health, Culture and Society* 3 (1): 95–111. https://doi.org/10.5195/hcs.2012.82.

Bonilla-Silva, Eduardo. 2021. *Racism Without Racists*. 6th ed. New York: Rowman & Littlefield.

Booth, Jeff. 2015. "Why Genuine Empathy Is Good for Business." *Fast Company*, October 19, 2015. https://www.fastcompany.com/3052337/why-genuine-empathy-is-good-for-business.

Bourdieu, Pierre. 1986. *Distinction: A Social Critique of the Judgement of Taste*. New York: Routledge.

Bourdieu, Pierre. 1997. "The Forms of Capital." In *Education: Culture, Economy, Society*, edited by A. H. Halsey, Hugh Lauder, Phillip Brown, and Amy Stuart Wells. Oxford University Press.

Brower, Tracy. 2021. "Empathy Is The Most Important Leadership Skill According to Research." *Forbes*, September 19, 2021. https://www.forbes.com/sites/tracybrower/2021/09/19/empathy-is-the-most-important-leadership-skill-according-to-research/?sh=278cac8d3dc5.

Brown, David West. 2006. "Girls and Guys, Ghetto and Bougie: Metapragmatics, Ideology, and the Management of Social Identities." *Journal of Sociolinguistics* 10 (5): 596–610. https://doi.org/10.1111/j.1467-9841.2006.00297.x.

Bureau of Labor Statistics. 2024. "Union Members Summary." https://www.bls.gov/news.release/union2.nr0.htm.

Calarco, Jessica. 2011. "'I Need Help!' Social Class and Children's Help-Seeking in Elementary School." *American Sociological Review* 76 (6): 862–882. https://doi.org/10.1177/0003122411427177.

Calarco, Jessica. 2018. *Negotiating Opportunities: How the Middle-Class Secures Advantages in School*. New York: Oxford University Press.

Canning, Elizabeth, Jennifer LaCrosse, Kathryn Kroeper, and Mary Murphy. 2020. "Feeling Like an Imposter: The Effect of Perceived Classroom Competition on the Daily Psychological Experiences of First-Generation College Students." *Social Psychological and Personality Science* 11 (5): 647–657. https://doi.org/10.1177/1948550619882032.

Canning, Elizabeth A., Makita White, and William B. Davis. 2024. "Growth Mindset Messages from Instructors Improve Academic Performance Among

First-Generation College Students." *CBE—Life Sciences Education* 23 (2): ar14. https://doi.org/10.1187/cbe.23-07-0131.

Carter, Prudence. 2005. *Keepin' It Real: School Success Beyond Black and White*. New York: Oxford University Press.

Cartier, Marie. 2012. "Le Caring, Un Capital Culturel Populaire?" *Actes de La Recherche En Sciences Sociales* 1–2 (191–192): 106–113. https://doi.org/10.3917/arss.191.0106.

Ceballo, Rosario, Laura K. Maurizi, Gloria A. Suarez, and Maria T. Aretakis. 2014. "Gift and Sacrifice: Parental Involvement in Latino Adolescents' Education." *Cultural Diversity and Ethnic Minority Psychology* 20 (1): 116–127. https://doi.org/10.1037/a0033472.

Cech, Erin. 2021. *The Trouble with Passion: How Searching for Fulfillment at Work Fosters Inequality*. Oakland: University of California Press.

Center for First-Generation Student Success. n.d. "Use of Student Support Services Among Freshman First-Generation College Students." Accessed June 29, 2024. https://firstgen.naspa.org/files/dmfile/NASPA_FactSheet-03_FIN.pdf.

Chang, Janet, Shu-wen Wang, Colin Mancini, Brianna McGrath-Mahrer, and Sujey Orama de Jesus. 2020. "The Complexity of Cultural Mismatch in Higher Education: Norms Affecting First-Generation College Students' Coping and Help-Seeking Behaviors." *Cultural Diversity and Ethnic Minority Psychology* 26 (3): 280–294. https://doi.org/10.1037/cdp0000311.

Cheadle, Jacob, and Paul Amato. 2010. "A Quantitative Assessment of Lareau's Qualitative Conclusions About Class, Race and Parenting." *Journal of Family Issues* 32 (5): 679–706. https://doi.org/10.1177/0192513X10386305.

Chetty, Raj, Nathaniel Henderen, Patrick Kline, Emmanuel Saez, and Nicholas Turner. 2014. "Is the United States Still a Land of Opportunity? Recent Trends in Intergenerational Mobility." *NBER* Working Paper 19844. https://doi.org/10.3386/w19844.

Cocks, Jay. 1983. "Chilling Out on Rap Flash." *Time Magazine*, March 21, 1983. https://time.com/vault/issue/1983-03-21/page/90/.

Collins, Kristina, Erica Price, Lisa Hanson, and Dianne Neaves. 2020. "Consequences of Stereotype Threat and Imposter Syndrome: The Personal Journey from STEM-Practitioner to STEM-Educator for Four Women of Color." *Journal of Culture and Education* 19 (4): 161–180.

Collins, Patricia Hill, and Sirma Bilge. 2020. *Intersectionality*. Hoboken, NJ: John Wiley & Sons.

Cooper, Frank. 2012. *Professional Boundaries in Social Work and Social Care: A Practical Guide to Understanding, Maintaining and Managing Your Professional Boundaries*. Philadelphia: Jessica Kingsley Publishers.

Cottingham, Marci. 2016. "Theorizing Emotional Capital." *Theory and Society* 45: 451–470. https://doi.org/10.1007/s11186-016-9278-7.

Covington, Martin V. 1992. *Making the Grade: A Self-Worth Perspective on Motivation and School Reform*. New York: Cambridge University Press.

Coy, Patrick. 2022. "Co-Optation." In *The Wiley-Blackwell Encyclopedia of Social and Political Movements*, edited by D. A. Snow, D. Porta, B. Klandermans, and D. McAdam. Hoboken, NJ: Wiley-Blackwell.

Credé, Marcus. 2018. "What Shall We Do About Grit? A Critical Review of What We Know and What We Don't Know." *Educational Researcher* 47 (9): 606–611. https://doi.org/10.3102/0013189X18801322.

Credé, Marcus, Michael Tynan, and Peter Harms. 2017. "Much Ado About Grit: A Meta-Analytic Synthesis of the Grit Literature." *Journal of Personality and Social Psychology* 113 (3): 492–511. https://doi.org/10.3102/0013189X18801322.

Crew, Teresa. 2024. *The Intersections of a Working-Class Academic Identity: A Class Apart*. Leeds, UK: Emerald Publishing. https://bookstore.emerald.com/the-intersections-of-a-working-class-academic-identity.html.

Cuff, Benjamin, Sarah Brown, Laura Taylor, and Howat Douglas. 2016. "Empathy: A Review of the Concept." *Emotional Review* 8 (2): 144–153. https://doi.org/10.1177/1754073914558466.

Darling-Hammond, Linda. 2010. "Structured for Failure: Race, Resources, and Student Achievement." In *Doing Race: Essays for the 21st Century*, edited by Hazel Rose Markus and Paula Moya. New York: W. W. Norton & Company.

Davis, Scott, and Jessica Rizk. 2018. "The Three Generations of Cultural Capital Research: A Narrative Review." *Review of Educational Research* 88 (3): 331–365. https://doi.org/10.3102/0034654317748423.

Dawson, Lyndon, Barlow Soper, and Charles Pettijohn. 1992. "The Effects of Empathy on Salesperson Effectiveness." *Psychology & Marketing* 9 (4): 297–310. https://doi.org/10.1002/mar.4220090404.

Dean, Paul, and Claudia Kelly. 2020. "Educational Travel for First-Generation Students." *Teaching Sociology* 48 (4): 341–352. https://doi.org/10.1177/0092055X20952826.

Decety, Jean. 2020. "Empathy in Medicine: What It Is, and How Much We Really Need It." *American Journal of Medicine* 133 (5): 561–566. https://doi.org/10.1016/j.amjmed.2019.12.012.

De Keere, Kobe. 2020. "Finding the Moral Space: Rethinking Morality, Social Class, and Worldviews." *Poetics* 79. https://doi.org/10.1016/j.poetic.2019.101415.

Deroche, Christina. 2014. "Label, Stigma, and Sick Roles in a Therapeutic Culture: The Case of Developmental Coordination Disorder." PhD diss., McMaster University, Hamilton, Ontario, Canada.

Dews, C. L., and Carolyn Lest Law. 1995. *This Fine Place So Far from Home: Voices of Academics from the Working-Class*. Philadelphia: Temple University Press.

Dieterich-Ward, Allen. 2017. "'We've Got Jobs. Let's Fight for Them': Coal, Clean Air, and the Politics of Antienvironmentalism." *Ohio Valley History* 17 (1): 6–28.

Duckworth, Angela. 2016. *Grit: The Power of Passion and Perseverance*. New York: Simon and Schuster.

Durkee, Myles I., and Katherine Mangan. 2023. "Race on Campus: The Taxing Performances of Code Switching." *Chronicle of Higher Education*, January 10, 2023. https://www.chronicle.com/newsletter/race-on-campus/2023-01-10.

Edgerton, Jason D., and Lance W. Roberts. 2014. "Cultural Capital or Habitus? Bourdieu and Beyond in the Explanation of Enduring Educational Inequality." *Theory and Research in Education* 12 (2): 193–220. https://doi.org/10.1177/1477878514530231.

Farkas, George, Robert P. Grobe, Daniel Sheehan, and Yuan Shuan. 1990. "Cultural Resources and School Success: Gender, Ethnicity, and Poverty Groups Within an Urban School District." *American Sociological Review* 55 (1): 127–142. https://doi.org/10.2307/2095708.

Fox, Aaron A. 2004. *Real Country: Music and Language in Working-Class Culture*. Durham, NC: Duke University Press.

Gilbert, Dennis. 2021. *The American Class Structure in an Age of Growing Inequality*. 11th ed. Thousand Oaks, CA: Sage.

Giroux, Henry A., and David E. Purpel. 1983. *The Hidden Curriculum and Moral Education: Deception Or Discovery?* Berkeley, CA: McCutchan Publishing Corporation.

Glass, Leah E. 2023. "Social Capital and First-Generation College Students: Examining the Relationship Between Mentoring and College Enrollment." *Education and Urban Society* 55 (2): 143–174. https://doi.org/10.1177/00131245221076097.

Glenn, James. 2020. *Wealth Inequality in America: Causes, Consequences and Solutions*. Cottonhall, CA: Pernsiero Press.

Goldman, Michael. 2005. *Imperial Nature: The World Bank and Struggles for Social Justice in the Age of Globalization*. New Haven, CT: Yale University Press.

Goldstein, Arnold P., and Gerald Y. Michaels. 2021. *Empathy: Development, Training, and Consequences*. New York: Routledge.

Goldstein, Thalia R., and Ellen Winner. 2012. "Enhancing Empathy and Theory of Mind." *Journal of Cognition and Development* 13 (1): 19–37. https://doi.org/10.1080/15248372.2011.573514.

Gordon, Milton. 2005. "The Nature of Assimilation." In *Incorporating Diversity: Rethinking Assimilation in a Multicultural Age*. New York: Routledge.

Goudeau, Sébastien, Nicole M. Stephens, Hazel R. Markus, Céline Darnon, Jean-Claude Croizet, and Andrei Cimpian. 2025. "What Causes Social Class Disparities in Education? The Role of the Mismatches between Academic Contexts and Working-Class Socialization Contexts and How the Effects of These Mismatches Are Explained." *Psychological Review* 132 (2): 380–403. https://doi.org/10.1037/rev0000473.

Goward, Shonda L. 2021. "Resilience and Grit Are for Rich People: How 'Making It' Through Higher Education Has Made Me Sick." In *Amplified Voices, Intersecting Identities: Volume 2*. Brill. https://doi.org/10.1163/9789004445253_023.

Gramsci, Antonio. 2011. *Prison Notebooks*. New York: Columbia University Press.

Hagler, Matthew A. 2023. "Mentoring First-Generation College Students: Examining Distinct Relationship Profiles Based on Interpersonal Characteristics, Support Provision, and Educational Capital." *Journal of Community Psychology* 51 (8): 3103–3120. https://doi.org/10.1002/jcop.23003.

Halewood, Michael. 2022. "'Class Is Always a Matter of Morals': Bourdieu and Dewey in Social Class, Morality, and Habit(Us)." *Cultural Sociology* 17 (3): 373–389. https://doi.org/10.1177/17499755221108135.

Halle, David. 1993. *Inside Culture: Art and Class in the American Home*. Chicago: University of Chicago Press.

Harackiewicz, Judith M., Elizabeth A. Canning, Yoi Tibbetts, Cynthia J. Giffen, Seth S. Blair, Douglas I. Rouse, and Janet S. Hyde. 2014. "Closing the Social Class Achievement Gap for First-Generation Students in Undergraduate Biology." *Journal of Educational Psychology* 106 (2): 375–389. https://doi.org/10.1037/a0034679.

Hart, Caroline Sarojini. 2016. "How Do Aspirations Matter?" *Journal of Human Development and Capabilities* 17 (3): 324–341. https://doi.org/10.1080/19452829.2016.1199540.

Heath, Shirley. 1983. *Ways with Words: Language, Life, and Work in Communities and Classrooms*. New York: Cambridge University Press.

Heath, Shirley Brice. 2012. *Words at Work and Play: Three Decades in Family and Community Life*. New York: Cambridge University Press.

Heath, Shirley Brice. n.d. "Shirley Brice Health." http://shirleybriceheath.net/.
Hernandez, Ivan, David Silverman, and Mesmin Destin. 2021. "From Deficit to Benefit: Highlighting Lower-SES Students' Background-Specific Strengths Reinforces Their Academic Persistence." *Journal of Experimental Social Psychology* 92.
Herrnstein, Richard J., and Charles A. Murray. 1994. *The Bell Curve: Intelligence and Class Structure in American Life*. New York: Free Press.
Hodgman, Matthew R. 2013. "Class, Race, Credibility, and Authenticity Within the Hip-Hop Music Genre." *Journal of Sociological Research* 4 (2): 402–413. https://doi.org/10.5296/jsr.v4i2.4503.
Holt, Douglas B. 1997. "Distinction in America? Recovering Bourdieu's Theory of Tastes from Its Critics." *Poetics* 2–3 (25): 93–120.
Hooks, Bell. 2014. *Teaching to Transgress: Education as the Practice of Freedom*. New York: Routledge.
Hurst, Allison L. 2010. *The Burden of Academic Success: Managing Working-Class Identities in College*. Lanham, MD: Lexington Books.
Illouz, Eva. 2008. *Saving the Modern Soul: Therapy, Emotions, and the Culture of Self-Help*. Berkeley: University of California Press.
Jack, Andrew Abraham. 2015. "(No) Harm in Asking: Class, Acquired Cultural Capital, and Academic Engagement at an Elite University." *Sociology of Education* 89 (1): 1–19. https://doi.org/10.1177/0038040715614913.
Jackson, Philip Wesley. 1990. *Life in Classrooms*. New York: Teachers College Press.
Jensen, Barbara. 2013. *Reading Classes: On Culture and Classism in America*. Ithaca, NY: ILR Press.
Jones, Susan R., Yoolee Choe Kim, and Kristan Cilente Skendall. 2012. "(Re-) Framing Authenticity: Considering Multiple Social Identities Using Autoethnographic and Intersectional Approaches." *Journal of Higher Education* 83 (5): 698–724.
Jussim, Lee, and Kent D. Harber. 2005. "Teacher Expectations and Self-Fulfilling Prophecies: Knowns and Unknowns, Resolved and Unresolved Controversies." *Personality and Social Psychology Review* 9 (2): 131–155. https://doi.org/10.1207/s15327957pspr0902_3.
Khan, Shamus Rahman. 2021. *Privilege: The Making of an Adolescent Elite at St. Paul's School*. Princeton, NJ: Princeton University Press.
King, Colby R., Jakari Griffith, and Meghan Murphy. 2017. "Story Sharing for First-Generation College Students Attending a Regional Comprehensive University: Campus Outreach to Validate Students and Develop Forms of Capital." *Teacher-Scholar: The Journal of the State Comprehensive University* 8 (1): 1. https://doi.org/10.58809/QFFH2531.
Kisida, Brian, Jay Greene, and Daniel Bowen. 2014. "Creating Cultural Consumers: The Dynamics of Cultural Capital Acquisition." *Sociology of Education* 87 (4): 281–295. https://doi.org/10.1177/0038040714549076.
Knudsen, Herman, Jens Lind, and Bjarke Refslund. 2023. "Denmark: Trade Unions Still Afloat at Ebb Tide." In *Trade Unions in the European Union*, edited by Jeremy Waddington, Torsten Müller, and Kurt Vandaele. Work & Society. Bruxelles: Peter Lang. https://www.etui.org/sites/default/files/2023-06/Chapter8_Denmark_Trade%20unions%20still%20afloat%20at%20ebb%20tide_2023.pdf.
Kozlowski, Karen Phelan. 2015. "Culture or Teacher Bias? Racial and Ethnic Variation in Student-Teacher Effort Assessment Match/Mismatch." *Race and Social Problems* 7 (1): 43–59. https://doi.org/10.1007/s12552-014-9138-x.

KPMG UK. 2022. "Social Mobility Progression Report 2022: Mind the Gap." London. https://assets.kpmg.com/content/dam/kpmg/uk/pdf/2022/12/social-mobility-progression-report-2022-mind-the-gap-brochure.pdf.

Kraus, Michael W., Stéphane Côté, and Dacher Keltner. 2010. "Social Class, Contextualism, and Empathic Accuracy." *Psychological Science* 21 (11): 1716–1723. https://doi.org/10.1177/0956797610387613.

Kraus, Michael W., Paul Piff, Rodolfo Mendoza-Denton, Michelle L. Rheinschmidt, and Dacher Keltne. 2012. "Social Class, Solipsism, and Contextualism: How the Rich Are Different from the Poor." *Psychological Review* 119 (3): 546–572. https://doi.org/10.1037/a0028756.

Kugelmass, Heather. 2016. "'Sorry, I'm Not Accepting New Patients': An Audit Story of Access to Mental Health Care." *Journal of Health and Social Behavior* 57 (2): 168–183. https://doi.org/10.1177/0022146516647098.

Kundu, Anindya, Yimeng Liu, and June Ahn. 2024. "'I Got It from My Mama:' The Influence of Working-Class Parents on Young People's Cultural Capital for Success in School and Work." *Equity in Education & Society* 3 (3): 297–316. https://doi.org/10.1177/27526461231170233.

Kusserow, Adrie. 2012. "When Hard and Soft Clash: Class-Based Individualism in Manhattan and Queens." In *Facing Social Class: How Societal Rank Influences Interaction*, edited by S. T. Fiskie and H. Markus. New York: Russell Sage Foundation.

Lacy, Karyn R. 2004. "Black Spaces, Black Places: Strategic Assimilation and Identity Construction in Middle-Class Suburbia." *Ethnic and Racial Studies* 27 (6): 908–930. https://doi.org/10.1080/0141987042000268521.

Lahire, Bernard. 2003. "From the Habitus to an Individual Heritage of Dispositions. Towards a Sociology at the Level of the Individual." *Poetics* 31 (5): 329–355. https://doi.org/10.1016/j.poetic.2003.08.002.

Lamont, Michèle. 1992. *Money, Morals, Manners: The Culture of the French and the American Upper-Middle-Class*. Chicago: University of Chicago Press.

Lamont, Michèle. 2000. *The Dignity of Working Men: Morality and the Boundaries of Race, Class, and Immigration*. New York and Cambridge, MA: Russell Sage Foundation and Harvard University Press.

Lampert, Jo, Bruce Burnett, and Stevie Lebhers. 2016. "'More Like the Kids than the Other Teachers': One Working-Class Pre-Service Teacher's Experiences in a Middle-Class Profession." *Teaching and Teacher Education* 58: 35–42. https://doi.org/10.1016/j.tate.2016.04.006.

Lareau, Annette. 2011. *Unequal Childhoods: Class, Race, and Family Life*. Berkeley: University of California Press.

Lareau, Annette, and Vanessa Muñoz. 2012. "'You're Not Going to Call the Shots': Structural Conflicts Between the Principal and the PTO at a Suburban Public Elementary School." *Sociology of Education* 85 (3): 201–218. https://doi.org/10.1177/0038040711435855.

Latimer, Jeff, Craig Dowden, and Danielle Muise. 2005. "The Effectiveness of Restorative Justice Practices: A Meta-Analysis." *Prison Journal* 85 (2): 127–144. https://doi.org/10.1177/0032885505276969.

Laurison, Daniel, and Sam Friedman. 2024. "The Class Ceiling in the United States: Class-Origin Pay Penalties in Higher Professional and Managerial Occupations." *Social Forces* 103 (1): 22–44. https://doi.org/10.1093/sf/soae025.

Leondar-Wright, Betsy. 2014. *Missing Class: Strengthening Social Movement Groups by Seeing Class Cultures*. Ithaca, NY: ILR Press.

Levon, Erez, Devyani Sharma, and Christian Ilbury. 2022. *Speaking Up: Accents and Social Mobility*. London: Sutton Trust.

Lin, Nan. 1999. "Social Networks and Status Attainment." *Annual Review of Sociology* 25 (August): 467–487. https://doi.org/10.1146/annurev.soc.25.1.467.

Lobb, Andrea. 2017. "Critical Empathy." *Constellations: An International Journal of Critical and Democratic Theory* 24 (4): 594–607. https://doi.org/10.1111/1467-8675.12292.

Loewen, James. 2007. *Likes My Teacher Told Me: Everything Your American History Textbook Got Wrong*. New York: New Press.

Löffler, Charlotte, and Tobias Greitemeyer. 2023. "Are Women the More Empathetic Gender? The Effects of Gender Role Expectations." *Current Psychology* 42: 220–231. https://doi.org/10.1007/s12144-020-01260-8.

Lorde, Audre. 1984. "The Master's Tools Will Never Dismantle the Master's House." In *Sister Outsider: Essays and Speeches*. Berkeley, CA: Crossing Press.

Lubrano, Alfred. 2004. *Limbo: Blue-Collar Roots, White Collar Dreams*. Hoboken, NJ: John Wiley & Sons.

Luczaj, Kamil. 2023. "Social Class as a Blessing in Disguise? Beyond the Deficit Model in Working-Class and Higher Education Studies." *Equality, Diversity and Inclusion* 42 (2): 193–209. https://doi.org/10.1108/EDI-02-2022-0040.

Macdonald, Brandie. 2022. "Pausing, Reflection, and Action: Decolonizing Museum Practices." *Journal of Museum Education* 47 (1): 8–17. https://doi.org/10.1080/10598650.2021.1986668.

Maciel, Andre F. 2017. "The Cultural Tensions Between Taste Refinement and American Middle-Class Masculinity." In *Untapped: Exploring the Cultural Dimensions of Craft Beer*, edited by Nathaniel Chapman, J. Slade Lellock, and Cameron Lippard. Morgantown: Western Virginia University Press.

Manning, Alex. 2019. "The Age of Concerted Cultivation: A Racial Analysis of Parental Repertoires and Childhood Activities." *Du Bois Review* 16 (1): 5–35. https://doi.org/10.1017/S1742058X19000080.

Margolis, Eric, Michael Soldatenko, Sandra Acker, and Marina Gair. 2001. "Peekaboo: Hiding and Outing the Curriculum." In *The Hidden Curriculum in Higher Education*, edited by E. Margolis. New York: Routledge.

Marks, Abigail, Esme Terry, Jesus Canduela, Arek Dakessian, and Dimitris Christopoulos. 2023. "Feminized Cultural Capital at Work in the Moral Economy: Home Credit and Working-Class Women." *Gender, Work & Organization* 30 (1): 1–17. https://doi.org/10.1111/gwao.12892.

Markus, Hazel Rose. 2010. "Who Am I? Race, Ethnicity, and Identity." In *Doing Race: 21 Essays for the 21st Century*, edited by H. Markus and P. Moya. New York: W. W. Norton & Company.

Markus, Hazel Rose, and MarYam Hamedani. 2007. "Sociocultural Psychology: The Dynamic Interdependence Among Self Systems and Social Systems." In *Handbook of Cultural Psychology*, edited by S. Kitayama and D. Cohen. New York: Guilford.

Martin, Georgianna, and Sonja Ardoin. 2023. *Social Class Supports: Programs and Practices to Serve and Sustain Poor and Working-Class Students Through Higher Education*. New York: Taylor & Francis.

Massey, Douglas S., and Magaly Sanchez R. 2010. *Brokered Boundaries: Immigrant Identity in Anti-Immigrant Times*. New York: Russell Sage Foundation.

McCabe, Janice. 2016. *Connecting in College: How Friendship Networks Matter for Academic and Social Success.* Chicago: University of Chicago Press.

McCarty, Alyn. 2016. "Child Poverty in the United States: A Tale of Devastation and a Promise of Hope." *Sociology Compass* 10 (7): 623–639. https://doi.org/10.1111/soc4.12386.

McCluney, Courtney L., Myles I. Durkee, Richard E. Smith, Kathrina J. Robotham, and Serenity Sai-Lai Lee. 2021. "To Be, or Not to be . . . Black: The Effects of Racial Codeswitching on Perceived Professionalism in the Workplace." *Journal of Experimental Social Psychology* 97 (November): 104199. https://doi.org/10.1016/j.jesp.2021.104199.

McCoy, Selina, Delma Byrne, and Joanne Banks. 2012. "Too Much of a Good Thing? Gender, 'Concerted Cultivation' and Unequal Achievement in Primary Education." *Childhood Indicators Research* 5: 155–178. https://doi.org/10.1007/s12187-011-9118-2.

McEvoy, Charlotte, Victoria Clarke, and Zoe Thomas. 2021. "'Rarely Discussed but Always Present': Exploring Therapists' Accounts of the Relationship Between Social Class, Mental Health and Therapy." *Counseling Psychotherapy Research* 21 (2): 324–334. https://doi.org/10.1002/capr.12382.

Meltzer, James. 1978. "A Semiotic Approach to Suitability for Psychotherapy." *Psychiatry* 41 (4): 360–376. https://doi.org/10.1080/00332747.1978.11023995.

Metzgar, Jack. 2021. *Bridging the Divide: Working-Class Culture in a Middle-Class Society.* Ithaca, NY: Cornell University Press.

Milne, Emily, and Janice Aurini. 2015. "Schools, Cultural Mobility, and Social Reproduction: The Case of Progressive Discipline." *Canadian Journal of Sociology* 40 (1): 51–74. https://doi.org/10.29173/cjs20891.

Miranda, Alexis R., Amaya Perez-Brumer, and Brittany M. Charlton. 2023. "Latino? Latinx? Latine? A Call for Inclusive Categories in Epidemiologic Research." *American Journal of Epidemiology* 192 (12): 1929–1932. https://doi.org/10.1093/aje/kwad149.

Morris, Edward W. 2005. "'Tuck In That Shirt!' Race, Class, Gender, and Discipline in an Urban School." *Sociological Perspectives* 48 (1): 25–48. https://doi.org/10.1525/sop.2005.48.1.25.

Morton, Jennifer. 2019. *Moving Up Without Losing Your Way.* Princeton, NJ: Princeton University Press.

Morton, Jennifer M. 2014. "Cultural Code-Switching: Straddling the Achievement Gap." *Journal of Political Philosophy* 22 (3): 259–281. https://doi.org/10.1111/jopp.12019.

Mukherjee, Utsa, and Ravinder Barn. 2021. "Concerted Cultivation as a Racial Parenting Strategy: Race, Ethnicity and Middle-Class Indian Parents in Britain." *British Journal of Sociology of Education* 42 (4): 521–536. https://doi.org/10.1080/01425692.2021.1872365.

Munoz, Carlos. 2007. *Youth, Identity, Power: The Chicano Movement.* Brooklyn, NY: Verso Books.

National Association of Colleges and Employers. 2023. *Job Outlook 2024.* https://www.naceweb.org/docs/default-source/default-document-library/2023/publication/research-report/2024-nace-job-outlook.pdf?sfvrsn=57be133e_5.

Newman, Lainey, and Theda Skocpol. 2023. *Rust Belt Union Blues: Why Working-Class Voters Are Turning Away from the Democratic Party.* New York: Columbia University Press.

Nguyen, Thai-Huy, and Bach Mai Dolly Nguyen. 2018. "Is the 'First-Generation Student' Term Useful for Understanding Inequality? The Role of Intersectionality in Illuminating the Implications of an Accepted—Yet Unchallenged—Term." *Review of Research in Education* 42 (1): 146–176. https://doi.org/10.3102/0091732X18759280.

Nunn, Lisa. 2021. *College Belonging: How First-Year and First-Generation Students Navigate Campus Life*. New Brunswick, NJ: Rutgers University Press.

Oakes, Jeannie. 2005. *Keeping Track: How Schools Structure Inequality*. 2nd ed. New Haven, CT: Yale University Press.

Obermiller, Phillip, and Michael Maloney. 2016. "The Uses and Misuses of Appalachian Culture." *Journal of Appalachian Studies* 22 (1): 103–112. https://doi.org/10.5406/jappastud.22.1.0103.

Ogbar, Jeffrey O. G. 2019. *Black Power: Radical Politics and African American Identity*. Baltimore, MD: Johns Hopkins University Press.

Osborne, Melissa. 2024. *Polished: College, Class, and the Burdens of Social Mobility*. Chicago: University of Chicago Press.

O'Shea, Sarah, and Janine Delahunty. 2019. "'That Working-Class Ethic . . . Where There's a Will There's a Way:' A Strengths-Based Approach to Developing Employable Scholars." In *Employability via Higher Education: Sustainability as Scholarship*, edited by Alice Diver. Cham, Switzerland: Springer International Publishing. https://doi.org/10.1007/978-3-030-26342-3_11.

Patillo, Mary. 2013. *Black Picket Fences: Privilege and Peril among the Black Middle-Class*. 2nd ed. Chicago: University of Chicago Press.

Peckham, Irv. 1995. "Complicity in Class Codes: The Exclusionary Function of Education." In *This Fine Place So Far from Home*, edited by C. Dews and C. Law. Philadelphia: Temple University Press.

Pendergast, Donna, Jeanne Allen, Glenda McGregor, and Michelle Ronksley-Pavia. 2018. "Engaging Marginalized, 'At-Risk' Middle-Level Students: A Focus on the Importance of a Sense of Belonging at School." *Education Sciences* 8 (3): 138. https://doi.org/10.3390/educsci8030138.

Peterson, Richard A., and Roger M. Kern. 1996. "Changing Highbrow Taste: From Snob to Omnivore." *American Sociological Review* 61 (5): 900–907. https://doi.org/10.2307/2096460.

Pisarcik, Ian. 2024. "Women Outnumber Men in US Law School Classrooms, but Statistics Don't Tell the Full Story." *Jurist News*, January 17, 2024. https://www.jurist.org/commentary/2024/01/women-outnumber-men-in-us-law-school-classrooms-but-statistics-dont-tell-the-full-story/.

Portes, Alejandro, and Min Zhou. 1993. "The New Second Generation: Segmented Assimilation and Its Variants." *ANNALS of the American Academy of Political and Social Science* 530 (1): 74–96.

Ready, Douglas, and David Wright. 2011. "Accuracy and Inaccuracy in Teachers' Perceptions of Young Children's Cognitive Abilities: The Role of Child Background and Classroom Contexts." *American Educational Research Journal* 48 (2): 335–360. https://doi.org/10.3102/0002831210374874.

Reardon, Sean F. 2011. "The Widening Academic Achievement Gap Between the Rich and the Poor: New Evidence and Possible Explanations." In *Wither Opportunity? Rising Inequality, Schools, and Children's Life Chances*, edited by Greg J. Duncan and Richard J. Murnane. New York: Russell Sage Foundation.

Reilly, Iona Burnell. 2022. *The Lives of Working Class Academics: Getting Ideas Above Your Station*. Bingley, UK: Emerald Group Publishing.

Reynolds, John R., and Michael Parrish. 2018. "Natural Mentors, Social Class, and College Success." *American Journal of Community Psychology* 61 (1–2): 179–190.

Richards, Bedelia, and Lauren Camuso. 2015. "Cultural Capital in the Classroom: The Significance of Debriefing as a Pedagogical Tool in Simulation-Based Learning." *International Journal of Teaching and Learning in Higher Education* 27 (1): 94–103.

Riddell, Sheila. 1992. *Gender and the Politics of Curriculum*. New York: Routledge.

Ridgeway, Cecilia, and Susan Fisk. 2012. "Class Rules, Status Dynamics, and 'Getaway' Interactions." In *Facing Social Class: How Societal Rank Influences Interaction*, edited by S. T. Fiske and H. R. Markus. New York: Russell Sage Foundation.

Riess, Helen. 2017. "The Science of Empathy." *Journal of Patient Experience* 4 (2): 74–77. https://doi.org/10.1177/2374373517699267.

Rivera, Lauren. 2012. "Hiring as Cultural Matching: The Case of Elite Professional Service Firms." *American Sociological Review* 77 (6): 999–1022. https://doi.org/10.1177/0003122412463213.

Ruffins, Fath D. 1994. "'Lifting as We Climb': Black Women and the Preservation of African American History and Culture." *Gender & History* 6 (3): 376–396. https://doi.org/10.1111/j.1468-0424.1994.tb00208.x.

Rutherford, Markella B. 2011. "The Social Value of Self-Esteem." *Society* 48 (5): 407–412. https://doi.org/10.1007/s12115-011-9460-5.

Sayer, Andrew. 2011. "Class and Morality." In *The Handbook of the Sociology of Morality*, edited by Steven Hitlin and Stephen Vaisey. New York: Springer.

Scerri, Andy. 2019. "Moralizing About Politics: The White Working-Class 'Problem' in Appalachia and Beyond." *Journal of Appalachian Studies* 25 (2): 202–221. https://doi.org/10.5406/jappastud.25.2.0202.

Schuette, Anthony. 2023. *Navigating the Enrollment Cliff in Higher Education*. Round Rock, TX: Trellis Company. https://eric.ed.gov/?id=ED628984.

Schumann, William, and Rebecca Adkins Fletcher. 2016. *Appalachia Revisited: New Perspectives on Place, Tradition, and Progress*. Lexington: University Press of Kentucky.

Sharps, Daron L., and Cameron Anderson. 2021. "Social Class Background, Disjoint Agency, and Hiring Decisions." *Organizational Behavior and Human Decision Processes* 167 (November):129–143. https://doi.org/10.1016/j.obhdp.2021.08.003.

Sheppard, Keith, Peter Dominick, and Zvi Aronson. 2003. "Preparing Engineering Students for the New Business Paradigm of International Teamwork and Global Orientation." In *Enhancement of the Global Perspective for Engineering Students by Providing an International Experience*, edited by Carl McHargue and Eleanor Baum. New York: Engineering Conferences International. https://dc.engconfintl.org/enhancement/27.

Sherman, Rachel. 2017. *Uneasy Street: The Anxieties of Affluence*. Princeton, NJ: Princeton University Press.

Simpson, Ruth, Jason Hughes, and Natasha Slutskaya. 2016. "White Working Class Masculinities and Dirty Work." In *Gender, Class and Occupation: Working Class Men Doing Dirty Work*, edited by Ruth Simpson, Jason Hughes, and Natasha Slutskaya. London: Palgrave Macmillan UK. https://doi.org/10.1057/978-1-137-43969-7_5.

Sirin, Selcuk R. 2005. "Socioeconomic Status and Academic Achievement: A Meta-Analytic Review of Research." *Review of Educational Research* 75 (3): 417–453. https://doi.org/10.3102/00346543075003417.

Slater, Graham B. 2022. "Terms of Endurance: Resilience, Grit, and the Cultural Politics of Neoliberal Education." *Critical Education* 13 (1): 1–16. https://doi.org/10.14288/ce.v13i1.186530.

Smith, Barbara Ellen. 2020. *Digging Our Own Graves: Coal Miners and the Struggle over Black Lung Disease*. Chicago: Haymarket Books.
Smith, Buffy. 2015. *Mentoring At-Risk Students Through the Hidden Curriculum of Higher Education*. Lanham, MD: Lexington Books.
Snyder, Benjamin H. 2022. "Precarious Futures: How White-Collar Workers Experience Unemployment." In *Working in America*, 5th ed., edited by Amy Wharton, New York: Routledge.
Somers, Patricia, Shawn R. Woodhouse, and James E. Cofer. 2004. "Pushing the Boulder Uphill: The Persistence of First-Generation College Students." *Journal of Student Affairs Research and Practice* 41 (3): 811–828. https://doi.org/10.2202/1949-6605.1353.
Sommet, Nicolas, Alain Quiamzade, Mickaël Jury, and Gabriel Mugny. 2015. "The Student-Institution Fit at University: Interactive Effects of Academic Competition and Social Class on Achievement Goals." *Frontiers in Psychology* 6 (June). https://doi.org/10.3389/fpsyg.2015.00769.
Song, Juyoung. 2018. "Critical Approaches to Emotions of Non-Native English Speaking Teachers." *Chinese Journal of Applied Linguistics* 41: 453–467. https://doi.org/10.1515/cjal-2018-0033.
Soria, Krista, Brad Weiner, and Elissa Lu. 2014. "Financial Decisions Among Undergraduate Students from Low-Income and Working-Class Social Class Backgrounds." *Journal of Student Financial Aid* 44 (1). https://doi.org/10.55504/0884-9153.1037.
Soto-Luna, Isabel. 2023. "Hispanic, Latine, Latinx How Monolithic Terminology Can Amplify and Erase Millions of Voices." In *Serving Hispanic, Latine, and Latinx Students in Academic Libraries*, edited by Isabel Soto-Luna and Sommer Browning. Sacramento, CA: Litwin Books.
Stahl, Garth. 2018. "Aspiration Paradoxes: Working-Class Student Conceptions of Power in 'Engines of Social Mobility.'" *International Journal of Qualitative Studies in Education* 31 (7): 557–571. https://doi.org/10.1080/09518398.2017.1286404.
Statistica. 2022. "Share of High School Graduates Enrolled in College in the United States from 2000 to 2020, by Family Income Quartile." https://www.statista.com/statistics/782387/college-enrollment-by-family-income-quartile-us/.
Stephens, Nicole M., Stephanie A. Fryberg, and Hazel Rose Markus. 2011. "When Choice Does Not Equal Freedom: A Sociocultural Analysis of Agency in Working-Class American Contexts." *Social Psychological and Personality Science* 2 (1): 33–41. https://doi.org/10.1177/1948550610378757.
Stephens, Nicole M., Stephanie A. Fryberg, and Hazel Rose Markus. 2012a. "It's Your Choice: How the Middle-Class Model of Independence Disadvantages Working-Class Americans." In *Facing Social Class: How Societal Rank Influences Interaction*, edited by S. T. Fiske and H. R. Markus. New York: Russell Sage Foundation.
Stephens, Nicole M., Stephanie A. Fryberg, Hazel Rose Markus, Camille S. Johnson, and Rebecca Covarrubias. 2012b. "Unseen Disadvantage: How American Universities' Focus on Independence Undermines the Academic Performance of First-Generation College Students." *Journal of Personality and Social Psychology* 102 (6): 1178–1197. https://doi.org/10.1037/a0027143.
Stephens, Nicole M., MarYam G. Hamedani, and Mesmin Destin. 2014. "Closing the Social-Class Achievement Gap: A Difference-Education Intervention Improves First-Generation Students' Academic Performance and All Students' College Transition." *Psychological Science* 25 (4): 943–953. https://doi.org/10.1177/0956797613518349.

Stephens, Nicole M., Sarah Townsend, Hazel Rose Markus, and L. Taylor Phillips. 2012. "A Cultural Mismatch: Independent Cultural Norms Produce Greater Increases in Cortisol and More Negative Emotions Among First-Generation College Students." *Journal of Experimental Social Psychology* 48 (6): 1389–1393. https://doi.org/10.1016/j.jesp.2012.07.008.

Stiles, Stefanie. 2017. "Blue-Collar Advantage: How Working-Class Academics Can Bring Us Together." *Times Higher Education (THE)*, April 25, 2017. https://www.timeshighereducation.com/blog/blue-collar-advantage-how-working-class-academics-can-bring-us-together.

Stockfelt, Shawanda. 2016. "Economic, Social and Embodied Cultural Capitals as Shapers and Predictors of Boys' Educational Aspirations." *Journal of Educational Research* 109 (4): 351–359. https://doi.org/10.1080/00220671.2014.968911.

Strauss, Claudia. 2004. "Is Empathy Gendered, and, if So, Why? An Approach from Feminist Psychological Anthropology." *Ethos* 32 (4): 432–457. https://doi.org/10.1525/eth.2004.32.4.432.

Stuber, Jenny Marie. 2011. "Integrated, Marginal, and Resilient: Race, Class, and the Diverse Experiences of White First-Generation College Students." *International Journal of Qualitative Studies in Education* 24 (1): 117–136. https://doi.org/10.1080/09518391003641916.

Tatarlar, Ceren Deniz, and A. Güldem Cerit. 2016. "Relationship Between Empathy Skill Levels and Job Selection: A Study on Business Administration Students." *Marmara Journal of Pure and Applied Sciences* 1: 1–6. https://doi.org/10.7240/mufbed.67483.

Tatum, Katharine, and Irene Browne. 2019. "The Best of Both Worlds: One-Up Assimilation Strategies among Middle-Class Immigrants." *Poetics* 75 (August): 101317. https://doi.org/10.1016/j.poetic.2018.08.002.

Taylor, Yvette. 2008. "'That's Not Really My Scene': Working-Class Lesbians In (and Out of) Place." *Sexualities* 1 (5): 523–546. https://doi.org/10.1177/1363460708094266.

Telles, Edward E., and Vilma Ortiz. 2008. *Generations of Exclusion: Mexican-Americans, Assimilation, and Race.* New York: Russell Sage Foundation.

Terry, Josh. 2020. "Politicians Have Always Misunderstood Springsteen's 'Born in the U.S.A.'" *Vice* (blog). October 5, 2020. https://www.vice.com/en/article/pkyjvn/misunderstood-bruce-springsteens-born-in-the-usa-trump.

Tønnessen, Marianne, Kjetil Telle, and Astri Syse. 2016. "Childhood Residential Mobility and Long-Term Outcomes." *Acta Sociologica* 59 (2): 113–129. https://doi.org/10.1177/0001699316628614.

Torche, Florencia. 2011. "Is a College Degree Still the Great Equalizer? Intergenerational Mobility Across Levels of Schooling in the United States." *American Journal of Sociology* 117 (3): 763–807. https://doi.org/10.1086/661904.

Toussaint, Eric. 2023. *The World Bank: A Critical History.* London: Pluto Press.

Tracey, Monica, and John Baaki. 2022. *Cultivating Professional Identity in Design.* New York: Routledge.

Van Bommel, Tara. 2021. "The Power of Empathy in Times of Crisis and Beyond." *Catalyst.* https://www.catalyst.org/reports/empathy-work-strategy-crisis/.

Van Galen, Jane. 2020. "Mediating Stories of Class Borders: First-Generation College Students, Digital Storytelling, and Social Class." In *Routledge International Handbook of Working-Class Studies*, edited by Michele Fazio, Christie Launius, and Tim Strangleman. New York: Routledge.

Vannini, Phillip, and Alexis Franzese. 2008. "The Authenticity of Self: Conceptualizations, Personal Experience, and Practice." *Sociology Compass* 2 (5): 1621–1637. https://doi.org/10.1111/j.1751-9020.2008.00151.x.

Wagner, Thomas E., Phillip J. Obermiller, Melinda B. Wagner, and Mike Maloney. 2013. "Fifty Years of Appalachian Advocacy: An Interview with Mike Maloney." *Appalachian Journal* 40 (3/4): 174–218.

Walpole, MaryBeth. 2003. "Socioeconomic Status and College: How SES Affects College Experiences and Outcomes." *Review of Higher Education* 27 (1): 45–73. https://doi.org/10.1353/rhe.2003.0044.

Walther, Joachim, Shari Miller, and Nicola Sochacka. 2017. "A Model of Empathy in Engineering as a Core Skill, Practice Orientation, and Professional Way of Being." *Journal of Engineering Education* 106 (1): 123–148. https://doi.org/10.1002/jee.20159.

Warde, Alan. 2006. "Cultural Capital and the Place of Sport." *Cultural Trends* 15 (2–3): 107–122. https://doi.org/10.1080/09548960600712827.

Warner, Catharine, and Melissa Milkie. 2013. "Cultivating Gendered Talents? The Intersection of Race, Class, and Gender in the Concerted Cultivation of U.S. Elementary Students." In *Notions of Family: Intersectional Perspectives (Advances in Gender Research* vol. 17), edited by M. Kohlman, D. Krieg, and B. Dickerson. Leeds, UK: Emerald Group Publishing Limited.

Watson, Gerald. 2005. "The Hidden Curriculum in Schools: Implications for Lesbian, Gay, Bisexual, Transgender, and Queer Youth." *Alternate Routes: A Journal of Critical Social Research* 21: 18–39.

We Are Somebody. n.d. "Our Mission." Accessed April 26, 2025. https://wearesomebody.org/.

Weinger, Susan. 1998. "Poor Children 'Know Their Place': Perceptions of Poverty, Class and Public Messages." *Journal of Sociology and Social Welfare* 25 (2): 100–118.

Wilkinson, Richard, and Kate Pickett. 2011. *The Spirit Level: Why Greater Equality Makes Societies Stronger*. New York: Bloomsbury Publishing USA.

Williams, Joan. 2012. "The Class Culture Gap." In *Facing Social Class: How Societal Rank Influences Interaction*, edited by S. Fiske and H. Markus. New York: Russell Sage Foundation.

Willis, Roxana. 2020. "'Let's Talk About It': Why Social Class Matters to Restorative Justice." *Criminology & Criminal Justice* 20 (2): 187–206. https://doi.org/10.1177/1748895818804307.

Working Class Studies Association. n.d. "About." https://workingclassassn.org/about/.

World Economic Forum. 2020. *The Global Social Mobility Report 2020: Equality, Opportunity and a New Economic Imperative*. Geneva, Switzerland: World Economic Forum. https://www.weforum.org/publications/global-social-mobility-index-2020-why-economies-benefit-from-fixing-inequality/.

Wren, David J. 1999. "School Culture: Exploring the Hidden Curriculum." *Adolescence* 34 (135): 593–596.

Wright, Erik Olin. 2000. *Class Counts*. New York: Cambridge University Press.

Yosso, Tara J. 2005. "Whose Culture Has Capital? A Critical Race Theory Discussion of Community Cultural Wealth." *Race, Ethnicity and Education* 8 (1): 69–91.

Yu, Kyoung-Hee. 2016. "Immigrant Workers' Responses to Stigmatized Work: Constructing Dignity Through Moral Reasoning." *Journal of Industrial Relations* 58 (5): 571–588. https://doi.org/10.1177/0022185615609204.

Zembylas, Michalinos. 2007. "Emotional Capital and Education: Theoretical Insights from Bourdieu." *British Journal of Educational Studies* 55: 443–463. https://doi.org/10.1111/j.1467-8527.2007.00390.x.

Zeng, Wen, Dallin George Young, Catherine Hartman, and Isaac Portillo. 2022. *Using Data and Evidence to Lead Holistic Advising Redesign: A Guidebook for Campus Leaders for Promoting Consistent, Coherent, and Collaborative Data Use in Advising: Vol. 3: Improving the Human Resources Needed to Use Data More Strategically.* Columbia: University of South Carolina, National Resource Center for The First-Year Experience and Students in Transition.

Zumbrunn, Sharon, Courtney McKim, Eric Buhs, and Leslie Hawley. 2014. "Support, Belonging, Motivation, and Engagement in the College Classroom: A Mixed Method Study." *Instructional Science* 42 (5): 661–684. https://doi.org/10.1007/s11251-014-9310-0.

Index

The letter t following a page number denotes a table. The letter n following a page number denotes an endnote.

accomplishment of natural growth, 21, 24
achievement: academic achievement gap, 37–38, 142; costs of achievement culture, 77, 124, 130; identity, and, 48; as a value, 11, 30–31, 33t, 34, 77, 124
American Dream, 1, 8, 9, 15; missing, what is, 1, 4, 62
Anyon, Jean, 42–43
Appalachia, 98, 99, 135; diversity of, 28, 83, 138; stereotypes of, 4
assimilation, 117; definition, 118; into middle-class culture, 118–120, 130; resistance to, 120–121; strategic assimilation, 121–123; into whiteness, 120
authenticity. *See* working-class values: authenticity

belonging, 25, 28, 49, 77, 143; academic, 22, 26, 39, 44, 48, 53, 74, 77; class, 1, 4, 26, 51, 122, 124; working-class value, 27
Bernstein, Basil, 25–26
bougie, 28, 108, 109, 127
Bourdieu, Pierre, 11

Calarco, Jessica, 41
class and: academic achievement, 37; childrearing, 10, 20–24, 31; college enrollment, 45; contradictory class locations, 6–7; definition, 5–7; economic inequality, 8; educational funding, 38; independence vs. interdependence, 25, 46, 68, 74, 76–77, 113, 135; language, 10, 21–22, 25–26, 33t, 39–40, 80; self-confidence and self-doubt, 3, 23, 47–49; self-identity, 7; stereotypes, 4, 58, 66, 67, 79, 83, 92, 93, 144. *See also* belonging; tastes; values; working-class cultural capital
classism, 2, 15, 52; defined, 37; in education, 36–37, 40, 42, 43–44; in professions, 51
code-switching, 16; burdens of, 93–94; "clear-eyed," 134–135; definition, 91; racial, 121. *See also* working-class cultural capital: code-switching
college. *See* higher education
competitiveness: as a middle-class value, 20, 21, 25, 31, 33t, 52, 74, 77, 119; in college and professional offices, 48
complicity, 16, 118, 123–127, 132
concerted cultivation, 21, 22, 24, 39, 46, 118, 122
constraint, sense of, 11, 22–23, 33t, 34, 48, 61, 94, 103, 113, 136
consumption, 3, 129
cooptation, 118, 127–131
cross-class coalitions, 100. *See also* working-class cultural capital: bridging

cultural capital: definition, 11, 20; programs for building, 24, 126; and social mobility, 11–12, 22, 23, 24, 34, 38. *See also* working-class cultural capital

cultural mismatch, 1, 2, 15, 112, 118, 120; definition, 37; in education, 38, 40–44, 45; in professions, 49–53; teaching about, 142; values, of, 31

culture, definition, 10. *See also* cultural capital; cultural mismatch; working-class cultural capital

culture shock, 108, 141

"deficit lens" of working-class background, 11, 147; critique of, 12, 140; in higher education, 140; in hiring, 144

dispositions, 16; definition, 102; in the hidden curriculum, 38, 39, 45; middle-class, 47, 102–103; and social mobility, 101, 103, 113, 162n1. *See also* working-class cultural capital: dispositions

empathy: acquisition of, 39, 58, 60, 62, 71; definition, 58; lack, of, 51, 58, 62, 64, 66–67. *See also* working-class cultural capital: empathy

engineering, 124–126, 149

entitlement, sense of, 33t, 77; asking for what one wants, 22, 34, 44, 58, 61, 102; critique of, 109, 113, 122, 123; for higher position and resources, 44, 51, 106; when interacting with authority figures, 10, 22, 52, 136

first-generation students: academic preparation, 45; advice for, 136–137; barriers navigating higher education, 75, 87; "buying in" vs. "selling out", 141; career advising, 68, 88–90, 137; cultural mismatch, 1, 49, 52–53, 86, 140–142; definition, 7; discrimination, 144–145; educational attainment, 67, 141, 142; educational travel, 9, 137; fear of failure, 47; financial aid, 75, 137; hard work ethic, 106; importance of asking for help, 136, 143; imposter syndrome, 48; interaction with professors, 136, 143; job interviews, 52, 113; learning the hidden curriculum, 45–47, 141, 142; mentoring by first-gen faculty and staff, 67–70, 88–90, 123, 143; programming for, 59, 126, 140–143; resilience, 111; self-confidence, 136–137; sense of belonging, 49, 135, 142, 143; as straddlers, 5; summer bridge programs, 142; teaching methods, 70–71; use of campus resources, 47; work experiences during college, 49, 68. *See also* working-class cultural capital

gender: cultural capital, 24, 28, 61; discrimination, 94–95, 144, 145; education, 44, 48, 61, 69, 94; imposter syndrome, 48, 61; representation of, 129, 150; socialization, 32, 44, 71, 79, 84, 104

hard work, 11; costs of, 103, 106–107, 139. *See also* working-class values: hard work

Heath, Shirley, 39–40, 161n9

hidden curriculum: definition, 38, 159n6; higher education, 45–47, 49, 87–88, 141, 143; K–12 schooling, 38–44

higher education: debt, 13, 137, 139–140; financial aid, 45, 47, 75, 137; recommendations for, 140–143; selecting a college, 3, 13, 45, 64, 75, 87; selecting a major, 68, 76, 88, 89, 94, 104, 127; social experiences, 4, 142. *See also* first-generation students; hidden curriculum: higher education

hiring discrimination: class, 144–145; gender, 144–145; race, 8–9, 144

humility. *See* working-class values: humility

imposter syndrome, 47–49, 51, 53

individualism: in education, 43, 46, 71, 74; in language, 10, 25, 79; as a value, 11, 25, 27, 48, 79, 120. *See also* class: independence vs. interdependence; race: individualistic vs. group-based culture; solipsism

inside-outside strategy, 129, 130

intersectionality, 138, 145, 151, 154; definition, 11. *See also* race; gender; sexuality

Jensen, Barbara, 26, 39, 78–80, 121, 149, 153

Lamont, Michèle, 29–32, 34
language. *See* class: language; working-class cultural capital: language and communication
Lareau, Annette, 20–23, 31, 39, 41, 69, 154
Leondar-Wright, Betsy, 80–81, 144, 154
Lorde, Audre, 129–130
Lubrano, Alfred, 5, 10, 22, 50, 51, 52, 81, 138, 149

mentoring, 112, 113, 128, 135; children, 59, 60; first-gen students, 14, 49, 61, 68–69, 69–70, 94, 135, 137; peer, 142
morality, traditional, 32, 40, 84. *See also* values
Morton, Jennifer, 134–135

networks, 119, 142; academic support networks, 45, 47, 48, 88; difficulties in, 47, 49, 52; professional networking, 47, 52, 58, 69, 93, 132, 146

Osborne, Melissa, 141–142

poverty: definition, 7, 157n8; display of, 66; global, 104; organizing against, 81, 86, 108, 123–125, 134; shame of, 74, 127; stereotypes of, 4; surviving, 63; time, 49
precarity, 139
pride, working-class, 2, 7, 12, 77, 100, 128; in helping others, 92; reclaiming, 119, 122, 123, 131–132, 135, 143; strengths of working-class background, 15, 57, 63, 91, 101; working-class values, 2
privilege, class, 19–20, 58, 70, 76, 108, 139–140; invisibility of, 58, 144. *See also* white privilege

race, assimilation, 120, 121–122; authenticity, 28; cultural capital, 23–24, 28, 89–90; discrimination, 8–9, 32, 51, 63, 68, 95–96; economic inequality, 7, 8–9; education, 39–40, 44, 48, 61, 63, 89–90; individualistic vs. group-based culture, 28; help-seeking, 136; labor market discrimination, 8–9; Latine vs. Latino/a/x, 157n5; mentoring, 59, 60, 135; neighborhoods, 83, 121; social mobility, 9; values, 31–32. *See also* white privilege

research methodology, 14–15, 147–151
resilience: critique of, 111, 112–113; as a value, 11. *See also* working-class values: resilience; working-class cultural capital: dispositions

self-actualization, 11, 30, 31, 33t, 122, 131
"selling out," 130–131, 141
sexuality: class diversity, 11, 27, 32, 135; discrimination, 61, 84, 145; hidden curriculum, 44; identity, 122, 138
shame, working-class, 53, 99, 130, 144; accepting help, 79; lack of resources, 3; language abilities, 92, 101; public assistance, 127; resisting, 120; wanting to escape, 5, 119, 124
social capital, 58, 70
social democratic policies, 128, 130, 133–134
social mobility: cross-country comparisons, 9; rates, 8–9. *See also* upward mobility; first-generation students
social safety net, 4, 29, 134, 139
solipsism, 51
story-telling, 39, 135, 146
straddlers, 4, 29; belonging, 1, 15, 117, 143; burnout, 139; class uplift, 12, 16, 67, 101, 127, 129–131, 140, 146; definition, 5; identity, 138–139; pride, 57; unease in the middle class, 31, 49–50, 51, 52. *See also* assimilation; complicity; cooptation; first-generation students; working-class cultural capital
strengths, working-class. *See* working-class cultural capital

tastes: belonging, 27, 122; class differences, 10, 25, 27, 33t, 70; conflict, 79–80, 121; cultural capital, 34, 52, 73, 120, 121; race, 121. *See also* assimilation
time poverty, 49
Turner, Nina, 15, 47, 85, 101, 127–131, 134, 135, 149

unions: higher wages, 2, 13, 29, 94, 97; organizing, 101, 122; solidarity, 32, 91; unionization rates, 9
upward mobility, costs of, 82, 138–139, 140–142. *See also* first-generation students; social mobility

values: definition, 28–29; durability, 32, 33t, 84; explanations, 29–32; hidden curriculum, 38, 45; middle-class, 30–31, 33t, 34, 77; professional office, 50; social mobility, 34, 37, 51, 57, 130; values affirmation activity, 142, 143. *See also* assimilation; working-class values

white privilege, 4, 63, 90, 110

working-class cultural capital: bridging, 97–100; code-switching, 90–93, 99, 101, 120, 146; conflict mediation, 94–97; definition, 57; dispositions, 102–114, 135, 145; empathy, 60–61, 64–67, 69–72, 89, 108, 120, 123, 129; group-orientation, 74–78, 105, 107; language and communication, 73–74, 79–81, 82–84, 85, 88–90, 92–94, 99–100, 108–109, 145; translation, 87–90

working-class culture: devaluation, 89, 118, 120, 124, 126; invisibility, 78, 83, 84–85. *See also* working-class cultural capital; working-class values

working-class values: authenticity, 29, 33t, 107, 109–110, 117, 124, 129, 135, 145; community, 2, 75, 77, 79; directness or straightforwardness, 11, 29, 31, 33t, 34, 50, 117; family, 2, 21, 29, 33t, 80; hard work, 2, 29, 33t, 46, 100, 103–107, 139; honesty, 29, 50, 52; humility, 11, 29, 33t, 52, 69, 77, 107, 110, 117, 118, 122, 124; integrity, 2, 11, 29, 33t, 34, 124; practicality, 16, 27, 29, 33t, 103, 105–106, 113, 120, 145; resilience, 11, 16, 29, 33t, 60, 77, 111–113, 120, 145; responsibility, 29, 30, 33t, 41, 131, 134

World Bank, 125

About the Author

PAUL DEAN is a professor of sociology and social justice at Ohio Wesleyan University, an award-winning instructor, and a proud first-generation graduate. In addition to his research on working-class first-gen students, he has served as director of faculty development and is a leader in first-gen student pedagogy. He is a speaker, consultant, and workshop facilitator helping faculty, staff, and university administrators to better support first-gen students throughout higher education. Dean is coauthor of two other books, *Globalization: A Basic Text* and *Globalization: The Essentials*. Read more about Dean at drpauldean.com.